STAR TREK PSYCHOLOGY

The Mental Frontier

edited by
Travis Langley, PhD

#STpsych

An Imprint of Sterling Publishing Co., Inc.
1166 Avenue of the Americas
New York, NY 10036

STERLING and the distinctive Sterling logo are registered trademarks of Sterling Publishing Co., Inc.

ISBN 978-1-4549-1842-4

Distributed in Canada by Sterling Publishing
c/o Canadian Manda Group, 664 Annette Street
Toronto, Ontario, Canada M6S 2C8
Distributed in the United Kingdom by GMC Distribution Services
Castle Place, 166 High Street, Lewes, East Sussex, England BN7 1XU
Distributed in Australia by NewSouth Books
45 Beach Street, Coogee, NSW 2034, Australia

For information about custom editions, special sales, and premium and corporate purchases, please contact Sterling Special Sales at 800-805-5489 or specialsales@sterlingpublishing.com.

Manufactured in Canada

2 4 6 8 10 9 7 5 3 1

www.sterlingpublishing.com

IMAGE CREDITS

Deposit Photos: ©edvard76 267

Shutterstock: ©A-Digit 157, ©A-spring 11, ©Dencg 135, ©Lonely 9, ©Losw 83, ©Vadim Sadovski 172–173, ©Lucky Team Studio 95, ©Oorka 122–123, ©Robert Voight 109

iStockphoto: ©4x6 39, 125, 213, ©Rossella Apostoli 147, ©Artbyjulie 69, ©Alex Belomlinsky 201, ©Chipstudio 229, ©Dondesigns 51, ©Pete Draper 226–227, ©Henrik5000 66–67, ©Anna Rassadnikova 231, ©Juliar Studio 23 (right), ©Lazarev 175, ©Oberart 239, ©Paha_L 187, ©Pixitive 23 (left)

Dedication

To Ed O'Neal
and all the other mentors and educators
who help our missions begin.

CONTENTS

ACKNOWLEDGMENTS

The Crew

The journey of a thousand miles may begin with a single step,[1] but no sojourner makes the trip with neither assistance during the years leading up to that journey nor encounters with others along life's way. A lone astronaut in a space station, physically distant from everyone else, got up there through the efforts of many, gets information and other assistance from people down below, and one day will leave orbit to rejoin the population below. Star Trek has never been about one person's lonely passage through the vacuum of space, and no book becomes real without the weight of past efforts to push it forward, the work of everyone involved in turning thought into text, and the attention of the audience it ultimately will reach.

After *Batman and Psychology: A Dark and Stormy Knight*, Star Trek was going to be the topic of my next book. Things happen in the publishing industry, though, and new books had to wait. *Star Trek Psychology: The Mental Frontier* has finally arrived thanks to many fine folks at Sterling Publishing: Ardi Alspach, Toula Ballas, Michael Cea, Diana Drew, Lisa Geller, Marilyn Kretzer, Sari Lampert, Eric Lowenkron, Rodman Neumann, Blanca Oliviery, Lauren Tambini, Theresa Thompson, and especially Connie Santisteban and Kate Zimmermann. During the time that passed between my first book's release and when our Popular Culture Psychology series for Sterling began with *The Walking Dead Psychology: Psych of the Living Dead*, I got to know other psychology professionals, my fellow "psych geeks" who also love to analyze one fantastic topic after another because they're fans of the fiction and of human nature. They know that the mental universe is a fascinating frontier to explore. Without them, this series could not exist. I thank them all and make special note of Janina Scarlet, who has contributed to every single book in this series so far. I could not ask for more enthusiastic, conscientious editorial assistants than Mara Wood and Janina's frequent co-author, Jenna Busch.

Starship Con

I met many of our writers through conventions. They know their psychology, they know their fandoms, and they know how to bring these together in ways that are both interesting and informative for audiences of all kinds. I thank Nicholas Langley and Matthew Smith, whose work led me to my first Comic-Con and therefore launched this long voyage of ours. I thank the organizers of the Comic Arts Conference (Peter Coogan, Randy Duncan, Kate McClancy), San Diego Comic-Con International (Eddie Ibrahim, Gary Sassaman, Cathy Dalton, Laura Jones, Sue Lord, Adam Neese, Amy Ramirez, Chris Sturhann), New York Comic Con (Lance Fensterman), Los Angeles Comic Con (Stan Lee, Regina Carpinelli, Jade Cresko, Keith Tralins), the Hero Round Table (Matt Langdon), River City Expo (Brent Douglass), so many Wizard World cons (Christopher Jansen, Peter Katz, Ryan Ball, Donna Chin, Shelby Engquist, Danny Fingeroth, Tony B. Kim, Mo Lightning, Madeleine McManus, Jerry Milani, Mai Nguyen, Alex Rae, Katie Ruark, Aaron Sagers, Brittany Walloch), and more.

Starship Henderson

Henderson State University has provided so much support for this work. Through groups such as our Comic Arts Club and the Legion of Nerds, our students prove that geeky passions go together with higher learning. Nerds learn! Our administrators—President Glendell Jones, Provost Steve Adkison, Dean John Hardee—encourage creative ways of teaching. Huie Library's director Lea Ann Alexander and staff keep the shelves full of unusual resources, notably (but not only) in our impressive graphic novel reading room. David Bateman, Lecia Franklin, Carolyn Hatley, Ermatine Johnston, and Salina Smith help me and my students go all the places we need to go. Millie Bowden, Denise Cordova, Renee Davis, Sandra D. Johnson, Dylan Taylor, Connie Testa, Flora Weeks, and many other staff members make sure other essentials get done. Our faculty writers group (Angela Boswell, Matthew Bowman, Martin Halpern, Vernon Miles, David Sesser, Michael Taylor, Suzanne Tartamella, Melanie Wilson Angell) reviewed portions of this manuscript. My fellow psychology faculty members offer abundant encouragement and insights of their own: Chair Aneeq Ahmad, Rafael Bejarano, Emilie Beltzer, Rebecca Langley, Paul Williamson. Departed colleagues Marian Breland Bailey[2] (who was behaviorist B. F. Skinner's second graduate student) and Erwin Janek supported exploration and a bit of misbehavior, encouraging us to find new ways to discuss and apply psychology outside the academic world.

Starship Langley

Rebecca Manning Langley deserves the fleet's highest honors for being my colleague, sounding board, best friend, wife, and partner in all things in this universe. Our sons Nicholas and Alex each played critical roles in the journey that led to this series of books. Katrina Hill, Marko Head, and Renee Couey have, too. My parents Lynda and Travis Sr. not only let me be me when I was growing up but also encouraged my roaming imagination in more ways than they know. Cousin Michael French had *Star Trek* comic books and toys before I ever did, and he really should live closer so we can hang out and ramble on about heroes and villains today.

Starship Web

Facebook friends and a Twitter legion help us brainstorm, find facts, and have fun—including Matt Beard, Chris Murrin, Helen South, and more who have helped us confirm or refute sources and quotes. We always check original sources, and yet online databases such as Memory Alpha sometimes help us find the right episode, movie, or book. Folks at OuterPlaces.com (Kieran Dickson, Chris Mahon, Louis Monoyudis, Janey Tracey) have joined us in our excursions, and everybody at NerdSpan (Dan Yun, Ian Carter, Ashley Darling, Keith Hendricks, Iain McNally, Alex Langley, Lou Reyna, Garrett Steele, and more) deserves a salute. Because I also discovered a number of our writers from among my fellow *Psychology Today* bloggers, I thank my editor there, Kaja Perina.

Benevolent Invaders

My literary agent, Evan Gregory with the Ethan Ellenberg Literary Agency, handles many details. We thank FirstGlance Photography's Bill Ostroff and everyone who shot our author photos. Jeffrey Henderson, Dustin McGinnis, Fermina San Juan, Don and DeeDee Sims, Bethany Souza, and others serves as our writers' muses, founts of knowledge, devil's advocates, partners in crimes, and emotional support. Lesley Aletter, Bob Bailey, Eric Bailey, Nic Baisley, Ray Bradbury, Benjamin Cruz, Carrie Goldman, Clare Kramer, Ralph McKenna, Marc Nadel, Adam Savage, Darian Sisson, Chris Spatz, Dean Stockwell, David Stoddard, Michael Uslan, Dolf Zillmann, and Phil Zimbardo deserve mention for reasons diverse and sometimes hard to explain.

Travis Langley and Patrick Stewart (Captain Jean-Luc Picard) share a laugh before a Wizard World Austin Comic Con panel. Photo by Alex Langley.

Enterprising Individuals

Fans owe the thousands of people who have worked on the Star Trek franchise over the years. I'm honored to count *Deep Space Nine*'s "Dabo girl" Chase Masterson and *Star Trek* original series antagonist Lee Meriwether among my friends. (When I refer to her character as a villain, though, Lee explains why she does not call Losira evil no matter how many crew members she killed.) For sharing their thoughts and time with us, we thank them along with Scott Bakula, LeVar Burton, Jonathan Frakes, Gates McFadden (although we mainly discussed superheroes), William Shatner, Sir Patrick Stewart, and especially Nichelle Nichols and Walter Koenig. The many people we know who have continued the Trek tradition through conventions, comic books, novels, audio plays, fan films, and stage shows include Grant Imahara, Eric Scull, Michele Specht, Len Wein, Marv Wolfman, and the man who got to punch Captain Kirk, our foreword's author, Chris Gore. We thank keeper of the flame Rod Roddenberry, and we can never say enough to recognize his father, Gene Roddenberry, for sharing these voyages with us all.

References

Breland, K., & Breland, M. (1961). The misbehavior of organisms. *American Psychologist, 16*(11), 681–684.

Gillaspy, A., & Bihm, E. (2002). Marian Breland Bailey (1920–2001). *American Psychologist, 57*(4), 292–293.

Lao-Tze (n.d.). *The Tao Te Ching* (trans. F. H. Balfour). Sacred Texts: http://www.sacred-texts.com/tao/ttx/ttx02.htm.

Notes

1. "The journey of a thousand miles begins under your feet," ". . . with a foot's pace," or ". . . with a single step," depending on the translation—Lao-Tze (n.d.), sometime between the fourth and sixth centuries BCE.
2. Breland & Breland (1961); Gillaspy & Bihm (2002).

FOREWORD

A Prescription for the Final Frontier

CHRIS GORE

"We did it! We landed on the moon!"

One of my earliest memories is of hearing my dad in front of the TV scream with joy that we landed on the moon. He had a passion for NASA's mission of space exploration, along with science and computers. Dad was particularly excited about a TV show that envisioned humans traveling the galaxy and solving problems. So it's no surprise that my father's obsessions rubbed off on me as we enjoyed watching reruns of the original *Star Trek* series together when I was growing up. The conversation that followed each episode was a perfect way for Dad and I to talk about the possibility of life on other planets, the differences between right and wrong, and girls.

I grew up in the Detroit area, and my father worked in the auto industry, which was pretty common. But his job was different from those on the assembly line because it involved computers, which was very rare at the time. He often would return home from work with a box of paper punch cards used to feed data into the room-size computers at his office. As we watched that evening's original *Star Trek* series rerun, I would use those punch cards to create crayon drawings of the travels of the crew of the starship *Enterprise* along with Kirk, Spock, and McCoy. I vividly recall my father taking me to work one Saturday for a big surprise: He powered up a computer view screen as we sat down to play *Star Trek*. It was a text-based game, and I gasped as the words "You have left dry dock" appeared before my eyes. Epic adventures involving new star systems and clashes with the Klingons all took place in text form. Not only was my father my hero; he was an original nerd. In that simpler time of scheduled television viewings in the 1970s (pre–VCR/DVR/Internet), watching *Star Trek* with my dad was everything.

My parents divorced when I was nine years old, and it was reruns of *Star Trek* that helped me deal with the pain of his departure. In the absence of my father, Captain Kirk became my surrogate TV dad. The idea of feeling as if one has been "adopted" by a TV father may be more common than people imagine. In that era, divorce became the new normal, as every kid on my block seemed to have a father who all but disappeared from the family equation. If you do the math, TV screens spend almost as much time with children as actual parents do. But it was not the worst upbringing when you consider that the best episodes of Trek are filled with good role models and healthy life lessons. Captain Kirk became a father figure, and if given the order, I would follow him to the ends of the galaxy.

With all due respect to the cool factor of transporters, phasers, starships, and all the tech of Trek, at the core of every great Star Trek story is a struggle involving morality and how we deal with human emotions. For this reason, Star Trek's worldwide popularity has transcended cultural and language barriers. The debates over choices involving the correct course of action in a volatile situation help us to define who we are as individuals, as a society, and as a species in a larger, still unexplored galaxy.

I feel it's important to note that I am not a psychologist. I am just one among millions who have been profoundly affected by Star Trek. And I can personally attest to the healing power of particular episodes. If you find yourself struggling with an issue in life, you'll find solace through the characters and stories in Star Trek. By binge watching one of the many Trek series, you may even find answers to life's difficult questions. I believe it's even possible to prescribe certain Star Trek episodes to help deal with a specific challenge.

For me, the original series always had a cure for my ills. Bothered by bullies? Try watching original series episode "Shore Leave" and see Kirk deal with Finnegan, his nemesis from Starfleet Academy.[1] It's cathartic to watch Kirk best this annoying bully. Bothered by racist bullies? Watch "Balance of Terror" and notice how Kirk deals with a bigoted crew member who begins to question the loyalties of Spock.[2] If you think your wedding is going poorly, try seeing what Spock must deal with in "Amok Time."[3] Trust me, you've got it easy. If you're looking for a laugh, try "The Trouble with Tribbles," which also accurately predicted our love for all things cute in the galaxy.[4] And while a broken heart is never easy to heal, the sacrifice Kirk makes in "The City on the Edge of Forever" is a thing of beauty.[5] It may even bring you to tears.

I find almost any Star Trek episode to be a good cure for a hangover since we know it's all going to turn out fine in the end. It is just as easy to get a hangover by playing a Star Trek drinking game. Dead red shirt, drink.[6] Kirk kisses a girl, drink.[7] McCoy says, "He's dead, Jim,"[8] drink. Star Trek truly is all-purpose in its healing abilities.

In my travels I have found Star Trek fans to be thinkers, explorers, and questioners of things—basically, my kind of people. I find it easy to connect with Trek fans because I have been one since I was very young. I often think fondly about my dad, who introduced me to the show that continues to boldly go. And I believe that generations of fans are bound by our collective adoptive TV father embodied by one James T. Kirk. Through Star Trek, we are united in our passion for unraveling the larger questions of our place in the universe. We are all a part of this great exploration in the continuing human adventure . . . which is only just beginning.

Chris Gore is a writer and comedian who turned his passion for geek culture into a diverse career. He created *Film Threat*, the influential magazine and website that championed independent movies and was also the co-founder of *Sci-Fi Universe* magazine. His published works include the books *The 50 Greatest Movies Never Made* (St. Martin's Press), *The Complete DVD Book* (Michael Wiese Publications), and *The Ultimate Film Festival Survival Guide* (Random House). Chris has hosted television shows on FX, Starz, and IFC as well as appearing on G4TV's *Attack of the Show!* where he covered movies through his popular DVDuesday segment. He co-wrote and produced the feature comedy *My Big Fat Independent Movie*. Chris counts his cameo as an alien dissident who nearly kills Captain Kirk in an episode of *Star Trek Continues* as his crowning achievement as a Trek fan.

References

Bailey, M. (n.d.). *Analytics according to Captain Kirk*. Matt Bailey: http://www.sitelogic-marketing.com/analytics-according-to-captain-kirk/.

MeTV (2016, April 25). *The 19 women Kirk kissed on "Star Trek."* MeTV: http://www.metv.com/stories/video-the-19-women-kirk-kissed-on-star-trek.

Notes

1. *Star Trek* episode 1–15, "Shore Leave" (December 29, 1966).
2. *Star Trek* episode 1–14, "Balance of Terror" (December 15, 1966).
3. *Star Trek* episode 2–1, "Amok Time" (September 15, 1967).
4. *Star Trek* episode 2–15, "The Trouble with Tribbles" (December 29, 1967).
5. *Star Trek* episode 1–28, "The City on the Edge of Forever" (April 6, 1967).
6. Of the 59 crew members shown to die in the original series, 73 percent were wearing red shirts (Bailey, n.d.). The red shirt/dead crewman trope begins in *Star Trek* episode 1–7, "What Are Little Girls Made Of?" (October 20, 1966).
7. Kirk kissed 19 women during the original series (MeTV, 2016), starting with Andrea in *Star Trek* episode 1–7, "What Are Little Girls Made Of?" (October 20, 1966).
8. Variations of this begin in the first episode aired, *Star Trek* episode 1–1, "The Man Trap" (September 8, 1966). McCoy first utters the full "He's dead, Jim," in episode 1–5, "The Enemy Within" (October 5, 1966).

INTRODUCTION

A Galaxy of Lights

TRAVIS LANGLEY

"This is the light of the mind. . . ."
—poet Sylvia Plath[1]

"There are four lights!"
—Captain Jean-Luc Picard[2]

In a vacuum, light travels 186,282 miles in one second: 299,792 kilometers. We don't see Alpha Centauri, our sun's nearest neighbor among the stars, as it is now. We don't know what it is doing at this very moment. More than four years ago, it emitted the light that's reaching us today. More than 50 years ago, while Gene Roddenberry was unleashing his ground-breaking science fiction series upon our world, the gravity of a large planet orbiting the star 51 Pegasi made that star wobble in a way our instruments can detect right now. So which is reality, the stars as they were then or as they are—*if* they still are—right now? The light we see from the past is the part that affects us. Perception is reality, as they say.

Star Trek starts with stars, tiny lights in the dark void. Because a few of those lights move toward the edge of the screen like objects we're sailing past, we get a sense of moving forward through the universe before Kirk calls space "the final frontier" and the *Enterprise* zooms our way.[3] We're not moving through the stars, not in that sense, and yet visual illusions help us feel like we are—a trick of the lights. We are moving through the stars in a broader sense in that we're on a planet with a 24-hour spin as it circles a star and that star takes us through a galaxy that is itself moving through the universe, but that's not what we perceive. Watching TV, we perceive ourselves sitting in one spot. It takes the illusion, the fiction, to give us a feeling of the trek we're actually taking.

Speculative fiction (science fiction, fantasy, horror, any fiction that speculates about fantastic variations on reality) can take a harder look at life than other genres of fiction do. The original *Star Trek* explored civil rights, race relations, international relations, and complicated moral dilemmas no other show dared touch. "It appealed to people who were thinking differently," Rod Roddenberry has said of his father's creation, "whether it was college students who were protesting the war or mixed-race couples or just people with different ideas."[4] The many series, films, novels, comics, and games have tackled issues big and small, although they did not remain alone in the wilderness as other programs began doing so as well. Above all, Star Trek seeks out the human elements of life's adventure. While exploring the reaches of outer space, Star Trek always explores the humanity of our inner space.

In addition to its well-known looks at *interpersonal* relations (those between people), Star Trek also looks at *intrapersonal* knowledge of oneself. Whereas Spock regularly struggles with his human side and often seeks to suppress it, nonbiological beings would strive to achieve greater humanity: an android, a hologram, a computer. Even among the humans, characters would wrestle with themselves. What is human, and what is real? When Kirk thinks he loves a woman because the Tantalus device has implanted a *pseudomemory*, a vivid yet false recollection, he feels those emotions nonetheless.[5] When Spock thinks he has killed Kirk, he briefly lives in a personal reality in which he has slain his captain and he feels wracked with guilt until he learns that McCoy helped Kirk fake the death.[6] When an alien probe makes Picard experience a lifetime in 25 minutes, he has trouble readjusting to being captain of the *Enterprise* because in his memory, he has been away for a lifetime—and a very full lifetime at that. He has also learned to play an ancient flute proficiently—a lingering sign of how the 25-minute fiction affected his real life.[7] More than once, characters consider the possibility that holographic events have reality of their own[8] and, in a rare moment of metafiction, touch upon the possibility that their own lives are some form of fiction.[9] "Reality" can be difficult to hold on to. An interrogator attempting to break Picard's will tries to get him to say he sees five lights behind him when there are only four. Although Picard never admits this to anyone but his ship's counselor, he begins to see five.[10]

The continuing mission cycles. Its reality changes and yet retains qualities we still call Star Trek in every incarnation. Kirk, then Picard, then Sisko, and then Janeway[11] lead crews and expand their known universe before the saga goes back to an earlier time when Captain Archer begins the trek.[12] In the movies the cycle then winds up with Kirk setting foot on his *Enterprise* for the first time,[13] whereas *Star Trek: Discovery* takes the trek along an alternate path toward the original series.[14] No trek goes from A to B. Even the straightest path has different routes that lead to it, offers choices along the way, and opens onto infinite possibilities afterward. Thanks to time travelers' interference, a new Kirk played by Chris Pine may grow up differently from the original played by William Shatner, but whether we view these two Kirks' lives as alternate timelines or simply different fictions, each is as real as we let him be. He means something to us. His journey matters. Because Kirk is fictional, the Kirk in each person's head is a personal fiction. Your Kirk may not be my Kirk, each Kirk can change, and therefore the number of Kirks can exceed the number of us thinking about him or any other character.

"The brain is wider than the sky."
—poet Emily Dickinson (1830–1886)[15]

The human brain has about 100 billion cells.[16] Each *neuron* (nerve cell) functions when an electric charge of sufficient strength travels through it—lighting it up, so to speak. That many stars fill the Milky Way galaxy we inhabit.[17] At least 20 times that many galaxies make up this universe,[18] and who knows how many universes there may be? There are many lights—infinitely many, for all we know. We can look up into the starry night to behold the pinpoints of light, consider the vastness of what little we see, and contemplate how much more lies beyond. Because a person's brain has a galaxy of neurons, we might also look out as if peering at a great brain all around us and maybe get a glimmer of our own brains' cosmic potential.

The characters in Star Trek explore the Milky Way and know only portions of it, much the way we know only portions of the mysteries of the human mind. In this book, we explore these mysteries by exploring Star Trek's characters and stories. Through more than a dozen movies and the better part of a thousand television episodes, not to mention a persistent stream of novels, comic books, games, and fan fiction, Star Trek characters explore the range of human behavior itself—not only the "new frontier" that President John F. Kennedy mentioned when inspiring travel into space but the mental frontier as well.[19] The stories are always about understanding people.

"What was once the furthest outpost on the old frontier of the West will be the furthest outpost on the new frontier of science and space."
—U. S. President John F. Kennedy[20]

"Imagination frees the mind."
—Captain Kathryn Janeway[21]

References

Dickinson, E. (1863/2003). CXXVI. In M. D. Bianchi (Ed.), *The poems of Emily Dickinson*. State College, PA: Pennsylvania State University.

Hibberd, J. (2016, August 10). *Star Trek: Major details revealed about new TV show*. Entertainment Weekly: http://ew.com/article/2016/08/10/star-trek-tv-series/.

Howell, E. (2014, May 21*). How many stars are in the Milky Way?* Space: http://www.space.com/25959-how-many-stars-are-in-the-milky-way.html.

Kennedy, J. F. (1962, September 12). Speech at Rice University. Transcript at NASA: http://er.jsc.nasa.gov/seh/ricetalk.htm.

Langley, T. (2012). *Star Trek: The mental frontier*. Psychology Today: https://www.psychologytoday.com/blog/beyond-heroes-and-villains/201209/star-trek-the-mental-frontier.

Lynn, S. J., Rhue, J. W., Myers, B. P., & Weekes, J. R. (1994). Pseudomemory in hypnotized and simulating subjects. *International Journal of Clinical & Experimental Hypnosis, 42*(2), 118–129.

Maloney, D. (2013, May 13). *Star Trek's history of progressive values—and why it faltered on LGBT crew members*. Wired: http://www.wired.com/2013/05/star-trek-lgbt-gay-characters/.

Mastin, L. (2010). *Neurons & synapses*. The Human Memory: http://www.human-memory.net/brain_neurons.html.

NASA (2016, October 13*). Hubble reveals observable universe contains 10 times more galaxies than previously thought*. NASA: https://www.nasa.gov/feature/goddard/2016/hubble-reveals-observable-universe-contains-10-times-more-galaxies-than-previously-thought.

Plath, S. (1961/1983). The moon and the yew tree. In T. Hughes (Ed.), *The collected poems—Sylvia Plath* (pp. 172–173).

Notes

1. *Star Trek: The Next Generation* 6–11, "Chain of Command" part 2 (December 21, 1992).
2. Plath (1961/1981), p. 172.
3. Beginning in *Star Trek* episode 1–1, "Where No Man Has Gone Before" (September 22, 1966).
4. Maloney (2013).
5. *Star Trek* episode 1–9, "Dagger of the Mind" (November 3, 1966).
6. *Star Trek* episode 2–1, "Amok Time" (September 15, 1967).
7. *Star Trek: The Next Generation* episode 5–25, "The Inner Light" (June 1, 1992).
8. e.g., *Star Trek: The Next Generation* episode 2–3, "Elementary, My Dear Data" (December 1988); *Star Trek: Voyager* episode 5–8, "Nothing Human" (December 2, 1998).
9. *Star Trek: Deep Space Nine* episode 6–13, "Far Beyond the Stars" (February 11, 1998).
10. *Star Trek: The Next Generation* episode 6–1, "Chain of Command" part 2 (December 21, 1992).
11. Beginning, respectively, in *Star Trek* episode 1–1, "Where No Man Has Gone Before" (September 22, 1966); *Star Trek: The Next Generation* episode 1–1, "Encounter at Farpoint" (September 28, 1987); *Star Trek: Deep Space Nine* episode 1–1, "Emissary" (January 3, 1993); *Star Trek: Voyager* episode 1–1, "Caretaker" (January 16, 1995).

12. *Enterprise* episode 1–1, "Broken Bow," part 1 (September 26, 2001).
13. *Star Trek* (2009 motion picture).
14. Dickinson (1863/2003), p. 74.
15. Hibberd (2016).
16. Mastin (2010).

17. Howell (2014).
18. NASA (2016).
19. Langley (2012).
20. Kennedy (1962).
21. *Star Trek: Voyager* episode 5–6, "Timeless" (November 18, 1998).

Left to right in foreground: NASA administrator Dr. James D. Fletcher, DeForest Kelley (who played Dr. Leonard "Bones" McCoy), George Takei (Mr. Sulu), James Doohan (Chief Engineer Montgomery "Scotty" Scott), Nichelle Nichols (Lt. Uhura), Leonard Nimoy (Mr. Spock), Star Trek creator Gene Roddenberry, U. S. Rep. Don Fuqua, and Walter Koenig (Ensign Pavel Chekov) with the space shuttle *Enterprise* in 1976. Source: NASA.

The ship sets sail, whether across waters or through the void between stars, every voyage a mystery and no two voyages the same. Explorers ready themselves to brave tempests and monsters of the deep between islands or between worlds, but why?

I

LAUNCH TIME

We explore environments, experiences, and ideas. What drives us to venture out in the first place, and why are some more ready than others to go forth? Do our rewards for exploration come from outside ourselves or from within?

•1•

Why We Go: The Psychology of Exploration in Star Trek

CLAY ROUTLEDGE

"They used to say that if man was meant to fly, he'd have wings. But he did fly. He discovered he had to."
—James Kirk[1]

". . . an endless series of daily choices and decisions in each of which one can choose to go back toward safety or forward toward growth. Growth must be chosen again and again; fear must be overcome again and again."
—psychologist Abraham Maslow[2]

We are explorers by nature. As a species, humans are curious, creative, and hungry for novelty. We want to learn more about the world around us and ourselves. Exploration is a fundamental part of human psychology. That being said, our explorative nature does not always come easy and is not without psychological cost. Star Trek provides an excellent platform for fans to consider the complexities of the psychology of exploration. Star Trek has always been about exploration—and not just space exploration but also exploring different cultures and ideas, and even turning inward and exploring one's own assumptions about the world and our deepest fears.

The Multifaceted Nature of Exploration

The crew of each *Enterprise* is charged with a mission to explore new worlds. Leaving on such a journey into the unknown is how people typically think about exploration. To explore means to physically go somewhere that you have not been before, right? Well, yes. That is one kind of exploration. But, for psychologists, exploration is much more complex. For example, according to psychologists Jeff Green and Keith Campbell, there are three different types of exploration: environmental, social, and intellectual.[3]

Environmental exploration is what most people typically call to mind when they think about exploration. It involves people's interest in exploring the physical world around them, which could include traveling abroad or something as simple as finding a new trail to hike. Humans settled a good portion of our planet because of this attraction to environmental exploration. If we were not explorers of the environment by nature, our ancestors may have never left Africa.

This inherent motive to want to know what is beyond that next ridge is also the reason humans want to explore outer space. Most of us won't likely get to travel to new worlds, but our attraction to this type of environmental exploration is a common theme in science fiction. When Kirk takes on a new life as a Starfleet admiral, overseeing training instead of captaining a ship and exploring space, his good friend Dr. McCoy knows that Kirk is best suited to be an explorer and pleads with him to get a new command and get back out exploring space in a starship before it is too late.[4] Fans identify with Kirk because as humans we understand the attraction to environmental exploration.

On the surface, Star Trek may seem primarily about environmental exploration because it so prominently features ships traveling through space on missions to seek out new worlds. However, as most fans can attest, Star Trek is as focused—or even more focused—on social exploration and intellectual exploration.[5] *Social exploration* concerns people's desire to experience new relationships and interpersonal experiences. This might involve making new friends, attending parties or other social events even though you do not know many people there, or striking up a conversation with a stranger on the bus or plane. *Intellectual exploration* refers to people's desire to think about and experience new theories, ideas, and traditions. This might involve learning about different cultures or taking a class on a topic that interests you but that you know little about.

Star Trek's emphasis on social and intellectual exploration is evidenced by the mission statement, which says the mission is not only to "explore strange new worlds" (environmental exploration) but also to "seek out new life, new civilizations."[6] In other words, the goal is to explore new social connections with other intelligent life forms and alternative ways of thinking about the world.

Many psychologists have argued that humans are social animals with a powerful need to belong.[7] As an android who does not experience emotion (until he eventually gets the emotion chip[8]) but endeavors to be more humanlike, Data continuously seeks out opportunities to experience different kinds of relationships. He understands that social exploration

Exploring Death in the *Kobayashi Maru*

The *Kobayashi Maru*, a simulation exercise that Starfleet officer cadets participate in during their training, involves a no-win situation in which there is no way to save their ship from destruction or their crew from death.[9] So what is the value of such a simulation? Research on *posttraumatic growth*[10] suggests that the *Kobayashi Maru* may help to promote psychological health and resilience. Posttraumatic growth is positive psychological change that can result from struggling with highly challenging, traumatic life crises. People forced to cope with loss and the prospect of death often later report a greater sense of meaning, respect for life, and personal strength.[11] Because most people prefer to avoid thinking about loss and death, simulations such as the *Kobayashi Maru* may be valuable because they force participants to confront these existential fears. Therapists use imagination exercises (e.g., *imaginal exposure therapy* in which clients imagine facing aversive stimuli[12]) because confronting fears may ultimately make people mentally stronger with a greater appreciation for life.

is a crucial component of being human. For instance, Data unsuccessfully attempts to pursue a romantic relationship with his shipmate, Jenna D'Sora, in a uniquely android way—by creating a romantic relationship subroutine.[13] The unique benefit of being an android is that when Data gets dumped, he simply has to delete the subroutine.

When humans lack social relationships or feel socially excluded and lonely, they suffer from various forms of psychological distress and are likely to engage in maladaptive behavior.[14] Specifically, loneliness is a major risk factor for depression and anxiety.[15] In addition, experiences of social exclusion, such as being rejected by friends, increase feelings of meaninglessness and hostility and decrease self-control as well as empathy toward others.[16] Social exploration is important for psychological health; it helps people forge new social connections and thus reduces the likelihood of loneliness and feelings of exclusion. While Data may not be able to appreciate the emotional consequences of failing to connect with others, he understands that social exploration is an important part of what it means to be human.

Star Trek: The Next Generation provides an excellent and humorous example of intellectual exploration when, as part of an officer-exchange program, Commander Riker is assigned as first officer of a Klingon ship. To fit in with his new Klingon crew, Riker must explore and embrace various aspects of Klingon culture, including establishing respect through physical violence and eating exotic foods, such as bregit lung and rokeg blood pie. Riker does his best.

What Drives Exploration?

Motivation

What makes people want to explore in the first place? Humans might be explorers because we are naturally curious and psychological research has revealed quite a bit about the inherent nature of human curiosity. *Curiosity* is the "recognition, pursuit, and intense desire to explore novel, challenging, and uncertain events."[17] Psychologists also assert that curiosity is intrinsically motivated. *Intrinsic motivation* involves people doing something because they find it personally enjoyable and fulfilling and not because of an external motivator such as money or social pressure.

Self-reported curiosity correlates positively with happiness and other indicators of psychological well-being, such as how satisfied people say they are with their lives.[18] It feels good to be curious. Psychologists also argue that curiosity is an important driver of personal growth.[19] From this perspective, human exploration is a fundamental component of cognitive and emotional development.

Star Trek affirms this view of exploration as intrinsically motivated and important for personal growth. The Federation does not use money, so starship crew members are explorers because they are intrinsically motivated and desire to learn and grow, not because they seek economic gain. Captain Picard attempts to explain this idea to a man from the twentieth century who had been recently awakened from cryogenic suspension by saying, "We have eliminated hunger, want, the need for possessions."[20] They seek *intrinsic rewards*, experiences they can value for the sake of the experiences themselves, instead of *extrinsic rewards* that would simply help them get something else.

Personality

Humans may be explorers by nature, but, like other psychological traits, the proclivity to explore varies from person to person. The personality factor that best captures this individual difference in exploration is *openness to experience*. Openness to experience, or what psychologists sometimes simply refer to as openness, is considered one of the core dimensions of personality, along with *extraversion*, *neuroticism*, *conscientiousness*, and *agreeableness*.[21] Openness reflects the extent to which people are adventurous and interested in new ideas and experiences. People who enjoy traveling, meeting people from diverse backgrounds, trying new foods, learning new languages, and starting new hobbies tend to rank high on openness and thus are likely natural explorers.

Captain Picard, for example, constantly strives to learn about and experience new cultures. He expresses open-mindedness when confronted with an idea or tradition that he is unfamiliar with and may even find disagreeable, and he regularly encourages his crew to do the same. This trait helps make him an excellent starship captain. A more lighthearted example of Picard's desire for open-mindedness among his crew occurs when Worf protests the unique cultural tradition of a Betazoid wedding involving all attendants being nude. Picard, in contrast, proclaims that all crew members who attend will follow the tradition.[22]

Some people are less naturally disposed to exploration. Those who prefer routines and become anxious when thinking about trying something different tend to be low on openness. Dr. McCoy may be low on openness, certainly lower than Kirk or Picard, and thus does not have a strong disposition for exploration. McCoy is often portrayed as being fearful of adventure. In fact, psychologists might describe him as being high in *neuroticism*, a trait reflecting someone who chronically worries or is generally anxious.[23] Neuroticism correlates negatively with curiosity and exploration.[24] Dr. McCoy's aversion to exploration is beautifully captured by a statement he makes to Kirk regarding his anxiety about space travel: "Space is disease and danger wrapped in darkness and silence."[25]

Psychological Barriers to Exploration

Ask any developmental psychologist how babies and children learn and that psychologist will emphasize the importance of exploration for cognitive, social, and emotional development. Once human babies become mobile, they typically turn into little adventurers with a strong desire to discover the world around them. As kids get older, they engage in more social and intellectual exploration through formal education and more informally by experimenting with different types of social roles and interactions. However, there are mental states that reduce people's desire to go out and experience new things.

Fear and anxiety are perhaps the biggest mental roadblocks to exploration. Studies show that higher levels of anxiety are associated with lower levels of environmental, social, and intellectual exploration.[26] Research also indicates that fear-evoking experiences, such as thinking about death or terrorism, decrease exploratory behavior.[27] The character Reginald Barclay's fear of transporters keeps him from going on a mission that requires transporter travel to a planet, until he ultimately receives help confronting his fear from ship counselor Deanna Troi and Transporter Chief O'Brian.[28]

Because fear and anxiety undermine exploration, infants and adults are most inclined to explore when they feel safe and secure.[29] According to *attachment theory*, close relational bonds provide people with the psychological security needed to facilitate exploration. Indeed, infants and toddlers are most likely to explore their environment when they have a *secure attachment style*, which reflects a close bond with a primary caregiver that is established by the caregiver acting as a reliable source of comfort when the child is emotionally or physically distressed.[30] Similarly, adults report high levels of environmental, social, and intellectual exploration if they score high on secure adult attachment, which is the extent to which people perceive relationship partners as sources of emotional comfort and psychological security.[31]

The assertion advanced by attachment theory that the security provided by close relational bonds promotes exploration is echoed in Star Trek. Starship crews act like families. They spend years in close proximity, living, working, and socializing together. Life aboard a starship such as the *Enterprise* involves uncertainty and risk. The *Enterprise* regularly investigates previously unexplored cosmic phenomena and travels to worlds inhabited by life that is unfamiliar to and sometimes hostile toward the ship's crew. The close relationships crew mates enjoy provide the secure psychological foundation needed for the crew to complete their mission and explore.

Truth in Trek

Humans are naturally motivated to explore. It is in our DNA. The mandate of Starfleet exemplifies this aspect of human nature. Starfleet is, at its core, about exploration and thus, in terms of capturing the psychology of exploration, Star Trek gets it right. Some people are more inclined to explore than others. These people are high in traits related to openness to experience. Different Star Trek characters illustrate this individual difference. There are also situations that diminish our tendency to explore. When we are anxious or afraid, we tend not to seek out new experiences. In Star Trek, the universe can be a scary place. Uncertainty and death are everywhere. But, like real humans, the characters in Star Trek often overcome their fears and find the mental fortitude to move forward.

References

Baumeister, R. F., Brewer, L. E., Tice, D. M., & Twenge, J. M. (2007). Thwarting the need to belong: Understanding the interpersonal and inner effects of social exclusion. *Social and Personality Psychology Compass, 1*(1), 506–520.

Baumeister, R. F., & Leary, M. (1995). The need to belong: Desire for interpersonal attachments as a fundamental human motivation. *Psychological Bulletin, 117*(3), 497–529.

Bowlby, J. (1988). *A secure base: Parent-child attachment and healthy human development.* London, UK: Routledge.

Cacioppo, J. T., Hughes, M. E., Waite, L. J., Hawkley, L. C., & Thisted, R.A. (2006). Loneliness as a specific risk factor for depressive symptoms: Cross-sectional and longitudinal analyses. *Psychology & Aging, 21*(1), 140–151.

Freedman, S. A., Hoffman, H. G., Garcia-Palacio, A., Weiss, P. L., Avitzour, S., &

Josman, N. (2010). Prolonged exposure and virtual reality–enhanced imaginal exposure for PTSD following a terrorist bulldozer attack: A case study. *Cyberpsychology, Behavior, & Social Networking, 13*(1), 95–101.

Green, J. D., & Campbell, K. W. (2000). Attachment and exploration in adults: Chronic and contextual accessibility. *Personality & Social Psychological Bulletin, 26*(4), 452–461.

Kashdan, R. B., Rose, P., & Fincham, F. D. (2004). Curiosity and exploration: Facilitating positive subjective experiences and personal growth opportunities. *Journal of Personality Assessment, 82*(3), 291–305.

Kashdan, T. B., & Silvia, P. J. (2009). Curiosity and interest: The benefits of thriving on novelty and challenge. In S. J. Lopez and C. R. Snyder (Eds.), *The Oxford handbook of positive psychology* (pp. 367–374). New York, NY: Oxford University Press.

Maslow, A. H. (1966). *The psychology of science: A reconnaissance.* New York, NY: Harper & Row.

McCrae, R. R., & Costa, R. T. (1990). *Personality in adulthood.* New York, NY: Guilford.

Routledge, C., Juhl, J., & Vess, M. (2010). Divergent reactions to the terror of terrorism: Personal need for structure moderates the effects of terrorism salience on worldview-related attitudinal rigidity. *Basic & Applied Social Psychology, 32*(3), 243–249.

Tarrier, N., & Humphreys, L. (2000). Subjective improvement in PTSD patients with treatment by imaginal exposure cognitive therapy: Session by session changes. *British Journal of Clinical Psychology, 39*(1), 27–34.

Tedeschi, R. G., & Calhoun, L. G. (2004). Posttraumatic growth: Conceptual foundations and empirical evidence. *Psychological Inquiry, 15*(1), 1018.

Notes

1. *Star Trek* episode 2–20, "Return to Tomorrow" (February 9, 1968).
2. Maslow (1966), p. 22.
3. Green & Campbell (2000).
4. *Star Trek II: The Wrath of Khan* (1982 motion picture).
5. Green & Campbell (2000).
6. Starting with *Star Trek* episode 1–03, "Where No Man Has Gone Before" (September 22, 1966).
7. e.g., Baumeister & Leary (1995).
8. *Star Trek: Generations* (1994 motion picture).
9. *Star Trek II: The Wrath of Khan* (1982 motion picture); Star Trek (2009 motion picture).
10. Tedeschi & Calhoun (2004).
11. Tedeschi & Calhoun (2004).
12. Freedman et al. (2010); Tarrier & Humphreys (2000).
13. *Star Trek: The Next Generation* episode 4–25, "In Theory" (June 3, 1991).
14. Baumeister et al. (2007).
15. Cacioppo et al. (2006).
16. Baumeister et al. (2007).
17. Kashdan & Silvia (2009).
18. Kashdan et al. (2004).
19. Kashdan & Silvia (2009).
20. *Star Trek: The Next Generation* episode 1–26, "The Neutral Zone" (May 16, 1988).
21. McCrae & Costa (1990).
22. *Star Trek: Nemesis* (2002 motion picture).

23. McCrae & Costa (1990).
24. Kashdan et al. (2004).
25. Star Trek (2009 motion picture).
26. Green & Campbell (2000).
27. Routledge et al. (2010).
28. *Star Trek: The Next Generation* episode 6–2, "Realm of Fear" (October 11, 1992).
29. Green & Campbell (2000).
30. Bowlby (1988).
31. Green & Campbell (2000).

Trying to deter bullying may be less effective than trying to build heroes in everyday life. Either attempt at intervention carries challenges. At what point is it best to keep out of other people's affairs, and when should we step in? Psychology is surprisingly short on research into bullying and heroism, but does offer lessons on how to stop standing by.

•2•

Bullies, Heroes, and the Bystander Directive: Barriers in Exploring What Brings Out the Best and Worst in Us

Travis Langley

"You were innocent bystanders for decades as the Cardassians took our homes, as they violated and tortured our people in the most hideous ways imaginable. As we were forced to flee."

—Bajoran refugee Keeve Falor to Captain Picard[1]

"If you are neutral in situations of injustice, you have chosen the side of the oppressor. If an elephant has its foot on the tail of a mouse and you say you are neutral, the mouse will not appreciate your neutrality."

—Bishop Desmond Tutu[2]

Bullies bad, heroes good—simple enough, right? Then why don't we have more empirical evidence showing us how to reduce bullying and promote heroism? There is some solid research, to be sure, but too little in light of how much importance people assign to these issues. Star Trek has often played out stories of bullies and heroes on an interstellar scale—"bullies" possibly being more accurate than "villains" for many of the franchise's antagonists, given how many believe themselves to be in the right. Despite difficulties putting ideas about bullies and heroes to a scientific test, we may gain some insights about both from what researchers have learned about bystanders.

Bullying

People debate the effectiveness of anti-bullying programs.[3] One study of seven thousand teens attending nearly two hundred schools found that those attending schools that implemented bullying prevention programs experienced *more* peer victimization, rather than less, which some interpreted as meaning the anti-bullying efforts were making things worse.[4] That interpretation might be a mistake. The mere fact that variables coincide does not prove that either causes the other. Looking at a *correlation*, a statistic identifying that variables are related, does not reveal how that relationship is created. "Correlation is not causality," Spock points out to *Enterprise* crew members in a 1970s educational PSA.[5] Maybe variable A (anti-bullying program) somehow caused variable B (the bullying), but maybe B caused A. Having a higher-than-average number of potential bullies at a school might be what prompts the bullying prevention efforts in the first place. Knowing which one happened first, though, still does not reveal that one caused the other. As Spock adds, "Just because one event follows another on a number of occasions does not mean the first event caused the second."[6] Some other factor (variable C) may have caused both. More likely, though, many other factors played a role in both elevating the levels of bullying and inspiring anti-bullying efforts. In some cases, there may only be an *illusory correlation*,[7] in which variables that seem related really are not. Among other things, bullying awareness efforts may simply increase the number of reports of bullying.

Most of the evidence regarding bullying must be correlational, however, due to the ethical and practical difficulties in conducting experiments to determine which variables cause bullying. Experimentally assigning one-third of students to watch pro-bullying videos, one-third to watch anti-bullying videos, and one-third (the *control group*, as opposed to the two *experimental groups*) to watch a video on an unrelated topic would be dangerous, ill-advised, and potentially grounds for legal action. "Genuine research takes time," Dr. Beverly Crusher says when admonishing a doctor whose medical experiments endanger lives, "sometimes a lifetime of painstaking, detailed work in order to get any results."[8]

One of the most bullied characters in any Star Trek series may be *Star Trek: Deep Space Nine*'s Rom, the unassertive Ferengi whose brother Quark regularly berates him. Despite his strengths and talents, Rom often appears—like many victims of emotional abuse[9]—to be anxious, unhappy, unconfident, and low in self-esteem.[10] Not every abused, bullied, or otherwise mistreated person internalizes the experience or relives the suffering, but plenty do.[11] Overcoming these difficulties can be hard without changes in circumstances, and is complicated by the fact that the sheer experience of being victimized alters the victim's brain, even if abuse is not physical.[12] Repeatedly failing in efforts to get the bullying to stop can train the person to feel powerless (*learned helplessness*) and give up. Encouragement from others can help (as Kirk apparently believes every time he encourages the local population to stand up to those who would oppress them[13]). Even among those who suffer the worst, though, plenty rise up and grow and become healthy, successful people.[14] In time, Rom stands up

Bullied, Brave, and Beautiful Inside

I'm grateful that Leeta and Rom's story line was so popular and is so enduring with the fans. I think the reason is that Leeta and Rom's love is a very Star Trek story. We all want to be seen for who we really are inside, to be acknowledged as being worthy of love and of cherishing, despite those who might brand us as unworthy, not socially skilled enough or accomplished enough or pretty enough or smart enough or cool enough. It hurts when the world judges, invalidates, and dismisses us.

And then when someone comes along and sees who we really are, and sees the goodness buried deep inside that pain, suddenly there is hope. And within that hope, beautiful things happen, and we grow and gain confidence and accomplish amazing things in the light of love. Rom was always brave, deep down, but when he was oppressed by Quark, his courage was hidden, even from himself.[15] Leeta saw in Rom what he couldn't see in himself, and she loved him unflinchingly, standing up for him and their love even in the toughest of times.[16] Rom was pretty enough on the inside that Leeta loved—and was wildly attracted to—his outside, too.[17] And Rom loved Leeta in a pure way, also wanting to give and not just take, unlike so many people Leeta had encountered, especially given that she had escaped from occupied Bajor.[18]

Watching Rom, we learn that underdogs can win. That if, right now, you're feeling like the kid brother who always gets the short end of the deal—but you have a good heart and truly care about doing the right things—there may be love and respect and life better than you ever dreamed, just around the corner. Leeta and Rom's story is a message of hope, and Star Trek is about hope.

—Chase Masterson
(Leeta on *Star Trek: Deep Space Nine*)

for both himself and others,[19] proves he can be heroic,[20] marries the bar's bright and beautiful Dabo girl, Leeta,[21] and rises to a position of importance among the Ferengi people.[22]

One reason some anti-bullying efforts might be less successful than hoped for may be that focusing on stopping bullying stresses the bullying itself. A discussion about that very concern during a New York Comic Con anti-bullying panel led *Deep Space Nine*'s Chase Masterson and her fellow co-founders of the Pop Culture Anti-Bullying Coalition to transform the organization into the Pop Culture Hero Coalition.[23] When programs only look at how to oppose bullying, they may fail to promote more positive behaviors. Like *authoritarian parenting*, a rigid "zero tolerance" style of disciplining children, it emphasizes the negative rather than the positive. A rigid authoritarian approach may teach rigidity and aggressiveness, fostering the potential to bully.[24] *Authoritative parenting*, on the other hand, also exerts discipline but with tolerance, patience, and instruction on what to do, not just what not to do.[25] *Permissive parenting*, in which parents are involved without exerting discipline or control, and *uninvolved parenting*, in which parents do not interact much with their children, offer no lessons for preventing bullying and fail to curtail the escalation of impulsive aggression, thereby allowing children to become bullies.[26] Perhaps the most extreme case of a child who has received permissive parenting in Star Trek is the bratty Trelane, who has been raised as a spoiled child and lives on a planet constructed for his own amusement. Permissive parenting having allowed him to turn into a bully, Trelane manipulates Kirk and his crew with his seemingly unlimited power until others of his own race finally intervene much later than they should have.[27]

Heroism

Heroic acts might not be any easier to study than bullying. *Heroism* (pro-social behavior that voluntarily turns values and ideals into action despite personal risk[28]) often must be investigated after the fact. Creating an experimental situation with enough *experimental realism* (getting participants to engage in psychological processes during an experiment similar to those they'd experience in other situations) to see who would rise to the occasion during a crisis poses serious ethical problems. *Deception*, deliberately misleading participants, may be involved. Someone who knows the crisis is not real may not be any more worried than someone enjoying a holodeck adventure (that is, until the safety protocols fail yet again).

Two prominent psychologists turned the focus of their work from looking at the dark side of human nature to the light. Martin E. P. Seligman, known for studying the causes and consequences of learned helplessness,[29] founded *positive psychology* on the belief that psychology overemphasizes the worst parts of human nature to the neglect of trying to understand the best.[30] While other science fiction franchises might view humankind with cynicism and pessimism, focusing on the worst human qualities and the failure of human systems, Star Trek spotlights strengths that positive psychologists look for in us all (wisdom, courage, justice, temperance, transcendence, humanity itself[31]). Soon, Philip Zimbardo—best known for his prison simulation study, which showed how the situation could bring out cruelty in a number of participants[32]—launched the Heroic Imagination Project so that he, too, might investigate the better side of human nature.[33]

Heroism is more than helping. Helping is an important part of it, to be sure. Captain Kirk tells social worker Edith Keeler that a "classic" twenty-first-century novel follows the theme of offering help.[34] Kirk, however, must choose between allowing McCoy to help Keeler herself by saving her life or going to heroic lengths to make sure she dies in order to restore history and save the lives of millions (as discussed in the sidebar, "Psychology's Final Frontier: Understanding Heroism"). Many studies in psychology have investigated *altruism* (helping others at a cost or risk to oneself[35]) and our views on it, but the field has barely explored[36] the overlapping yet more complex concept of heroism.

Heroes can be distinguished by many criteria. For example, is the person called to be a hero because of morality (e.g., saints) or competence (e.g., sports stars)? Many fantastic heroes, like

Psychology's Final Frontier: Understanding Heroism

Dr. McCoy accidentally injects himself with a chemical that causes *paranoid psychosis* (severe loss of contact with reality). Subsequently traveling through time to 1930, delusional McCoy disrupts events in a way that will erase all Starfleet achievements from history unless Kirk and Spock can restore the timeline, and that restoration will require a tragic cost.[37] Transcending loss and adhering to principle in the face of crisis are foundations of heroic action.[38] A *heroic stance* informs every encounter, even if the crew's stories—any record of their existence—might be lost to the nameless void.

In response to World War II, twentieth-century psychologists often focused on understanding evil. While Joseph Campbell and others explored heroism using mythic and narrative psychology,[39] relatively few researchers studied the extreme good in human nature using empirical methods. This has changed with recent studies on heroism that differentiate it from other topics like altruism.[40] *Everyday heroism*, the idea that anyone can be a hero if prepared to act in crises, was introduced along with the notion that we have to foster a "heroic imagination" in ourselves.[41] Stories like the award-winning episode "The City on the Edge of Forever" offer just such a chance to consider how we would act when faced with the profound unknown. A large part of this heroic stance involves the ability to transcend fear and act based on a principle-driven or existential view of life: By preserving our ideals, our lives are meaningful even in the face of death.

—Zeno Franco

James Kirk and Hoshi Sato, embody both, regardless of areas where they could improve, but real-life figures can, too.[42] One criterion that figures into how a potential hero deals with bullies or avoids being a mere bystander is whether that person acts *reactively* (responding to circumstances as they arise, spontaneously, in the moment) or *proactively* (choosing to take action without waiting for a crisis to force a decision).[43] When delusional Dr. McCoy rushes to save Edith Keeler from being killed by a car in 1930, this is *reactive heroism*. After Spock and Kirk travel back to a point several days earlier, Spock says that they must prevent Dr. McCoy from saving her in order to restore the timeline and save many millions of lives—a plan for *proactive heroism.*[44] Proactively heroic acts do not all end in that kind of tragedy, of course. In one example among so many, Irena Sendler saved some 2,500 lives by proactively organizing a network to rescue Jewish children from the Warsaw ghetto.[45] Starfleet personnel who intervene in other people's fates to such a great extent, however, can find themselves in trouble for violating the Federation's first rule to avoid interfering—the Prime Directive.[46]

Standing By

Should technically developed cultures share their advancements with aboriginal peoples or even make contact with them in the first place? The risks may be great either way. Outside intervention can be horrible, such as when European exploration of the New World led to millions of deaths through disease, deprivation, and outright murder.[47] And yet outside intervention can be good. Consider how many millions of lives have been saved throughout the world by helping underdeveloped countries fight disease, famine, and pestilence of many kinds.[48] Which risk should we take? Starfleet and the Federation of Planets are supposed to abide by the Prime Directive as their guiding principle, a noninterference policy prohibiting interference in the social, cultural, and technological development of alien civilizations.[49] The Prime Directive allows its members to study other civilizations but mandates that they act as uninvolved observers of those civilizations' progress or even their downfall.[50] In essence, it orders them to be bystanders.

"The opposite of a hero isn't a villain; it's a bystander," asserts educator Matt Langdon,[51] who teaches pro-heroism (originally anti-bullying) workshops[52] and co-founded the Pop Culture

Hero Coalition with Chase Masterson and Carrie Goldman.[53] One of the phenomena most studied in social psychology, *bystander apathy* refers to people's frequent inaction and failure to help when help is needed.[54] Social psychologists have explored a wide range of situational influences (e.g., number of people present, familiarity with the person in need, previous assumption of responsibility[55]) and emotions (e.g., guilt, depression[56]) that can raise or lower the likelihood that anyone will step in.

Norms of helping make a difference as well. When the standard of behavior with a team or other group includes an expectation that helping is good, members of that team—or specific starship crew—may become more likely to help.[57] Kirk breaks the Prime Directive on numerous occasions, interpreting it loosely whenever he wants to help people, even though he values the directive's essential principle above his own life.[58] Because Kirk often discusses the issues with his crew when weighing whether or not to bend the rules,[59] involving them in the process creates a norm among themselves in which they accept that the Prime Directive will get violated. Norms change over time, though. Decades later, Picard considers the Prime Directive to be imperative because history has "proven again and again that whenever mankind interferes with a less developed civilization, no matter how well intentioned that interference may be, the results are invariably disastrous."[60]

Standing Up

Who will help and who will not? Before a particular situation arises, we might not know that even about ourselves. In the course of studying how to get people to stop being bystanders and become heroes, whether to prevent bullying or to help in other situations, Zimbardo came to see that people have to prepare for heroism, anticipate opportunities to be heroic, recognize them when they come, and do something about it—to be what psychologist Philip Zimbardo calls "heroes in waiting," waiting for the right moment, even if it only happens once in a lifetime.[61] He and other heroism researchers call on people to stand up, speak out, and take action, to become *positive deviants* by stepping apart from the crowd to do the right thing.[62]

Was Kirk more of a "hero in waiting" than Picard or Janeway because he seemed more ready to break rules to help others?[63] By adhering to a noninterference norm, might the later ones be better prepared to stay uninvolved?[64] A well-developed habit can be difficult to overcome when a situation requires a quick decision. Those who maintain a heroism heuristic, a mental shortcut of readiness to act heroically, may indeed be the greater "heroes in waiting." People who follow heuristics tend to be more effective in addressing problems that require quick answers, but then again, they also make more mistakes at other times. Action can be a mistake, but so can inaction. Which mistake do we risk making?

> *"I think you can't judge people by what they think or say—only by what they do."*
>
> —Kira Nerys[65]

> *"To be a hero, you have to learn to be a deviant, because you're always going against the conformity of the group. Heroes are ordinary people whose social actions are extraordinary. Who act."*
>
> —psychologist Philip Zimbardo[66]

References

Allison, S. T., & Goethals, G. R. (2011). *Heroes: What they do & why we need them.* New York, NY: Oxford University Press.

Ayenibiowo, K. O. (2011). Psychopathology of bullying and emotional abuse among school children. *IFE Psychologia, 19*(2), 127–141.

Baek, T. H., & Reid, L. N. (2013). The interplay of mood and regulatory focus in influencing altruistic behavior. *Psychology & Marketing, 30(8)*, 635–646.

Baldry, A. C., & Farrington, D. P. (2000). Bullies and delinquents: Personal characteristics and parental styles. *Journal of Community & Applied Social Psychology, 10*(1), 17–31.

Baumrind, D. (1966). Effects of authoritative parental control on child behavior. *Child Development, 37*(4), 887–907.

Baumrind, D. (1991). The influence of parenting style on adolescent competence and substance use. *Journal of Early Adolescence, 11*(1), 56–95.

Becker, S. W., & Eagly, A. H. (2004). The heroism of women and men. *American Psychologist, 59*(3), 163–178.

Brackett, M., & Divecha, D. (2013, September 6). *School anti-bullying programs ineffective.* Courant: http://www.courant.com/opinion/hc-op-brackett-school-bullying-programs-ineffectiv-20130906-story.html.

Brown, R. M. (1984). *Unexpected news: Reading the Bible with third world eyes.* Louisville, KY: Westminster John Knox Press.

Calvete, E. (2014). Emotional abuse as a predictor of early maladaptive schemas in adolescents: Contributions to the development of depressive and social anxiety symptoms. *Child Abuse & Neglect, 38*(4), 735–746.

Campbell, J. (1949). *The hero with a thousand faces.* Princeton, NJ: Princeton University Press.

Chakrabortty, A. (2010, March 8). *Brainfood: The psychology of heroism.* The Guardian: http://www.theguardian.com/science/2010/mar/09/brain-food-psychology-heroism.

Chao, R. K. (1994). Beyond parental control and authoritarian parenting style: Understanding Chinese parenting through the cultural notion of training. *Child Development, 65*(4), 1111–1119.

Clint, E. (2012, November 4). *The Prime Directive: Star Trek's doctrine of moral laziness.* Skeptic Link: http:// skepticink.com/incredulous/2012/11/04/the-prime-directive-star-treks-doctrine-of-moral-laziness/.

Duimering, P. R., & Robinson, R. B. (2007). Situational influences on team helping norms: Case study of a self-directed team. *Journal of Behavioral & Applied Management, 9*(1), 62–87.

Ellis, A., & Powers, M. G. (2000). *The secret of overcoming verbal abuse: Getting off the emotional roller coaster and regaining control of your life.* Chatsworth, CA: Wilshire.

Emdin, C. (2011, October 18). *5 reasons why current anti-bullying initiatives don't work.* Huffington Post: http://www.huffingtonpost.com/christopher-emdin/5-reasons-why-antibully in_b_1017810.html.

Espelage, D. L. (2012). Foreword. In C. Goldman (Author), *Bullied: What every parent, teacher, and kid needs to know about ending the cycle of fear* (pp. ix–x). New York, NY: HarperOne.

Farsides, T., Pettman, D., & Tourle, L. (2013). Inspiring altruism: Reflecting on the personal relevance of emotionally evocative prosocial media characters. *Journal of Applied Social Psychology, 43*(11), 2251–2258.

Forward, S. (2002). *Toxic parents: Overcoming their hurtful legacy and reclaiming your life.* New York, NY: Bantam.

Franco, Z. E., Blau, K., & Zimbardo, P. G. (2011). Heroism: A conceptual analysis and differentiation between heroic action and altruism. *Review of General Psychology, 15*(2), 99.

Franco, Z., & Zimbardo, P. (2006). The banality of heroism. *Greater Good, 3*(2), 30–35.

Gatto, J., Hartley, A., Langdon, M., Langley, T., Eckstein, A., Vega, E., Goldman, C., & Masterson, C. (2014, October). *End bullying now! Responding to cruelty in our culture.* New York Comic Con, New York, NY.

Georgiou, S. N. (2008). Parental style and child bullying and victimization experiences at school. *School Psychology of Education, 11*(3), 213–227.

Goldman, C. (2012). *Bullied: What every parent, teacher, and kid needs to know about ending the cycle of fear.* New York, NY: HarperOne.

Graham, S., & Juvonen, J. (1998). Self-blame and peer victimization in middle school: An attributional analysis. *Developmental Psychology, 34*(3), 587–599.

Grant, A. M., & Patil, S. V. (2012). Challenging the norm of self-interest: Minority influence and transitions to helping norms in work units. *Academy of Management Review, 37*(4), 547–568.

Harris, M. B. (1977). Effects of altruism on mood. *Journal of Social Psychology, 102*(2), 197–208.

Hauser, D. (n.d.). *Logical thinking.* Guide to Animated Star Trek: http://www.danhausertrek.com/AnimatedSeries/Logic.html.

Hero Construction Company (2015, January 21). *Philip Zimbardo and Matt Langdon at the Hero Round Table 2014.* https://www.youtube.com/watch?v=ujtkIaAfiSM.

Infurna, M. R., Reichi, C., Parzer, P., Schimmenti, A., Bifulco, A., & Kaess, M. (2016). Associations between depression and specific childhood experiences of abuse and neglect: A meta-analysis. *Journal of Affective Disorders, 190*(1), 47–55.

Jeong, S., & Lee, B. H. (2013). A multilevel examination of peer victimization and bullying preventions in schools. *Journal of Criminology,* article 735397. http://www.hindawi.com/journals/jcrim/2013/735397/.

Kaufmann, D., Gesten, E., Santa Lucia, R. C., Salsedo, O., Gobioff, G. R., & Gadd, R. (2000). The relationship between parenting style and children's adjustment: The parents' perspective. *Journal of Child & Family Studies, 9*(2), 231–245.

Lamborn, S. D., Mants, N. S., Steinberg, L., & Dornbusch, S. M. (1991). Patterns of competence and adjustment among adolescents from authoritative, authoritarian, indulgent, and neglectful families. *Child Development, 62*(5), 1049–1065.

Langdon, M. (n.d.). *Who we are. Hero Construction Company*: http://www.heroconstruction.org/who-we-are/.

Latané, B., & Darley, J. M. (1970). *The unresponsive bystander: Why doesn't he help?* New York, NY: Appleton-Century-Crofts.

Lee, S. W., Yoo, J. H., Kim, K. W., Lee, J., Kim, D., Park, H., Choi, J., & Jeong, B. (2015). Aberrant function of frontoamygdala circuits in adolescents with previous abuse experiences. *Neuropsychologica, 79*(part A), 75–85.

Luxenberg, H., Limber, S. P., & Olweus, D. (2014). *Bullying in U.S. schools: 2013 status report.* Center City, MN: Hazelden Foundation.

Massing-Schaffer, M., Liu, R. T., Kraines, M. A., Choi, J. Y., & Alloy, L. B. (2015). Elucidating the relation between childhood emotional abuse and depressive symptoms in adulthood: The mediating role of maladaptive interpersonal processes. *Personality & Individual Differences, 74*(1), 105–111.

McMillan, G. (2013, November 12). *10 reasons to love Rom, the greatest Star Trek character ever.* Wired: http://www.wired.com/2013/11/star-trek-rom-is-the-best/.

Miller, J. M., DiIorio, C., & Dudley, W. (2002). Parenting style and adolescent's reaction to conflict: Is there a relationship? *Journal of Adolescent Health, 31*(6), 463–468.

Moriarty, T. (1975). Crime, commitment, and the responsive bystander: Two field experiments. *Journal of Personality & Social Psychology, 31*(2), 370–376.

Mullen, B., & Johnson, C. (1990). Distinctiveness-based illusory correlations and stereotyping: A meta-analytic integration. *British Journal of Social Psychology, 29*(1), 11–28.

Pelham, B., & Blanton, H. (2013). *Conducting research in psychology: Measuring the weight of smoke* (4th ed.). Belmont, CA: Cengage.

Peterson, C., & Seligman, M. E. P. (2004). *Character strengths and virtues.* Washington, D.C.: American Psychological Association.

Piliavin, J. A., & Charng, H. (1990). Altruism: A review of recent theory and research. *Annual Review of Sociology, 16*(1), 27–65.

Pop Culture Hero Coalition (n.d.). *Mission and history.* Pop Culture Hero Coalition: http://www.popculturehero.org/#!about/c1enr.

Popova, M. (n.d.). *The Heroic Imagination Project.* Brain Pickings: http://www.brainpickings.org/2011/02/07/philip-zimbardo-heroic-imagination-project/.

Rachlin, H., & Locey, M. (2011). A behavioral analysis of altruism. *Behavioural Processes, 87*(1), 25–33.

Reed, K. P., Nugent, W., & Cooper, R. L. (2015). Testing a path model of relationships between gender, age, and bullying victimizations and violent behavior, substance abuse, depression, suicidal ideation, and suicide attempts in adolescents. *Children and Youth Services Review, 55*, 128–137.

Rooney, A. (2009). *Feeding the world.* Collingwood, Ontario, Canada: Small Apple Media.

Rubin, S. G. (2011). *Irena Sendler and the children of the Warsaw ghetto.* New York, NY: Holiday House.

Schwarz, L., Jennings, K., Petrillo, J., & Kidd, R. (1980). Role of commitments in the decision to stop a theft. *Journal of Social Psychology, 110*(2), 183–192.

Seligman, M. E. P., (1972). Learned helplessness. *Annual Review of Medicine, 23*(1), 407–312.

Seligman, M. E. P. (1998). Building human strength: Psychology's forgotten mission. *APA Monitor, 29*(1), 1.

Seligman, M. E. P., & Maier, S. F. (1967). Failure to escape traumatic shock. *Journal of Experimental Psychology, 74*(1), 1–9.

Seligman, M. E. P., Steen, T. A., Park, N., & Peterson, C. (2005). Positive psychology progress: Empirical validation of interventions. *American Psychologist, 60*(5), 410–421.

Stannard, D. E. (1993). *American holocaust: The conquest of the New World.* Oxford, UK: Oxford University Press.

Star Trek (2013, September). *Poll says captain with the most respect for the Prime Directive is . . .* Star Trek: http://www.startrek.com/article/poll-says-captain-with-the-most-respect-for-the-prime-directive-is.

Stemwedel, J. D. (2015, August 20). *The philosophy of Star Trek: Is the Prime Directive ethical?* Forbes: http://www.forbes.com/sites/janetstemwedel/2015/08/20/the-philosophy-of-star-trek-is-the-prime-directive-ethical/#307c0d7e642b.

TED (2008, September). *Philip Zimbardo on the psychology of evil: Subtitles and transcript.* TED: https://www.ted.com/talks/philip_zimbardo_on_the_psychology_of_evil/transcript.

Tottenham, B., Hare, T. A., Millner, A., Gilhooly, T., Zevin, J. D., & Casey, B. J. (2011). Elevated amygdala response to faces following early deprivation. *Developmental Science, 14*(2), 190–204.

Trowbridge, A. (2013, October 10). *Are anti-bullying efforts making it worse?* CBS News: http://www.cbsnews.com/news/are-anti-bullying-efforts-making-it-worse/.

Underwood, B., Froming, W. J., & Moore, B. S. (1977). Mood, attention, and altruism. *Developmental Psychology, 13*(5), 541–542.

Vigil, K. M. (2003). *Clean water* (2nd ed.). Corvallis, OR: Oregon State University Press.

Youngdahl, K., Hammond, B., & Sipics, M. (2013). *The history of vaccines.* Philadelphia, PA: The College of Physicians of Philadelphia.

Zimbardo, P. G. (1969). The human choice: Individuation, reason, and order versus deindividuation, impulse, and chaos. In W. J. Arnold & D. Levine (Eds.), *Nebraska Symposium on Motivation* (Vol. 17). Lincoln, NE: University of Nebraska Press.

Zimbardo, P. G. (1971, October 25). *The psychological power and pathology of imprisonment.* A statement prepared for the U.S. House of Representatives Committee on the Judiciary, Subcommittee No. 3: Hearings on Prison Reform, San Francisco, CA.

Zimbardo, P. G. (2007). *The Lucifer effect: Understanding how good people turn evil.* New York, NY: Random House.

Zimbardo, P. G. (n.d.). *Understanding heroism.* The Heroic Imagination Project: http://b.3cdn.net/raproject/ed834126c9c0786b1e_93m6i2aqj.pdf.

Notes

1. *Star Trek: The Next Generation* episode 5–03, "Ensign Ro" (October 7, 1991).
2. Quoted in Brown (1984), p. 19.
3. Brackett & Divecha (2013); Emdin (2011); Espelage (2012); Goldman (2012); Luxenberg et al. (2014).
4. Jeong & Lee (2013); Trowbridge (2013).
5. Hauser (n.d.).
6. Hauser (n.d.).
7. Mullen & Johnson (1990); Pelham & Blanton (2013).
8. *Star Trek: The Next Generation* episode 5–16, "Ethics" (February 29, 1992).
9. Ayenibiowo (2011); Calvete (2014); Massing-Schaffer et al. (2015).
10. *Star Trek: Deep Space Nine* episodes 1–11, "The Nagus" (March 21, 1993); 2–3, "The Siege" (October 10, 1993); 2–11, "Rivals" (January 2, 1994); McMillan (2013).
11. Graham & Juvonen (1998); Infurna et al. (2016); Reed et al. (2015).
12. Lee et al. (2015); Tottenham et al. (2011).
13. e.g., *Star Trek* episodes 1–26, "Errand of Mercy" (March 23, 1967); 2–19, "A Private Little War" (February 2, 1968).
14. Ellis & Powers (2000); Forward (2002); Goldman (2012).
15. *Star Trek: Deep Space Nine* episode 7–24, "The Dogs of Wars" (May 26, 1999).
16. *Star Trek: Deep Space Nine* episodes 5–26, "Call to Arms" (June 16, 1997); 6–6, "Sacrifice of Angels" (November 3, 1997).
17. *Star Trek: Deep Space Nine* episodes 5–7, "Let He Who Is Without Sin . . ." (November 11, 1966); 5–16, "Doctor Bashir, I Presume" (February 24, 1997); 5–20, "Ferengi Love Songs" (April 21, 1997).
18. *Star Trek: Deep Space Nine* episodes 3–22, "Explorers" (Mary 8, 1995); 3–25, "Facets" (June 12, 1995).
19. *Star Trek: Deep Space Nine* episodes 3–14, "Heart of Stone" (February 6, 1995); 3–23, "Family Business" (May 15, 1995).
20. *Star Trek: Deep Space Nine* episodes 6–4, "Behind the Lines" (October 20, 1997); 6–6, "Sacrifice of Angels" (November 3, 1997); 6–10, "The Magnificent Ferengi" (January 1, 1998).
21. *Star Trek: Deep Space Nine* episode 5–26, "Call to Arms" (June 16, 1997).
22. *Star Trek: Deep Space Nine* episode 7–24, "The Dogs of Wars" (May 26, 1999); McMillan (2013).
23. Gatto et al. (2014).
24. Baldry & Farrington (2000); Kaufmann et al. (2000).
25. Baumrind (1966; 1991); Chao (1994).
26. Georgiou (2008); Lamborn et al. (1991); Miller et al. (2002).
27. *Star Trek* episode 1–17, "The Squire of Gothos" (January 12, 1967).
28. Franco et al. (2011).

29. Seligman & Maier (1967); Seligman (1972).
30. Seligman (1998); Seligman et al. (2005).
31. Peterson & Seligman (2004).
32. Zimbardo (1969; 1971).
33. Popova (n.d.).
34. *Star Trek* episode 1–28, "The City on the Edge of Forever" (April 6, 1967).
35. Farsides et al. (2013); Piliavin & Charng (1990); Rachlin & Locey (2011).
36. Hero Construction Company (2015).
37. *Star Trek* episode 1–28, "The City on the Edge of Forever" (April 6, 1967).
38. Franco et al. (2011).
39. e.g., Campbell (1949).
40. Becker & Eagly (2004); Franco et al. (2011); Zimbardo (2007).
41. Franco & Zimbardo (2006).
42. Allison & Goethals (2011).
43. Rubin (2011); Zimbardo (n.d.).
44. *Star Trek* episode 1–28, "The City on the Edge of Forever" (April 6, 1967).
45. Zimbardo (n.d.).
46. *Star Trek* episodes 1–21, "The Return of the Archons" (February 9, 1967); 2–25, "Bread and Circuses" (March 15, 1968); 2–23, "The Omega Glory" (March 1, 1968).
47. Stannard (1993).
48. Rooney (2009); Vigil (2003); Youngdahl et al. (2013).
49. *Star Trek* episodes 1–21, "The Return of the Archons" (February 9, 1967); 2–23, "The Omega Glory" (March 1, 1968): 2–25, "Bread and Circuses" (March 15, 1968).
50. *Star Trek* episodes 1–21, "The Return of the Archons" (February 9, 1967); 2–25, "Bread and Circuses" (March 15, 1968).
51. Chakrabortty (2010).
52. Langdon (n.d.).
53. Pop Culture Hero Coalition (n.d.).
54. Latané & Darley (1970).
55. e.g., Moriarty (1975); Schwarz et al. (1980).
56. e.g., Baek & Reid (2013); Harris (1977); Underwood et al. (1977).
57. Duimering & Robinson (2007); Grant & Patil (2012).
58. *Star Trek* episodes 2–4, "Mirror, Mirror" (October 6, 1967); 2–5, "The Apple" (October 13, 1967); 2–23, "The Omega Glory" (March 1, 1968).
59. e.g., in *Star Trek* episode 1–21, "The Return of the Archons" (February 9, 1967).
60. *Star Trek: The Next Generation* episode 1–22, "Symbiosis" (April 18, 1988).
61. Zimbardo (n.d.).
62. Hero Construction Company (2015).
63. Star Trek (2013); Stemwedel (2015).
64. Clint (2012).
65. *Star Trek: Deep Space Nine* episode 5–15, "By Inferno's Light" (February 17, 1997).
66. TED (2008).

We ask questions about our own existence, trying to understand what we are and why. Existential psychology looks at how we find meaning in our lives and in the universe as we experience it for ourselves. The pursuit may be more important than the answers.

•3•

Quests and Questions: An Interview with Rod Roddenberry on the Human Experience

TRAVIS LANGLEY AND JENNA BUSCH

"Each of us, at some time in our life, turns to someone—a father, a brother, a god—and asks, 'Why am I here? What was I meant to be?'"
—Spock[1]

"One does not become fully human painlessly."
—existential psychologist Rollo May[2]

Who are we? Why are we? Where are we going? What does it all mean? Is there any point to it all? *Existential philosophy* (a.k.a. existentialism[3]) asks these questions about our existence, and *existential psychology* looks at why we ask them.[4] Existential psychologists like Rollo May argue that every person has the power to define one's individual existence.[5] Stressing the importance of *free will*,[6] they question the status quo by which professionals throughout the many areas of psychology look for causes behind our actions, thoughts, and feelings. They criticize the other areas of psychology as being too *deterministic*, for emphasizing myriad influences as if everything we do is ultimately determined by physical, social, and other factors.[7]

Gene Roddenberry asked existential questions. In presenting his optimistic view of where the human race could go and how to get there, *Star Trek* allowed him and his writers to explore the nature of contemporary human existence. In the 1960s, the television series *Star Trek* let them consider the path that might take the human race from Vietnam to Vulcan. The way their characters engage in philosophical debates when deciding their course of action is, in some ways, reminiscent of existential group therapy. Much as *existential therapists* help their patients look at life's problems philosophically,[8] Starfleet captains and their officers conduct strategy sessions by weighing facts and philosophy.

For a look into how *Star Trek* creator Gene Roddenberry and those who came after him used Gene's space-faring fiction to examine these questions and explore the real human condition, we went straight to the keeper of the flame.

The Human Experience

Gene's son Eugene "Rod" Roddenberry is the chief executive officer of Roddenberry Entertainment. He produced the documentary *Trek Nation* as a way to look at the life of his father and the value of the series, then eventually joined the production team for *Star Trek: Discovery*, the sixth live-action Star Trek TV series.[9] Rod Roddenberry spoke with us about why Star Trek has been so enduring, what it says about the human experience and the search for our own humanity, and why its characters are so iconic.

Busch: What do you think it says about the human experience that other shows haven't managed to capture?

Roddenberry: Nowadays, depending how deeply you want to look into it, I think a lot of shows capture it. Those shows that take the real things that have happened in law and crime and with criminals—the things that don't fall on one side or the other. Those shows do a great job of examining things that some of us don't know the right way to go on. What *is* the right way? I certainly don't want to say that Star Trek is the only one, but in terms of television, Star Trek was one of the first to question what it means to be human and look at things from different points of view. And really talk about ethics and right or wrong.

Thinking Four-Dimensionally

Existential psychologists offer a variety of views on how to examine human existence. Among them, existential therapist Emmy van Deurzen has proposed a model for looking at life along four fundamental "dimensions" of existence: physical, social, personal, and spiritual.[10] Star Trek explores them all. The way people experience and interpret these dimensions effectively defines each individual's own reality. In one person's reality, chocolate tastes better than it does in someone else's. For some, such as Gene Roddenberry, the future is brighter and more hopeful than it is for others, such as writers who expect a dystopian future. When Spock and McCoy debate an issue, both can be right because each of them is examining their shared situation as it fits his own subjective view, no matter how objective Spock might try to be. "Right" can mean something different to each person, depending on each individual's subjective reality. If everyone raised as a Vulcan existed in identical reality on all levels (personal, interpersonal, physical, and metaphysical) without the power of choice, they might never disagree with one another over matters of opinion—but they often do.[11]

Physical Dimension: What's All That?

In the *physical dimension*—the universe of concrete, tangible things—we relate to our environment, to the natural world, both around us and within our bodies.[12] Space exploration, while obviously about exploring the reaches of the natural universe, also requires consideration of our internal processes and needs. We cannot reach Mars, much less think to colonize it, without accounting for how to provide ourselves with sustenance (air, food, water), protection (from things like temperature extremes, radiation, maybe even disease), and other life-supporting necessities. As they explore their galactic environment, Star Trek characters repeatedly risk life and limb.

Their mission is not simply to map out planets and stars. Not one episode of any Star Trek series is ever entirely about exploring the physical universe. Nor does any episode focus mainly on internal physical reality. Even when disease or other physical need drives the plot, the real story is about character interactions. For example, when B'Elanna Torres and Tom Paris spend much of a *Voyager* episode with their spacesuits slowly running out of air as they float together in the void of space, the real story is about their relationship and B'Elanna's need to admit her feelings about that to Tom and even to herself.[13]

Star Trek's real mission is about van Deurzen's nonphysical dimensions—the social, psychological, and spiritual.

Social Dimension: Who Are They?

The *social dimension*—the ways in which we connect to others and interact with them, whether individually or collectively—includes how we identify ourselves in relation to them. Which specific individual, group, culture, or society do we include in "us," which do we distinguish as "them," and how do we treat them all? Love and hate, competition and cooperation, acceptance and rejection, connection and isolation all fall within this realm. Star Trek, however, quite often has been about breaking through the limits of such dichotomous thinking in interpersonal relations.

> **Roddenberry:** So many of us, including myself at times, need to pull our heads out of our collective asses, and realize what side of history we want to be on. The fear of things that are different, the fear of change that we all have, that "I'm not used to it, so I'm going to say no to it," we're looking at things the wrong way many times. We need to be inviting in things that are different. Opposing points of view. And if we can be rational and have discussions about these things, we're all going to grow and evolve from it. Even if we don't understand or believe the other person, just hearing that point of view will give us context, will give us room to evolve our own thinking. For me that's what Star Trek is about. Star Trek wasn't about aliens. It's seeking out new ideas in the universe and being open and excited about hearing those new ideas. Forgive me. I'm on a soapbox right now, but that's what Star Trek is to me. That's what excited me about the future. Racism in the sixties, feminism in the seventies or nineties, now it's marriage equality—the future is going to happen! I

> don't know why we're fighting it. We should just be welcoming all these new ideas. I don't understand the fright. Ethics, morals, whatever you want to call them. . . . I think they come from the inside. I think they come from a common sense of right and wrong. The classic phrase of "Do unto others as you would have them do to you"[14] makes perfect sense to me.

Psychologists studying social behavior look not only at direct social interactions between people but also at the ways in which people are influenced without direct connection. This includes the many ways in which individuals are affected by role models and other people they observe.

Psychological Dimension: Who Am I?

The *psychological dimension* is about self-perception and understanding, about relating to oneself and creating a personal world. How do we view ourselves as we were in the past, as we are now, and as we could be in the future?[15] Do we reconcile our contradictions or try not to think about them? In the original *Star Trek* series, the character who struggles the most with these questions is Spock. This son of two worlds reveres logic and yet repeatedly must learn lessons about his own emotional nature. "Logic is the beginning of wisdom," he decides as he grows older, "not the end."[16] Decades later, when Data asks Spock if he has missed his humanity, Spock indicates that he has reached a point of self-acceptance by saying simply, "I have no regrets," with no elaboration.[17]

> **Roddenberry:** You know what the weirdest thing is? In the sixties, Spock was the one that appealed most to women. Spock got the fan mail from the women.

Zhi Mian Existential Therapy

We often see examples of cross-species communication in Star Trek, but here on Earth we're still working on cross-cultural communication, also known as *cross-cultural dialogue*. To a futuristic Trekkie, cross-cultural dialogue may seem downright Stone Age, but for psychologists, it's an important way of learning about other people. A good example is the Chinese concept of *Zhi Mian*, a term meaning "to face directly." Psychologist Xuefu Wang used it when he developed *Zhi Mian therapy*—a psychological approach he explains as "facing life directly, facing oneself directly, and facing relationships directly."[18]

Does anything about this approach sound familiar? After engaging in cross-cultural dialogue, psychologists came to the conclusion that *Zhi Mian* is an indigenous Chinese form of existential therapy, and that existential therapy can be considered a Western form of *Zhi Mian* therapy. While engaging in their cross-cultural dialogue, psychologists had a "Spockian" encounter of sorts. They found out that, although it's "commonly asserted that the Chinese either do not have emotions or do not express emotions readily," while visiting an opera in China, a translator clarified the situation for them: "It is not that Chinese do not express emotions, but rather they do not express them in a manner such as is common in the United States."[19]

—Dana Klisanin

I don't know if they wanted to fix him because he was so emotionally unavailable or what it was.

Busch: It always felt to me like it was about the compassion that he had, even though he was stoic, there was still that side to him.

Roddenberry: I didn't know much about it, but I learned this from John [Champion] who does my *Mission Log* podcast. It kind of goes back to ethos, logos, and pathos—which is Kirk, Spock, and McCoy. They are a triumvirate. They are almost one person. Spock is the logic, McCoy is the emotion, and Kirk is the best of both worlds.

Spiritual Dimension: What's It All Mean?

The *spiritual dimension* provides meaning, an outlook for relating to the unknown, establishing principles, and developing a personal philosophy.[20] The person who can achieve all of these tends to have a greater sense of spirituality in life. Some find meaning through religion or other worldviews, while others find meaning through family or creativity.[21] It's about values. Many of those values involve the ways we determine right from wrong. Kirk and company repeatedly weigh issues of right and wrong, especially when debating whether to violate the Prime Directive by interfering with other worlds for the sake of the greater good.[22] In addition to our views on right and wrong, our sense of spirituality has a lot to do with how we see our own mortality—all of which comes together in the question of what it means to be human.

> **Roddenberry:** *Next Generation* is my favorite and Data is probably one of my favorite characters. What is Data, as a person? What is a person? So many people approach it in different ways, right? What is this thing called life? Is there a god? All of these questions. Is there an end? What happens when you die? Is there something beyond Earth? I think these are questions, no matter where you come from. You may not have all the same ones, but we all, in some ways, want to know what life is and why we're here. Is it something cosmic and supernatural? Are we just a virus on a planet? Are we one of millions and millions? Some people are too scared to think about that. It's a scary thing for them. I get excited by the future. In fact, I get *so* excited by the future—not just technology, because we have awesome technology—but I'm a true believer in that Star Trek future.

Vitality from Vietnam to Vulcan

Existential psychology earned its important place in the field of psychology by raising questions and challenging the rest of psychology to look closely at itself, for us all to challenge our own assumptions. Perhaps because it offers no answers or because it questions how applicable any research findings are to people's everyday lives, existential psychology does not shape a lot of the ongoing research in the science of psychology.[23] That does not change the fact that we keep asking the existential questions and we keep going after the answers. Gene Roddenberry himself valued the struggle to find meaning over the actual finding of it, saying, "It is the struggle itself that is most important. We must strive to be more than we are. It does not matter that we will not reach our ultimate goal. The effort itself yields its own reward."[24]

Busch: Why do you think Star Trek has endured for so many years and through so many incarnations?

Roddenberry: There is probably no one answer, but I think Star Trek really appeals to those who sort of think differently or feel differently or don't fit in and just approach things in a different way. It's everything from people who disagreed with Vietnam (and that's a huge part of it) and disagreed with the social injustices of the time, even today. I think people who disagreed with that saw *Star Trek* and saw this awesome future and said, "Why aren't we doing *that*?" I think that's just the message that has stood the test of time. Almost fifty years. People look at what's going on in the world and still say the same thing. Why aren't we doing that? I think Star Trek speaks to that person who questions the status quo.

Uhura, Too: A Word with Nichelle Nichols

Actress Nichelle Nichols played communications officer Uhura in the original *Star Trek* television series, *Star Trek: The Animated Series*, and six *Star Trek* motion pictures. After discussing and praising the actors who keep Uhura and other characters alive in newer films, Nichols shared her thoughts on Star Trek's cultural impact.

Nichols: Gene Roddenberry was such a genius. He gave us what we thrived for and didn't even know what we were thriving for, and that comes from me as a fan of the show as much as being in it. It was beautiful. It was a wonderful experience. What's so incredible about it is that it still is a wonderful experience and it still is a wonderful idea.

Langley: What does Star Trek say about human nature?

Nichols: We're not perfect. We have our ups and downs and faults, and Star Trek shows that beautifully. And it's optimistic. It says we have powers they haven't even discovered yet.

Langley: For all those ups and downs, do you feel that the characters inspired the fans as people in their own lives?

Nichols: I absolutely *know* that that's true because I've been told that enough times from the people.

—Travis Langley

References

Appignanesi, R., & Zarate, O. (2001). *Introducing existentialism.* Cambridge, UK: Icon.

Cooper, M. (2003). *Existential therapies.* London, UK: Sage.

Frankl, V. E. (1963). *Man's search for meaning.* Boston, MA: Beacon.

Frankl, V. E. (1967). *Psychotherapy and existentialism: Selected papers on logotherapy.* New York, NY: Simon & Schuster.

Hanly, C. M. T. (1979). *Existentialism and psychoanalysis.* New York, NY: International Universities Press.

Hoffman, L. (2012). *Second international conference on existential psychology: The meaning and inspirations of Zhi Mian.* APA Division 32: http://www.apadivisions.org/division-32/publications/newsletters/humanistic/2011/12/second-international-conference.aspx.

Hoffman, L., Wang, X., & Yang, M. (2011). *Existential psychology in China.* APA Division 32: http://www.apadivisions.org/division-32/publications/newsletters/humanistic/2011/04/existential-psychology.aspx.

La Cour, P., & Hvidt, N. C. (2010). Research on meaning-making and health in secular society: Secular, spiritual, and religious existential orientations. *Social Science & Medicine, 71*(1), 1292–1299.

Littleton, C. (2016, March 3). *'Star Trek' TV series beams up Rod Roddenberry, Trevor Roth as exec producers.* Variety: http://variety.com/2016/tv/news/star-trek-rod-roddenberry-cbs-all-access-1201721941/.

May, R. (1978). Foreword. In R. S. Valle & M. King (Eds.), *Existential-phenomenological alternatives in psychology* (pp. x–xii). New York, NY: Oxford University Press.

May, R. (1983). *The discovery of being: Writing in existential psychology.* New York, NY: Norton.

Norcross, J. C., Karpiak, C. P., & Santoro, S. O. (2005). Clinical psychologists across the years: The division of clinical psychology from 1960 to 2003. *Journal of Clinical Psychology, 61*(12), 1467–1483.

Schneider, K. J. (2015). The case for existential (spiritual) psychotherapy. *Journal of Contemporary Psychotherapy, 45*(1), 21–24.

Van Deurzen, E. (2002). *Existential counseling and psychotherapy in practice* (2nd ed.). London, UK: Sage.

Van Deurzen, E. (2009). Life is for living: Claiming past, present, and future. *Existential Analysis, 20*(2), 226–239.

Wnuk, M., & Marcinkowski, J. T. (2014). Do existential variables mediate religious-spiritual facts of functionality and psychological wellbeing? *Journal of Religion & Health, 53*(1), 56–67.

Zenou, T. (2013, May). *Star Trek into Darkness* [review]. Double Exposure: http://doubleexposurejournal.com/blog/star-trek-into-darkness/.

Notes

1. *Star Trek: The Motion Picture* (1979 motion picture).
2. May (1978), p. xii.
3. Appignanesi & Zarate (2001).
4. Frankl (1963).
5. May (1983).
6. Frankl (1967).
7. Hanly (1979).
8. Frankl (1967).
9. Littleton (2016).
10. Cooper (2003); van Deurzen (2002).
11. e.g., *Star Trek* episode 2–10, "Journey to Babel" (November 17, 1967); *Star Trek VI: The Undiscovered Country* (1991 motion picture).
12. Van Deurzen (2002).
13. *Star Trek: Voyager* episode 4–3, "Day of Honor" (September 17, 1997).
14. Luke 6:31.
15. Van Deurzen (2009).
16. *Star Trek VI: The Undiscovered Country* (1991 motion picture).
17. *Star Trek: The Next Generation* episode 5–8, "Unification" part II (November 11, 1991).
18. Hoffman (2012).
19. Hoffman et al. (2011).
20. Schneider (2015); van Deurzen (2002).
21. La Cour & Hvidt (2010); Wnuk & Marcinkowski (2014).
22. e.g., *Star Trek* episodes 2–21, "Patterns of Force" (February 16, 1968); 2–25, "Bread and Circuses" (March 15, 1968).
23. Norcross et al. (2005).
24. Zenou (2013).

We try to know who we are, but who we are keeps changing with experience and age. We try to know our place in the world, but does anyone really live in only one world?

•4•

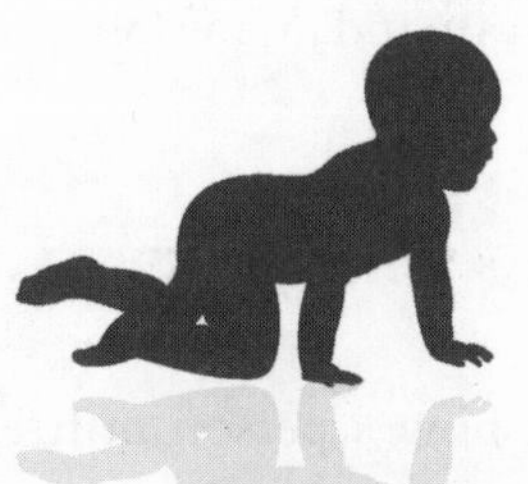

Child of Two Worlds: Understanding Development of Identity

ELIZABETH KUS
AND ALAN KISTLER

"You will always be a child of two worlds."
—Sarek[1]

"In the social jungle of human existence, there is no feeling of being alive without a sense of identity."
—developmental psychologist Erik Erikson[2]

It's one of the most important questions we ask ourselves, three words that can simultaneously request the most basic information and express a deep-seated need to define something that many believe can't ever be fully defined. It's a question both philosophical and psychological. Even if you think you answer it, that answer may change. To know who we are at any time, we may need to understand what has crafted our identity and how we develop it into something all our own. One character who symbolizes this question and the struggle for identity more than most is Spock, son of the Vulcan Sarek and the Earth human Amanda Grayson.[3]

Who Am I?

Simply put, *identity* is how a person utilizes to define himself or herself and how that person connects to others (both individually and as part of groups). Philosopher John Locke, whose ideas played an important role in leading to the creation of psychology as a distinct field,[4] looked at identity as a psychological continuity[5] in which there is a blank slate shaped by each person's experiences, sensations, and connections as well as that person's reflections on each of those elements. In this view, we are born without innate knowledge and a planned path toward who we might become; instead, later life experiences shape that path and guide us to develop into who we are.

Spock is a hybrid, the son of one Vulcan and one human parent. Although physically he looks like any other Vulcan, several stories refer to his behavior, particularly as a child, as a sign of his human biological heritage.[6] Along with this, Spock is told as a child that he must choose between two paths: One would follow the way of his father and the great Vulcan philosopher Surak; the other would follow his mother's way of life despite living among people who will not understand it.[7] This is an example of how individuals utilize experiences and knowledge that is gained in order to develop the self. Per Locke's view, Spock fills his blank slate and develops his sense of self by the way he connects to the various things that he takes in.

Stages of Development

Locke's philosophy on identity has similarities to psychologist Erik Erikson's views. Erikson posited that through eight stages of life, which occur at particular ages, human beings experience crises that lead to the development of aspects of identity. From birth to death, each stage allows for the resolution of its crisis with a positive or negative connotation. If a positive resolution is reached, the individual will move fluidly into the next stage, as appropriate, and continue developing his or her self. When a negative resolution is reached, the individual is likely to have difficulty in that area and later in his or her life.

Trust versus Mistrust (Birth–about 18 Months)

The first stage—from birth to 18 months—looks at trust and mistrust. The infant must gain an understanding that the parent or caregiver can be relied on to support and provide for them. But if the caregiver does not fulfill the infant's needs and provide shelter, food, and protection, trust does not develop and the growing child will develop an unconscious belief that others will fail him or her in a similar fashion. Because this idea develops at such an early age, it becomes a deep-rooted attitude that is difficult to change, leading to difficulty in developing intimacy with others. In one adventure, a Vulcan highly skilled in telepathy produces a vision of Sarek looking at the newly born Spock and remarking with shame that the boy is "so human."[8] This vision is likely formed not by literal memories Spock has but by impressions of a distant father in whom he (at least during infancy and childhood) perceives embarrassment and shame. Perhaps this is why for years Spock initially finds it difficult to admit feelings of friendship and love, even keeping his supportive mother at a distance.[9]

From Dr. Spock to Mr. Spock

Pediatrician Benjamin Spock rose to fame with his 1946 bestseller *Baby and Child Care*, which is full of child-rearing advice and encouragement for post–World War II baby boomers.[10] Spock recommended showing children nurturing and warmth at a time when other childcare books promoted a colder, more detached approach.[11] He opened with the simple yet powerful advice, "Trust yourself. You know more than you think you do."[12]

Improving the world in which he lived interested the renowned author. Alien worlds did not. When Dr. Spock told the actor who played TV's Mr. Spock that "science fiction has never beckoned to me," Leonard Nimoy replied, "By translating Earth problems into another time and place, you can draw an analogy that makes their reality striking."[13]

—T. L.

Autonomy versus Shame and Doubt (about ages 2–3)

The second stage occurs during early childhood, from about 2 to 3 years of age. This is when children examine their autonomy versus their feelings of shame and doubt, stepping away from their parents in the process. If this process is successful, their feelings of autonomy and pride will allow for further experimentation and independence. Failure leads to feelings of shame and guilt that will convince children that it is unwise to step outside their comfort zone and try new things. Spock's later behavior, such as his insistence on breaking rules and keeping secrets from his parents even when it results in punishment, makes it seems likely that he successfully explores his autonomy and pride during this stage.

Initiative versus Guilt (about ages 3–5)

The third stage occurs during the preschool years, ages 3 to 5 or 6. In this stage, it is imperative that children continue to explore their environment and collect new experiences so that they can continue learning. However, it is also important that boundaries be set so that they appreciate order, rules, and appropriate social behavior. When children fail to meet the rules and perceive that they have done wrong, they begin developing the first stages of self-evaluation that will continue through later stages. Defying the rules they're supposed to follow can lead to disapproval from the parent/caregiver and feelings of guilt in the child. As a child, Spock often disobeys rules, repeatedly exploring nearby mountains despite being told not to. When his mother, Amanda, sees him trying to act stiff-lipped though "anguished, because the other boys tormented you, saying that you weren't really Vulcan," she knows "that inside the human part of you was crying."[14] She shows both her *cognitive empathy*, knowing and understanding how someone else feels, and her *affective empathy*, feeling compassion for him and some distress in line with his own.[15] Soon before his death, Sarek admits to noticing these things as well and to having admired his son's will and endurance of punishments.[16]

Industry versus Inferiority (about age 6 to puberty)

Erikson referred to the fourth stage, when the child is attending school from ages 6 to 11, as "industry versus inferiority." Entering a new social and academic landscape, the growing individual must learn essentially to sink or swim. By "swimming," the child learns to achieve in the environment, gaining a sense of success and competence. "Sinking" leads to feelings of inferiority, leading the child perhaps to pull away from peers and situations rather than risk public failure and be seen as less than the others. In different stories, we see Spock often getting into fights as a child, as early as when he is five Vulcan years of age (though it's not specified how long that is in Earth years). He is mocked as an outsider from the group because of his mixed heritage and/or because he finds it more difficult to control and hide his emotions than the other children.[17] During such fights, children call him "barbarian" and "Earther," saying he will never be a true Vulcan.[18] Children in this stage also begin to learn the importance of their culture and self-efficacy.

Identity Achievement versus Role Confusion (Adolescence)

One of the most important points according to Erikson is the fifth stage, adolescence, which occurs from age 12 to the late teens or maybe early twenties. In this stage, the primary goal is to form an identity,[19] leading to its formation on the basis of experiences, peers, and sense of self. Typically, teenagers pull away from their parents and attempt to fit into the social groups around them. They ask "Who am I?" and seek answers through action, perhaps by changing their appearance or behavior in order to fit in with the crowd they've chosen. Additionally, with the onset of puberty and body changes, adolescents look to become comfortable with who they are shaping into, again asking "Who am I?" but this time reflecting on the self rather than the crowd around them. "A direction for my life had to be chosen," young Spock explains, regarding his own identity formation. "I chose Vulcan."[20]

At the age of seven Vulcan years, Spock undergoes a maturity test known as the *kahs-wan ordeal*, which sounds similar to some Earth customs that celebrate adolescence as a pathway to adulthood. Such *rites of passage* may help maintain the culture by locking a child into an identity status known as *foreclosure*, in which the individual commits to follow other people's plans for his or her life before that person has time to consider alternatives.[21] Afterward, young Spock chooses to adopt the Vulcan way of life, which is dedicated to following lessons of logic, peace, and emotional control.[22]

Intimacy versus Isolation (Early Adulthood)

The sixth stage is young adulthood, occurring from the twenties until around age 40 and involving the individual looking at intimacy versus isolation. People in this stage base their development on the trust, autonomy, and role developed previously: What needs does the person wish to fill with another? Someone who has successfully navigated the previous stages reaches this stage and is able to develop an intimate (emotionally, cognitively, and physically) relationship with others. Someone who has a negative experience at this stage is more likely to be isolated or have unfulfilling relationships.

Self-concept is a motivator throughout the stages. Individuals may define themselves as rebels, for example, and react in an opposite manner to what is expected when punished for breaking rules and boundaries. They may choose a pattern of behavior that is more personally meaningful, or they may choose a pattern of self-preservation in which they establish shallow and weak relationships lacking depth.[23]

It is during this stage that Spock leaves the nest of Vulcan, deciding not to join the Vulcan Science Academy and instead enlist in Starfleet, believing the latter will fulfill his needs, desires, and potential.[24] Whether he means to or not, this move creates a philosophical compromise between his human and Vulcan sides. After living his entire life on Vulcan up to that point, he now joins an organization that largely follows Earth-based structures and philosophies and has its headquarters on Earth.

In the alternate timeline of the newer films, Spock reaches the decision to join Starfleet on realizing that the senior academics of the Vulcan Science Academy do not and will not see him as an equal because of his heritage.[25] Here the negative experience can be argued to result in Spock isolating himself from Vulcan out of anger, but it can also be seen as evidence of his acting logically, choosing the life that has the greatest possibility for advancement. In Starfleet, he develops close friendships with James T. Kirk, Leonard McCoy, and Nyota Uhura, all of them human beings who hold different beliefs and sometimes find Spock frustrating but also support him in his life and goals.

Generativity versus Stagnation (Middle Adulthood)

The seventh stage, middle adulthood, occurs from around age 40 to age 60 and relates to generativity versus stagnation. Essentially, these individuals seek to create something that will outlive them and continue to carry their names through their children or their deeds. Failure here entails a poor connection to and involvement in the world around them.

From adolescence through these later stages, culture becomes a major piece in an individual's development. Spock, as an older man, takes on protégés such as Saavik, a Vulcan-Romulan hybrid who probably also has troubles and concerns about being accepted by Vulcans suspicious of hybrids and their ability to keep emotions in check.[26]

Spock experiences literal death and a traumatic resurrection, after which he undergoes mental and physical rehabilitation.[27] These experiences cause him to reflect on Vulcan culture and his entire life in a way he may not have done otherwise, examining the stages and crises he has gone through. In finding a balance between both his sides, in accepting his victories and errors from the previous stages, he becomes a more mature person who then sends a very human message to his mother, a message that would not come from a typical Vulcan seeking to avoid any display of emotion or subjectivity: "I feel fine."[28]

Ego Integrity versus Despair (Late Life)

The final stage, maturity, comes sometime in the years after age 60, although these ages become harder to define as a person gets older. (Erikson eventually decided he should add a ninth stage for extreme old age, when the individual has outlived the majority of people he or she has ever known, but he had not finished formulating his ideas about that before he himself died.[29])

The crisis in this stage is ego integrity versus despair, when individuals reflect on their lives and achievements. Success here leads to a feeling of fulfillment, whereas an unsuccessful response leads to feelings of despair, bitterness, and even regret.[30] In *Star Trek: The Next Generation*, Spock, now an ambassador for the Federation, attempts to teach Vulcan philosophies to the people of the Romulan Empire,[31] a role emulating both his mother (a teacher) and his father (an ambassador).[32] Here Spock continues to develop his cultural identity by sharing it with others and opening himself to their reactions.

After Spock finds himself in a newly created alternate timeline and soon afterward witnesses the destruction of Vulcan, he experiences despair and guilt over the destruction of those two worlds, which has made his people an "endangered species" and potentially shattered Vulcan culture. But rather than give in to despair and guilt, Spock Prime (as the older Spock from the original timeline's future is called from that point on) becomes proactive, ensuring that the new timeline's younger versions of himself and his friends still meet and become the heroes he knows they can and must be.[33]

Development of Identity

What are the components of identity? There are the innate feelings of self, of personality, that individuals are born with, but this is just a starting point for what makes people who they are. Locke and Erikson agreed that experiences shape much of who a person becomes, but those factors don't operate in a vacuum. Interest in a career path and finding a purpose in work play a role. Political and spiritual views shape viewpoints.

Relationship status, motivation to achieve, sexual orientation, gender, and culture all shape different aspects of identity, as do hobbies, personal entertainment interests, and body image.[34]

As people move through Erikson's stages, they begin (particularly starting in the adolescent stage) to categorize the groups around them—"school," "friends," "religion," and so on—and attempt to fit properly in each social group. They search for similarities and tighten their identification within that group or with those individuals as those similarities are seen as positives. However, if the similarities are seen as negative or if there are more things that differentiate the individuals, then there is movement away from that group or individuals.[35] It is within this categorization that the formation of one's true identity is born. Spock knows who he is when he leaves behind the fights with bullies and takes on the kahs-wan ordeal before he is supposed to. He knows who he is when he joins Starfleet rather than the Vulcan Science Academy. He knows who he is when he chooses time and time again to join his crewmates of the starship *Enterprise* in various adventures not just because it is his duty but also because they are his friends and family. He is Spock, child of two worlds, with all the experiences and lessons that entails.

> *"Put aside logic. Do what feels right."*
>
> —Spock Prime[36]

> *"The aim of life is self-development. To realize one's nature perfectly—that is what each of us is here for."*
>
> —playwright Oscar Wilde[37]

References

Erikson, E. H. (1968). *Identity, youth, and crisis.* New York, NY: Norton.

Erikson, E. H. (1998). *The life cycle completed* (extended version). New York, NY: Norton.

Fancher, R. E. (2000). Locke, John. In A. E. Kazdin (Ed.), *Encyclopedia of psychology* (vol. 5, pp. 66–68). Washington, DC: American Psychological Association.

Hidalgo, L. (2011). *Dr Spock's Baby and Child Care at 65.* BBC: http://www.bbc.com/news/world-us-canada-14534094.

Kroger, J. (2003). Identity development during adolescence. In J. Kroger (Ed.), *Discussions on ego identity* (pp. 1–20). Hillsdale, NJ: Erlbaum.

Leary, D. E. (1980). The intentions and heritage of Descartes and Locke: Toward a recognition of the moral basis of modern psychology. *Journal of General Psychology, 102*(2), 283–310.

Marcia, J. E. (1993). The relational roots of identity. In J. Kroger (Ed.), *Discussions on ego identity* (pp. 101–120). Hillsdale, NJ: Erlbaum.

Nimbalkar, N. (2011). John Locke on personal identity. *Mens Sana Monographs, 9*(1), 268–275.

Santrock, J. W. (2013). *Life-span development.* New York, NY: McGraw-Hill.

Shamay-Tsoory, S. G., Aharon-Peretz, J., & Perry, D. (2009). Two systems for empathy: A double dissociation between emotional and cognitive empathy in inferior frontal gyrus versus ventromedial prefrontal lesions. *Brain, 132*(3), 617–627.

Sokol, J. T. (2009). Identity development throughout the lifetime: An examination of Eriksonian theory. *Graduate Journal of Counseling Psychology, 1*(2), article 14. http://epublications.marquette.edu/gjcp/vol1/iss2/14.

Spock, B. (1946). *Baby and child care.* New York, NY: Duell, Sloan, & Pearce.

Spock, B., & Nimoy, L. (1979, July 15). Conversation piece: Dr. Spock & Mr. Spock. *Parade*, pp. 18, 20.

Stets, J. E., & Burke, P. J. (2000). Identity theory and social identity theory. *Social Psychology Quarterly 63*(3), 224–237.

Wilde, O. (1907). *The writings of Oscar Wilde* (vol. 6). New York, NY: Keller.

Notes

1. *Star Trek* (2009 motion picture).
2. Erikson (1968), p. 130.
3. *Star Trek* episode 2–10, "Journey to Babel" (November 17, 1967). *Star Trek: The Undiscovered Country* (1991 motion pictured).
4. Fancher (2000); Leary (1980).
5. Nimbalkar (2011).
6. *Star Trek* episode 2–10, "Journey to Babel" (November 17, 1967).
7. *Star Trek* episode 2–10, "Journey to Babel" (November 17, 1967).
8. *Star Trek V: The Final Frontier* (1989 motion picture).
9. *Star Trek* episodes 2–1, "Amok Time" (September 15, 1967); 2–10, "Journey to Babel" (November 17, 1967).
10. Spock (1946).
11. Hidalgo (2011).
12. Spock (1946), p. 3.
13. Spock & Nimoy (1979), p. 20.
14. *Star Trek* episode 2–10, "Journey to Babel" (November 17, 1967).
15. Shamay-Tsoory et al. (2009).

16. *Star Trek: The Next Generation* episode 5–7, "Unification," part 1 (November 4, 1991).
17. *Star Trek* episode 2–10, "Journey to Babel" (November 17, 1967).
18. *Star Trek: The Animated Series* episode 1–2, "Yesteryear" (September 15, 1973).
19. Sokol (2009).
20. *Star Trek: The Animated Series* episode 1–2, "Yesteryear" (September 15, 1973).
21. Kroger (2003); Marcia (1993).
22. *Star Trek: The Animated Series* episode 1–2, "Yesteryear" (September 15, 1973).
23. Sokol (2009); Stets & Burke (2000).
24. *Star Trek* episode 2–10, "Journey to Babel" (November 17, 1967).
25. *Star Trek* (2009 motion picture).
26. *Star Trek II: The Wrath of Khan* (1982 motion picture).
27. *Star Trek III: The Search for Spock* (1984 motion picture).
28. *Star Trek IV: The Voyage Home* (1986 motion picture).
29. Erikson (1998).
30. Erikson (1998).
31. *Star Trek: The Next Generation* episodes 5–7 and 5–8, 'Unification," parts 1 (November 4, 1991) and 2 (November 11, 1991).
32. *Star Trek* episode 2–10, "Journey to Babel" (November 17, 1967).
33. *Star Trek* (2009 motion picture).
34. Santrock (2013).
35. Stets & Burke (2000).
36. *Star Trek* (2009 motion picture).
37. Wilde (1907), p. 38.

Log File I

Star Trek and the Need for Excitement

TRAVIS LANGLEY

We need many things. Physically, we need air, water, food, sleep, protection from the elements, and more. Difficult as it might be to list all physical needs, whether conveniences for comfort or necessities for survival, psychological needs may be even harder to catalog. Sociologist-turned-psychologist Erich Fromm,[1] biologist-turned-psychologist Henry Murray,[2] and others each separately described psychological needs we have, the numbers of which keep varying depending on each theorist's experience, interpretation, and point of view. Among his, Fromm postulated a *need for excitement and stimulation*, meaning the need for a stimulating environment to activate a person's senses and brain activity in order to maintain optimal performance. Psychologist Marvin Zuckerman focused his work on understanding people who, like himself, yearn for arousal beyond the levels most people find optimal. Zuckerman referred to this need for novelty, variety, and excitement, along with an accompanying "willingness to take physical and social risks for the sake of such experiences,"[3] as *sensation seeking*.

Every Star Trek series tells exciting stories. None of the later programs, though, exemplify the need for excitement so clearly as the original *Star Trek*, in which a cowboy captain commands the *Enterprise* and episodes average more barroom brawls and other fight scenes than in any other Trek. While all starship personnel enter high-risk occupations, one captain in particular will be the first to set foot on new worlds and to charge into danger instead of running things from the comfort of his chair. James T. Kirk takes gambles, makes bluffs, provokes arguments, throws punches, beds women, and interferes with alien civilizations in violation (or in creative interpretation) of the Prime Directive more than any other series' captain.

Sensation seekers are not all the same. In addition to all their many other personality traits, they differ from each other in the ways they seek stimulation. Zuckerman eventually broke sensation seeking down into four components.[4]

- *Thrill and adventure seeking*—engaging in physical activities that involve danger, speed, height, and novelty. Newly demoted from the rank of admiral back to captain, Kirk climbs (and falls off) a mountain as Spock chides him for irresponsibility.[5]
- *Experience seeking*—seeking out variety in experiences through travel, exploration, art, or noncomformity. Though Archer and Picard explore, both maintain greater connection to Earth during their travels. Sisko works out of a space station. Janeway travels farther than any of the rest, but not voluntarily. No other starship captain leaves his ship to join an away mission so readily as does Captain James T. Kirk.
- *Disinhibition*—pursuing release in uninhibited social activities. All of the captains have some degree of inhibition. Great self-control is among the qualities that help them earn their leadership positions. While Kirk probably has more experiences with involuntary disinhibition, when alien manipulation or mysterious illnesses McCoy will cure within an hour alter his state of mind, even he does not choose this as a primary means of sensation seeking.
- *Boredom susceptibility*—restlessness and an aversion

Star Trek (1966–1969, 3 seasons, 79 episodes). Created by G. Roddenberry. Desilu, Norway, Paramount. Aired on NBC. (Although popularly called *Star Trek: The Original Series* throughout fandom to reduce confusion with the later shows and films, that was not its name.)

Star Trek: The Animated Series (1973–1974, 2 seasons, 22 episodes). Created by G. Roddenberry. Filmation, Norway Productions. Aired on NBC.

to routine, repetition, and predictability. Kirk shows greater patience when tension is high, waiting out an opponent because the situation is too precarious to bore him. Even so, he takes a lot of shortcuts when completing his missions.

A deeply principled man, Kirk never asks anyone to take a risk he would not take himself. He would score high in sensation seeking as a personality trait, and yet the need for excitement does not fully run his life. His intelligence, self-discipline, and many other qualities help maintain balance in his life.

References

Fromm, E. (1941). *Escape from freedom.* New York, NY: Holt, Rinehart & Winston.

Fromm, E. (1973). *The anatomy of human destructiveness.* New York, NY: Holt, Rinehart & Winston.

Murray, H. A. (1938). *Explorations in personality: A clinical and experimental study of fifty men of college age.* New York, NY: Oxford University Press.

Zuckerman, M. (1979). *Sensation seeking: Beyond the optimal level of arousal.* Hillsdale, NJ: Erlbaum.

Zuckerman, M. (1983). *Biological bases of sensation seeking, impulsivity, and anxiety.* Hillsdale, NJ: Erlbaum.

Notes

1. Fromm (1941, 1973).
2. Murray (1938).
3. Zuckerman (1979), p. 10.
4. Zuckerman (1983).
5. *Star Trek V: The Final Frontier* (1989 motion picture).

Science fiction uses the filter of unreality to look at life's reality from a new point of view. Every fantastic journey to planets faraway presents opportunities to shine lights upon the worlds within ourselves.

PART II

INNER WORLDS

The way we each answer the question of "Who am I?" includes comparisons and contrasts with others. "Who I am" includes some sense of "who I am not" and "who I used to be."

•5•

The Trek through Identity

ERIC D. WESSELMANN
AND J. SCOTT JORDAN

"They took everything I was. They used me to kill and destroy. And I could not stop them. I should have been able to stop them."

—Jean-Luc Picard[1]

"An identity is a definition, an interpretation, of the self . . . An identity crisis is not resolved by checking one's wallet for one's name and address. People who have problems with identity are generally struggling with the more difficult aspects of defining the self, such as the establishing of long-term goals, major affiliations, and basic values."

—social psychologist Roy F. Baumeister[2]

Humans are social animals. We have a fundamental need to forge meaningful relationships with others, much as we need food, water, and shelter.[3] Indeed, individuals who lack sufficient social relationships experience physical and psychological problems, even to the point of reducing their life expectancy.[4] Social connections do more than just satisfy one's need to belong; social relationships also provide individuals with a source of identity and a general sense of self.[5] Issues of belonging and identity are central to everyone's lives, and we can see our own successes, failures, and continued struggles reflected in various character arcs in Star Trek. For example, whereas Deep Space 9's commanding officer Sisko balances his roles and maintains a secure sense of self, Spock and Worf feel conflicted between roles and therefore each feels conflict in his identity. Even people who seem secure in who they are, like Captain Picard, may feel uncertainty about identity when external factors and events beyond their control inflict change upon them. Stories like these can illustrate what psychologists have learned about belonging and identity, and can help the audience reflect on and understand their own journeys through life.

The Self: "Who Am I?"

Many psychologists have argued about what the *self* conceptually is, but one common theme is that one's *self-concept* (how the person mentally perceives or describes him or herself[6]) has three primary levels: a personal level, a relational level, and a collective level.[7] Theorists disagree about which of these levels of self-concept dominates one's identity, but most agree that they are social in nature.[8]

Personal Level

The *personal level* involves defining the self by individual traits that differentiate one person from another.[9] For example, Benjamin Sisko has a personal self that is high in both *agency* (the ability to be decisive and make things happen) and *communion* (interpersonal warmth).[10] These traits are considered to be part of his personal self because they are part of how he interacts with the everyday world across situations, and they are part of how he introspectively defines himself.

Relational Level

The *relational level* involves defining oneself by the social roles and relationships in one's life.[11] For Sisko, two aspects of his relational self are his role as commander of Deep Space 9 and his role as a father. Both of these roles make different demands on the way he understands himself and how he chooses to interact with people. Sometimes they complement one another and other times they may conflict when he is forced to prioritize one role over another in any given situation.

Collective Level

Finally, the *collective level* involves defining oneself based on one's identification with larger groups and social categories (like gender, race, religion, or nationality).[12] Sisko's collective self focuses on how he experiences himself as both an African-American and as a human. His identity as an African-American emerges within the cultural context of his home planet, while his identity as a human emerges out of his interactions with life forms from other planets. These "selves" are different from his relational selves as a father and commander because collective selves are defined in terms of the broad social categories (i.e., in-groups and out-groups) to which one belongs. Identifying with these broad groups often results from but does not require actual interpersonal interaction with in-group members.[13]

Self-Identity Is Complex

Individuals' self-identities are complex. Not only are identities multifaceted, they also are dynamic, changing over time and sensitive to situational contexts.[14] Further, individuals strive to keep some sense of consistency between these different aspects of themselves, as well as between the types of selves they (and others) think they *should* be.[15] When individuals recognize that portions of their self-concept are inconsistent, they experience an unpleasant state of psychological and physiological arousal, called *cognitive dissonance*.[16]

As individuals work through their daily lives, conflicts are bound to emerge at each level (personal, relational, collective),[17] as well as between different levels. Spock's personal self, for example, seems to consistently struggle with reconciling his human emotionality and his Vulcan rationality. He also needs to cultivate smooth working relations with his crew mates, requiring him to maintain a consistent, stable relational self that deals with both the struggles of his personal self and the relational differences between his and his human shipmates' views on rationality versus emotionality. Spock also has to navigate the challenges presented by his collective, biracial identity (i.e., human and Vulcan).[18] The struggle between and within Spock's personal, relational, and collective selves is embodied in his struggle with *pon farr*, the Vulcan urge to mate.[19] Although Vulcan culture has developed rituals to help mitigate this mating drive, the humans Spock interacts with every day on the *Enterprise* are unaware

Microaggressions: Subtle Discrimination

Microaggressions are brief, often subtle (and sometimes unconscious) everyday comments, insults, or behaviors directed toward members of minority groups.[20] Verbal microaggressions often involve derogating someone's group membership, and range in severity from explicit insults (epithets or slurs) and subtle insensitive comments or questions (for example, suggesting that someone's achievements are due to affirmative action), to "backhanded compliments" that imply someone is exotic or a foreigner because of his or her group membership (like complimenting a non-Caucasian individual on speaking English well).[21] Even though many of these behaviors may seem innocuous, research suggests they can have severe, long-lasting psychological consequences on victims.[22]

Recently, psychologists have begun investigating microaggressions for bi- and multiracial individuals. Research suggests that these individuals experience both similar and unique microaggressions compared with individuals who are members of only one racial/ethnic group.[23] Any time someone treats biracial Spock as exotic or "different" because of his heritage, he may feel isolated or experience other negative feelings that microaggressions may prompt. Further, if he overhears a negative comment or joke about either Vulcans or humans, he may also experience a negative reaction.[24]

Sometimes individuals may even encounter microaggressions from members of their own families.[25] Worf, though technically adopted by humans, still experiences identity conflicts between his Federation loyalty and his Klingon heritage. Anytime a fellow Klingon (especially if it is a blood relative) questions his authenticity or lack of cultural knowledge, he likely feels isolated and devalued.[26]

of both this Vulcan struggle and the rituals Vulcans use to deal with it. This struggle results in an immense conflict among Spock's personal, relational, and collective selves, and ultimately results in his programming the ship to head to Vulcan against Kirk's orders.

Optimal Distinctiveness: How Much to Be Assimilated?

Another source of potential conflict within and between levels of self-concept is the degree to which we feel assimilated into our relationships as opposed to feeling unique or differentiated from others. *Optimal distinctiveness theory*[27] argues that both assimilation and distinctiveness are basic psychosocial needs that to continuously oppose one another. This persistent tension implies that one's daily life is geared toward finding a balance between assimilation and distinctiveness, and this tension can occur at multiple levels of self-concept.[28]

Perhaps nothing represents the struggle between these two opposite needs better than Picard's personal struggle following his period of assimilation by the Borg.[29] Once Picard escapes assimilation, he describes the experience as being part of a group mind, or a "collective."[30] Although Picard describes this experience as wholly negative, most individuals often seek events and experiences that allow them to dissolve their uniqueness and experience assimilation (for example, when they jump up and down in synchrony with strangers at a rock concert, or participate in collective cheering with strangers at a sporting event).

Picard finds such assimilation so appalling because of the hard work he has done his entire life to focus more on distinctiveness than assimilation. This becomes clear when Picard returns to his family vineyard following his escape from Borg assimilation.[31] As he and his brother work through the small talk of becoming reacquainted, the need for distinctiveness that originally compelled Picard to leave home and trek to the stars comes to the fore as his brother defends his own original need to assimilate into vineyard culture. As these two embodiments of assimilation and distinctiveness literally come to blows, it

Ostracism: The Social Death Penalty

Ostracism, being ignored and excluded, is a painful and common experience.[34] Colloquially, ostracism may be called "the silent treatment," "the cold shoulder," "excommunication," or "exile."[35] Ostracism has many negative psychological consequences (e.g., thwarting individuals' needs for belonging and self-esteem),[36] and it activates similar regions of the brain that physical pain does, suggesting that it literally causes individuals to feel pain.[37] Laboratory research demonstrates that participants are bothered by ostracism even when they are told explicitly that researchers purposely designed the study to ostracize them, or that the people ostracizing them are members of groups they would otherwise despise (for example, Ku Klux Klan members).[38]

Why does Worf willingly face ostracism by taking responsibility for his father's alleged treason, renouncing his Klingon affiliation, and allowing himself to be exiled?[39] Worf understands that if it becomes known that the most powerful family in Klingon society is responsible for the Khitomer betrayal, a civil war will ensue. *Relationship commitment* (whether it be to one person or a group) can motivate individuals to sacrifice for those to whom they are committed.[40] Worf takes the fall for Duras because he is committed to Klingon society, in spite of being raised by a human family.

becomes clear that Picard begins to find balance as his brother beats him into self-awareness.

Optimal distinctiveness theory argues that the best way to manage the tension between assimilation and distinctiveness is to find small groups in which your relational self can assimilate, while simultaneously being with others who (1) respect you as an individual, and (2) whose collective identities are clearly distinct from larger groups.[32] Eventually, Picard achieves balance and allows himself to assimilate positively with his subordinates by finally joining them in a card game, recognizing that he should have forged this relationship much earlier.[33]

Nostalgia: The Self's Journey Home

Another source of potential identity conflict is the changes individuals go through during various stages of development (infant, child, teenager, etc.), with each stage having its own unique trials and tribulations to be navigated.[41] When individuals look back on these different stages of life, not only do they notice these developmental changes, but they also notice discrepancies between their different levels of self-identity during these stages. How do individuals reconcile these differences and maintain a healthy level of identity coherence?

Psychologists have begun studying *nostalgia* as a potential answer to this question. Nostalgia is the experience of sentimental longing or desiring to connect with one's past.[42] When individuals experience nostalgia, they typically focus on memories as if they were narratives with themselves as protagonists, and usually involve interactions with close others or momentous life events influential to their self-identity. These memories are not uniformly positive and may involve some amount of ambivalence, especially if the memory involves struggles or negative experiences. However, when nostalgia involves negative memories, the narrative often closes with the individual triumphing over adversity and interpreting the initial struggles as necessary for developing virtue or future victories.[43]

Additionally, nostalgia functions as a reservoir of social connection and belonging, as well as positive feelings that can be used to bolster self-esteem after negative life events and identity threats, especially existential threats caused by thinking about one's own mortality.[44] This function of nostalgia is expressed uniquely when a time capsule's beam targets Picard and causes him to experience thirty years of someone else's life.[45] The time capsule's creators knew their sun was about to go supernova and destroy them. Faced with inevitable destruction, they found comfort in the idea that some future being would experience their culture via the capsule and, in a nostalgic sense, continue their lives.

Finally, nostalgia functions to maintain self-consistency across one's identity development, highlighting events that ultimately help individuals keep an overall *positive* self-identity.[46] Nostalgia's function is illustrated when Q allows Picard, who is critically injured, to travel back in time and change events in his past that he regretted and which would stop him from being injured in the present.[47] After Picard changes these events, Q gives him a glimpse of what life would have been like had he "played it safe" in his youth. Picard finds that, by changing those earlier events, his new life was boring and he would never be a captain, something he decided he could not tolerate. As such, he travels back and allows his original history to occur as it had, restoring the present and his self-consistency.

Your Continuing Mission

Individuals have powerful psychological needs linked to their relationships with others. In addition to simply satisfying one's core need to belong, individuals' social relationships and group memberships facilitate the development of self-identity, one that ideally involves positivity and consistency across various life events and domains. We may share similar identity challenges over the course of our lives, but each person's trek through these challenges is contextually unique. Given how central this trek is to our existence as persons, it seems our need to be with others will be with us into the foreseeable future, as well as into the final frontier, several centuries from now.

References

Baumeister, R. F. (1986). *Identity: Cultural change and the struggle for self.* New York, NY: Oxford University Press.

Baumeister, R. F., & Leary, M. R. (1995). The need to belong: Desire for inter-personal attachments as a fundamental human motivation. *Psychological Bulletin, 117*(3), 497–529.

Brewer, M. B. (1991). The social self: On being the same and different at the same time. *Personality & Social Psychology Bulletin, 17*(5), 475–482.

Brewer, M. B., & Gardner, W. (1996). Who is this "We"? Levels of collective identity and self representations. *Journal of Personality & Social Psychology, 71*(1), 83–93.

Brewer, M. B., & Pickett, C. L. (2002). The social self and group identification: Inclusion and distinctiveness motives in interpersonal and collective identities. In J. P. Forgas & K. D. Williams (Eds.), *The social self: Cognitive, interpersonal, and intergroup perspectives* (pp. 255–271). New York, NY: Psychology Press.

Brewer, M. B., & Roccas, S. (2001). Individual values, social identity, and optimal distinctiveness. In C. Sedikides & M. B. Brewer (Eds.), *Individual self, relational self, cognitive self* (pp. 219–237). Philadelphia, PA: Psychology Press.

Brown, U. M. (1995). Black/white interracial young adults: Quest for a racial identity. *American Journal of Orthopsychiatry, 65*(1), 125–130.

Cacioppo, J. T., & Patrick, W. (2008). *Loneliness: Human nature and the need for social connection.* New York, NY: Norton.

Chakraborty, A., & McKenzie, K. (2002). Does racial discrimination cause mental illness? *British Journal of Psychiatry, 180*(6), 475–477.

Clark, R., Anderson, N. B., Clark, V. R., & Williams, D. R. (1999). Racism as a stressor for African Americans: A biopsychosocial model. *American Psychologist, 54*(10), 805–816.

Eisenberger, N. I., Lieberman, M. D., & Williams, K. D. (2003). Does rejection hurt? An fMRI study of social exclusion. *Science, 302*(5643), 290–292.

Ellemers, N., & Haslam, S. A. (2012). Social identity theory. In P. A. M. Van Lange, A. W. Kruglanski., & E. T. Higgins (Eds.), *Handbook of theories of social psychology* (pp. 379–399). London, UK: Sage.

Ellemers, N., Spears, R., & Doosje, B. (2002). Self and social identity. *Annual Review of Psychology, 53*(1), 161–186.

Erikson, E. H. (1963). *Childhood and society.* New York, NY: Norton.

Festinger, L. (1962). Cognitive dissonance. *Scientific American, 207*(4), 93–102.

Forgas, J. P., & Williams, K. D. (2002). The social self: Introduction and overview. In J. P. Forgas & K. D. Williams (Eds.), *The social self: Cognitive, interpersonal, and intergroup perspectives* (pp. 1–18). New York, NY: Psychology Press.

Gonsalkorale, K., & Williams, K. D. (2007). The KKK won't let me play: Ostracism even by a despised outgroup hurts. *European Journal of Social Psychology, 37*(6), 1176–1186.

Higgins, E. T. (1987). Self-discrepancy: A theory relating self and affect. *Psychological Review, 94*(3), 319–340.

Juhl, J., Routledge, C., Arndt, J., Sedikides, C., & Wildschut, T. (2010). Fighting the future with the past: Nostalgia buffers existential threat. *Journal of Research in Personality, 44*(3), 309–314.

Linville, P. W. (1985). Self-complexity and affective extremity: Don't put all of your eggs in one basket. *Social Cognition, 3*(1), 94–120.

Linville, P. W., & Carlston, D. E. (1994). Social cognition of the self. In P. G. Devine, D. L. Hamilton, & T. M. Ostrom (Eds.), *Social cognition: Impact on social psychology* (pp. 143–193). San Diego, CA: Academic Press.

Markus, H., & Wurf, E. (1987). The dynamic self-concept: A social psychological perspective. *Annual Review of Psychology, 38*(1), 299–337.

Maslow, A. H. (1968). *Toward a psychology of being.* New York: Van Nostrand.

Nadal, K. L. (2011). The Racial and Ethnic Microaggressions Scale (REMS): Construction, reliability, and validity. *Journal of Counseling Psychology, 58*(4), 470–480.

Nadal, K. L., Sriken, J., Davidoff, K. C., Wong, Y., & McLean, K. (2013). Microaggressions within families: Experiences of multiracial people. *Family Relations, 62*(1), 190–201.

Nadal, K. L., Wong, Y., Griffin, K., Sriken, J., Vargas, V., Wideman, M., & Kolawole, A. (2011). Microaggressions and the multiracial experience. *International Journal of Humanities & Social Sciences, 1*(7), 36–44.

Root, M. P. P. (1998). Experiences and processes affecting racial identity development: Preliminary results from the biracial sibling project. *Cultural Diversity & Mental Health, 4*(3), 237–247.

Sedikides, C., & Brewer, M. B. (2001). Individual self, relational self, and collective self: Partners, opponents, or strangers? In C. Sedikides & M. B. Brewer (Eds.), *Individual self, relational self, cognitive self* (pp. 1–4). Philadelphia, PA: Psychology Press.

Sedikides, C., Wildschut, T., Arndt, J., & Routledge, C. (2008a). Nostalgia: Past, present, and future. *Current Directions in Psychological Science, 17*(5), 304–307.

Sedikides, C., Wildschut, T., Gaertner, L., Routledge, C., & Arndt, J. (2008b). Nostalgia as enabler of self-continuity. In F. Sani (Ed.), *Individual and collective self-continuity: Psychological perspectives.* Mahwah, NJ: Lawrence Erlbaum.

Steele, C. M., & Liu, T. J. (1983). Dissonance processes as self-affirmation. *Journal of Personality & Social Psychology, 45*(1), 5–19.

Sue, D. W., Capodilupo, C. M., & Holder, A. M. B. (2008). Racial microaggressions in the life experience of Black Americans. *Professional Psychology: Research & Practice, 39*(3), 329–336.

Sue, D. W., Capodilupo, C. M., Torino, G. C., Bucceri, J. M., Holder, A. M. B., Nadal, K. L., & Esquilin, M. (2007). Racial microaggressions in everyday life: Implications for clinical practice. *American Psychologist, 62*(4), 271–286.

Swann, W. B., Jr., Rentfrow, P. J., & Guinn, J. (2003). Self-verification: The search for coherence. In M. Leary & J. Tangney (Eds.). *Handbook of self and identity* (pp. 367–383). New York, NY: Guilford.

Van Lange, P. A. M., Rusbult, C. E., Drigotas, S. M., Arriaga, X. B., Witcher, B. S., & Cox, C. L. (1997). Willingness to sacrifice in close relationships. *Journal of Personality & Social Psychology, 72*(6), 1373–1395.

Wiggins, J. S. (1991). Agency and communion as conceptual coordinates for the understanding and measurement of interpersonal behavior. In D. Cicchetti & W. Grove (Eds.), *Thinking clearly in psychology: Essays in honor of Paul Everett Meehl* (pp. 89–113). Minneapolis, MN: University of Minnesota Press.

Wildschut, T., Sedikides, C., Arndt, J., & Routledge, C. (2006). Nostalgia: Content, triggers, functions. *Journal of Personality & Social Psychology, 91*(5), 975–993.

Williams, K. D. (2001). *Ostracism: The power of silence.* New York, NY: Guilford Press.

Williams, K. D. (2009). Ostracism: Effects of being excluded and ignored. In M. Zanna (Ed.), *Advances in experimental social psychology* (pp. 275–314). New York, NY: Academic Press.

Zadro, L., Williams, K. D., & Richardson, R. (2004). How low can you go? Ostracism by a computer is sufficient to lower self-reported levels of belonging, control, self-esteem, and meaningful existence. *Journal of Experimental Social Psychology, 40*(4), 560–567.

Zhou, X., Sedikides, C., Wildschut, T., & Gao, D. (2008). Counteracting loneliness: On the restorative function of nostalgia. *Psychological Science, 19*(10), 1023–1029.

Notes

1. *Star Trek: The Next Generation* episode 4–2, "Family" (October 1, 1990).
2. Baumeister (1986), p. 4.
3. Maslow (1968).
4. Baumeister & Leary (1995); Cacioppo & Patrick (2008).
5. Ellemers & Haslam (2012); Ellemers et al. (2002).
6. Linville & Carlston (1994); Markus & Wurf (1987).
7. Brewer & Gardner (1996); Forgas & Williams (2002).
8. Sedikides & Brewer (2001).
9. Brewer & Gardner (1996).
10. Wiggins (1991).
11. Brewer & Gardner (1996).
12. Brewer & Gardner (1996).
13. Ellemers & Haslam (2012); Sedikides & Brewer (2001).
14. Ellemers & Haslam (2012); Linville (1985); Markus & Wurf (1987).
15. Higgins (1987); Steele & Liu (1983); Swann et al. (2003).
16. Festinger (1962).
17. Brewer & Gardner (1996).
18. Brown (1995); Root (1998).
19. *Star Trek* episode 2–1, "Amok Time" (September 15, 1967).
20. Sue et al. (2007).
21. Nadal (2011); Sue et al. (2007).
22. Chakraborty & McKenzie (2002); Clark et al. (1999); Sue et al. (2008).
23. Nadal et al. (2011).
24. Nadal et al. (2011).
25. Nadal et al. (2013).
26. Nadal et al. (2013).
27. Brewer (1991).
28. Brewer & Roccas (2001); Brewer & Pickett (2002).
29. *Star Trek: The Next Generation* episodes 4–1, "The Best of Both Worlds," part 2 (September 24, 1990), and 4–2, "Family" (October 1, 1990); *Star Trek: First Contact* (1996 motion picture).
30. *Star Trek: First Contact* (1996 motion picture).
31. *Star Trek: The Next Generation* episode 4–2, "Family" (October 1, 1990).
32. Brewer (1991).
33. *Star Trek: The Next Generation* episode 7–26, "All Good Things . . ." (May 23, 1994).
34. Williams (2009).
35. Williams (2001).
36. Williams (2009).
37. Eisenberger et al. (2003).
38. Gonsalkorale, & Williams (2007); Zadro et al. (2004).
39. *Star Trek: The Next Generation* episode 3–17, "Sins of the Father" (March 19, 1990).
40. Van Lange et al. (1997).
41. Erikson (1963).
42. Sedikides et al. (2008a).

43. Wildschut et al. (2006).
44. Juhl et al. (2010); Wildschut et al. (2006); Zhou et al. (2008).
45. *Star Trek: The Next Generation* episode 5–25, "The Inner Light" (June 1, 1992).
46. Sedikides et al. (2008b).
47. *Star Trek: The Next Generation* episode 6–15, "Tapestry" (February 15, 1993).

Universal emotions common throughout our species are primal and yet key parts of what "humanity" means. After the original *Star Trek* series explored the value of emotions by featuring a half-human character struggling to suppress his feelings and stifle his humanity, the next series inverted that with an android character eager to understand feelings and to find out what it means to be human. Pinocchio wanted to be a real boy.

•6•

Emotion Data

JANINA SCARLET

"If being human is not simply a matter of being born flesh and blood, if it is instead a way of thinking, acting, and feeling, then I am hopeful that one day I will discover my own humanity."

—Data[1]

"We cannot selectively numb emotions. When we numb the painful emotions, we also numb the positive emotions."

—social work researcher Brené Brown[2]

Android Data devotes a lot of his attention and spends much of his time trying to comprehend and master human emotions—an effort that is contrary to what many humans do. Many people try to suppress their emotions and avoid thinking about them.[3] In fact, some believe that controlling or suppressing their emotions and relying only on logical processing is more helpful than feeling emotions.[4] Which is healthier—suppressing emotions, as many humans do, or experiencing them, as Data attempts to do?

Universal Emotions

Emotions are important for human survival in order to cope with life's various missions. They can also change a person's physiology. According to renowned emotions researcher Paul Ekman, humans are capable of experiencing numerous emotions. Six of these have often been identified as *universal emotions*, meaning that everyone feels them:

- happiness
- sadness
- fear
- anger
- surprise
- disgust[5]

All these emotions serve an important function in human survival. Despite being an android, Data is able to experience all six at different times throughout his stories.[6]

Happiness

Some cultures place great value on the pursuit of happiness. In other cultures—for example, in some Asian cultures—following social norms for the sake of everyone's benefit is generally considered more important than an individual's happiness.[7] Happiness can arise from a pleasurable event (*hedonic happiness*) or from following someone's core values (*eudaimonic happiness*). When *Enterprise* crew members are introduced to an addictive game, they become consumed by it, playing it instead of taking care of their own well-being[8]—an example of hedonic happiness. On the other hand, Data cries with happy tears when he finds his cat, Spot, whom he values—an example of eudaimonic happiness.[9] Eudaimonic happiness, more than hedonic happiness, produces a greater sense of well-being, a sense of meaning, a sense of inner peace and appreciation for life, as well as vitality and physical health outcomes.[10]

Sadness

The purpose of sadness might not be as clear as that of other universal emotions, yet this emotion is responsible for increasing the desire and the possibility for social connectedness.[11] Sadness can occur when someone experiences a loss, such as what fellow crew members experience when Tasha Yar dies.[12] Experiencing sadness allows people to process the saddening event and accept the social support needed for recovery. In addition, experiencing sadness—in particular when connecting with other people—allows the body to release *oxytocin*, a natural stress-fighting hormone[13] that helps soothe painful emotions and reduce stress.[14] Even though Data does not fully understand the purpose of having a service for Tasha after her death, he communicates to Captain Picard how empty his life will be without her. Through this communication, Data receives reassurance and support from his captain during that difficult time.[15]

Fear

Fears allows the individual to fight an attacker, flee from a situation, or freeze in place in order to ensure that individual's survival.[16] This response will trigger certain physiological responses, such as a rapid heart rate and elevated blood pressure. When Data finally gets an emotion chip installed, it allows him to experience a range of emotions, but he does not know how to handle them. Fear overwhelms him during a firefight and he freezes.[17] Data feels extremely guilty over this incident even though his response is quite natural. When people are in life-threatening situations, they may naturally experience fear, which as a form of self-preservation will cause a *fight-flight-freeze* response.[18]

Anger

Anger is sometimes considered to be a "dangerous" emotion because it can lead to aggression. However, the emotion of anger and the act of aggression are, in fact, different from one another. When an individual or that person's group members are threatened or insulted, the individual might become aggressive in order to maintain safety or social status.[19] Unknowingly controlled by his evil brother, Data gets angry over a Borg's killing of officer Corelki, then becomes aggressive and brutally kills one of the Borg.[20] The experience invigorates him.

Surprise

When someone has a set of expectations about how things will turn out but turns out to be mistaken, that individual is likely to experience surprise. This emotion offers humans and animals a number of benefits. The most important of these benefits may be enhanced ability to learn new information. Other benefits, like improved perception and physiological arousal, can allow the individual to learn a task better.[21] Data is surprised when he loses a game of poker to his crewmates.

However, this becomes an important opportunity for him to learn about bluffing.[22]

Disgust

Disgust triggers nausea, irritability, anger, or any combination of these feelings. When the bartender Guinan hands Data a drink while he is under the influence of a newly implanted emotion chip, he says that he hates it and is revolted by it, and he then orders another in order to experience that feeling again. Essentially, Data is feeling disgust.[23] Its main function for a biological organism would be to protect the individual from being poisoned. Disgust is also important when selecting a romantic partner or in social situations.[24] For example, when the ruler of Ligon II kidnaps Data's friend Tasha and tries to force her to marry him, her disgust for this ruler appropriately prevents her from seeing him as a potential mate.[25]

Emotion Avoidance and Suppression

Although some human emotions such as joy may be pleasant, many are difficult to experience. Some of these difficult emotions might produce uncomfortable changes in the person's physiology. For example, fear might produce shallow breathing, a rapid heart rate, and a release of adrenaline. This sensation may be unpleasant and even distressing. Ultimately, though, these emotions trigger an appropriate reaction that can potentially save that individual's life.[26] This is in some way what Data experiences when he feels fear for the first time.[27] This may also be what the Exocomps, sophisticated robots that become sentient, experience as well.[28] In both of these situations, these mechanical entities appear to experience fear or a similar emotion, causing them to act in the opposite way from which they were programmed in order to ensure self-preservation. For Data, this event leads him to experience another painful human emotion—guilt.[29]

Painful emotional experiences, such as guilt, depression, and anxiety, make it more likely that the individual will try to avoid these emotions or any experiences that might trigger these emotions (*experiential avoidance*). When people are anxious, for example, and are unwilling to experience a particular emotion, they are less able to achieve their goals.[30] When Data's friend Keiko is supposed to get married to transporter chief Miles O'Brien, she becomes anxious and gets "cold feet." She tells Data that she does not wish to marry O'Brien and initially breaks off the wedding as a way of trying to manage her emotions.[31]

After a life-threatening situation or trauma, an individual might experience a number of symptoms. *Hyperarousal* (an extreme state of alertness) and other trauma-related symptoms may make the person more irritable and more prone to anger or aggression.[32] Hyperarousal and other anxiety-related symptoms are usually the biggest reasons for *emotional numbing*, shutting down one's own emotional experiences in response to a traumatic event. For example, among female veterans who were sexual assault survivors, the women who showed the most extensive degree of hyperarousal after the traumatic experience also displayed the highest levels of emotional numbing. In turn, emotional numbing may be the top predictor of posttraumatic stress disorder (PTSD).[33]

Alexithymia, the inability to identify one's own emotions,[34] can lead to a worsening of emotion regulation. This, in turn, may make the individual more susceptible to developing a mental health disorder, such as PTSD and depres-

Courage and Vulnerability

Although many people strive to avoid experiencing emotions, emotions are actually adaptive for survival. For example, emotions allow individuals to get ready for action in threatening situations. In addition, emotions allow for specific physiological changes in the body that are necessary for the given situation.[37] The willingness to experience emotions and various emotional experiences are linked to improved mental health, higher self-esteem, and higher life satisfaction,[38] as well as reduced depression, anxiety, and PTSD.[39] Embracing and communicating one's emotions, as Data does when expressing how much he misses Tasha,[40] is a vulnerable experience. However, this vulnerability is also one of the most necessary components of healthy relationships and maintaining one's emotional health.[41] Data's constant inquiries regarding emotions and his willingness to admit when he is struggling may make him vulnerable,[42] but it also makes him more likable and more likely to get the help that he needs.

sion.[35] Despite the fact that he is an android, Data does not struggle with alexithymia. On the contrary, he readily learns about and experiences emotions. At one point, after having an emotion chip installed, he states that he has experienced 261 emotions.[36]

An Android's Humanity

Many people strive to avoid emotions by numbing or suppressing them. Emotional suppressing can make a person act and seem almost robotic. Data, on the other hand, is constantly trying to understand and experience emotions, potentially making him closer to a human being than some humans who try to suppress their feelings. At one point, Data has to prove that he is in fact a sentient being.[43] Captain Picard convinces a Starfleet judge that Data possesses intelligence and self-awareness, and demonstrates that no one can actually define the term *consciousness.* Data's emotional attachment to his medal and to Tasha's hologram demonstrate that his emotional state is akin to that of a healthy human being. And while Data may still be an android, he possesses what many androids do not—humanity. His emotional awareness and his willingness to experience emotions form a model from which many humans might benefit.

Overall, human beings who are able to experience their emotions tend to enjoy better mental health and respond better to stressful situations. Experiencing emotions allows people to get the help they need when they are struggling. Emotions help people protect their loved ones in the face of danger and let them savor life's happy moments. The irony is that the very control over one's emotions that many humans strive to achieve may be most harmful to their health. The willingness to experience emotions—all emotions, even those that make people feel vulnerable and cause pain at times—may actually be the healthiest action that people can take in the face of adversity.

It's all part of being human.

References

Badura, A. S. (2003). Theoretical and empirical exploration of the similarities between emotional numbing in posttraumatic stress disorder and alexithymia. *Journal of Anxiety Disorders, 17*(3), 349–360.

Baldwin, D. V. (2013). Primitive mechanisms of trauma response: An evolutionary perspective on trauma-related disorders. *Neuroscience & Biobehavioral Reviews, 37*(8), 1549–1566.

Bracha, H. S. (2004). Freeze, flight, fight, fright, faint: Adaptationist perspectives on the acute stress response spectrum. *CNS Spectrums, 9*(9), 679–685.

Brown, B. (2010). *The gifts of imperfection: Let go of who you think you're supposed to be and embrace who you are.* Center City, MN: Hazelden.

Brown, B. (2012). *Daring greatly: How the courage to be vulnerable transforms the way we live, love, parent, and lead.* New York, NY: Penguin.

Carmeli, A., Yitzhak-Halevy, M., & Weisberg, J. (2009). The relationship between emotional intelligence and psychological wellbeing. *Journal of Managerial Psychology, 24*(1), 66–78.

Donaldson-Feilder, E. J., & Bond, F. W. (2004). The relative importance of psychological acceptance and emotional intelligence to workplace well-being. *British Journal of Guidance & Counselling, 32*(2), 187–203.

Ekman, P. (1992). An argument for basic emotions. *Cognition & Emotion, 6*(3–4), 169–200.

Gilbert, P. (2009). Introducing compassion-focused therapy. *Advances in Psychiatric Treatment, 15(*3), 199–208.

Gray, H. M., Ishii, K., & Ambady, N. (2011). Misery loves company: When sadness increases the desire for social connectedness. *Personality & Social Psychology Bulletin, 37*(11), 1438–1448.

Grinde, B. (2002). Happiness in the perspective of evolutionary psychology. *Journal of Happiness Studies, 3*(4), 331–354.

Hayes, S. C., Luoma, J. B., Bond, F. W., Masuda, A., & Lillis, J. (2006). Acceptance and commitment therapy: Model, processes and outcomes. *Behaviour Research & Therapy, 44*(1), 1–25.

Kashdan, T. B., Barrios, V., Forsyth, J. P., & Steger, M. F. (2006). Experiential avoidance as a generalized psychological vulnerability: Comparisons with coping and emotion regulation strategies. *Behaviour Research & Therapy, 44*(9), 1301–1320.

Levine, D. S. (2008). Neural networks of human nature and nurture. *Avances en Psicología Latinoamericana, 26*(1), 82–98.

Meyer, E. C., Morissette, S. B., Kimbrel, N. A., Kruse, M. I., & Gulliver, S. B. (2013). Acceptance and Action Questionnaire—II scores as a predictor of posttraumatic stress disorder symptoms among war veterans. *Psychological Trauma: Theory, Research, Practice, & Policy, 5*(5), 521–528.

Monson, C. M., Price, J. L., Rodriguez, B. F., Ripley, M. P., & Warner, R. A. (2004). Emotional deficits in military-related PTSD: An investigation of content and process disturbances. *Journal of Traumatic Stress, 17*(3), 275–279.

Öhman, A., & Mineka, S. (2001). Fears, phobias, and preparedness: Toward an evolved module of fear and fear learning. *Psychological Review, 108*(3), 483–522.

Ryan, R. M., Huta, V., & Deci, E. L. (2008). Living well: A self-determination theory perspective on eudaimonia. *Journal of Happiness Studies, 9*(1), 139–170.

Schomaker, J., & Meeter, M. (2015). Short- and long-lasting consequences of novelty, deviance and surprise on brain and cognition. *Neuroscience & Biobehavioral Reviews, 55*, 268–279.

Sell, A. N. (2011). The recalibrational theory and violent anger. *Aggression & Violent Behavior, 16*(5), 381–389.

Song, L. Y., Singer, M. I., & Anglin, T. M. (1998). Violence exposure and emotional trauma as contributors to adolescents' violent behaviors. *Archives of Pediatrics & Adolescent Medicine, 152*(6), 531–536.

Taylor, G. J. (2000). Recent developments in alexithymia theory and research. *The Canadian Journal of Psychiatry/La Revue Canadienne de Psychiatrie, 45*(2), 134–142.

Tull, M. T., & Gratz, K. L. (2008). Further examination of the relationship between anxiety sensitivity and depression: The mediating role of experiential avoidance and difficulties engaging in goal-directed behavior when distressed. *Journal of Anxiety Disorders, 22*(2), 199–210.

Tull, M. T., & Roemer, L. (2007). Emotion regulation difficulties associated with the experience of uncued panic attacks: Evidence of experiential avoidance, emotional nonacceptance, and decreased emotional clarity. *Behavior Therapy, 38*(4), 378–391.

Tybur, J. M., Lieberman, D., & Griskevicius, V. (2009). Microbes, mating, and morality: individual differences in three functional domains of disgust. *Journal of Personality & Social Psychology, 97*(1), 103–122.

Zilboorg, G. (1943). Fear of death. *Psychoanalytic Quarterly, 12*, 465–475.

Notes

1. *Star Trek: The Next Generation* episode 4–11, "Data's Day" (January 7, 1991).
2. Brown (2010), p. 70.
3. Badura (2003).
4. Hayes et al. (2006).
5. Ekman (1992).
6. *Star Trek: The Next Generation* episodes 2–9, "The Measure of a Man" (February 13, 1989); 6–26 "Descent: Part I" (June 21, 1993); *Star Trek: Generations* (1994 motion picture).
7. Grinde (2002).
8. *Star Trek: The Next Generation* episode 5–6, "The Game" (October 28, 1991).
9. *Star Trek: Generations* (1994 motion picture).
10. Ryan et al. (2008).
11. Gray et al. (2011).
12. *Star Trek: The Next Generation* episode 1–23, "Skin of Evil" (April 25, 1988).
13. Levine (2008).
14. Gilbert (2009); Gray et al. (2011); Levine (2008).
15. *Star Trek: The Next Generation* episode 1–23, "Skin of Evil" (April 25, 1988).
16. Baldwin (2013).
17. *Star Trek: Generations* (1994 motion picture).
18. Bracha (2004); Öhman & Mineka (2001); Zilboorg (1943).
19. Sell (2011).
20. *Star Trek: The Next Generation* episode 6–26, "Descent: Part I" (June 21, 1993).
21. Schomaker & Meeter (2015).
22. *Star Trek: The Next Generation* episode 2–9, "The Measure of a Man" (February 13, 1989).
23. *Star Trek: Generations* (1994 motion picture).
24. Tybur et al. (2009).
25. *Star Trek: The Next Generation* episode 1–4, "Code of Honor" (October 12, 1987).
26. Ekman (1992).
27. *Star Trek: Generations* (1994 motion picture).
28. *Star Trek: The Next Generation* episode 6–9, "The Quality of Life" (November 14, 1992).
29. *Star Trek: Generations* (1994 motion picture).
30. Tull & Gratz (2008).
31. *Star Trek: The Next Generation* episode 4–11, "Data's Day" (January 7, 1991).
32. Song et al. (1998).
33. Tull & Roemer (2007).
34. Badura (2003); Taylor (2000).
35. Monson et al. (2004); Taylor (2000).
36. *Star Trek: Generations* (1994 motion picture).

37. Ekman (1992).
38. Carmeli et al. (2009); Donaldson-Feilder & Bond (2004).
39. Kashdan et al. (2006); Meyer et al. (2013).
40. *Star Trek: The Next Generation* episode 2–9, "The Measure of a Man" (February 13, 1989).
41. Brown (2010, 2012).
42. *Star Trek: The Next Generation* episode 4–11, "Data's Day" (January 7, 1991).
43. *Star Trek: The Next Generation* episode 2–9 "The Measure of a Man" (February 13, 1989).

Each of us is human, and each of us is alien. The human race needs diversity in skills, strengths, and interests, and yet appreciating that diversity can be difficult when someone differs from us in every one of those ways. When we find it hard to stay patient with those who are logical, literal, and socially out of sync, we may fail to discover what wondrous things they do for us all.

•7•

Gene Roddenberry Saw the Future . . . and the Future is Asperger's

FRANK GASKILL

". . . if we can't disguise you, we'll find some way of explaining you."
—Captain Kirk[1]

"Our civilization would be dull and sterile if we did not have and treasure people with Asperger's."
—clinical psychologist Tony Attwood[2]

I am a child psychologist who specializes in the area of Asperger's. People who have Asperger's tend to be above average in intelligence, demonstrate a special interest in a particular area within which they hyper-focus, and possess a deficit in social and nonverbal communication. All people with Asperger's—or *Aspies* for short—are different from one another. However, they do appear to share the common traits of social deficits, special interests, and higher intelligence.

I have been drawn to this population since my childhood. I was one of those kids obsessed with Star Trek, Rubik's cubes, and Dungeons & Dragons. My community of friends all seemed to be outsiders with similar interests. When we were together, we could speak our own nerdy language together. At the beginning of my professional career, I was drawn to this population of kids who were often bullied, considered strange, and generally excluded. Year after year I continue to see a common denominator that tends to be love of science fiction and fantasy. And the more I reflect on the Star Trek universe, the more Gene Roddenberry's predictions of the future make sense to me within the context of Asperger's.

The predictions and imaginative ideas from Star Trek are no longer science fiction but are now daily necessities and science fact, from mobile devices and tablet computers to Bluetooth headsets.[3] Tech predictions from Roddenberry go on and on;[4] what we take for granted now was pure science fiction when Star Trek began. However, the greatest prediction from the Star Trek universe and the mind of Roddenberry is neither future tech nor brave new worlds. His greatest foresight, as I see it, was how the invaluable mind of an individual with Asperger's dominates our society's past, present, and future. Roddenberry's future is not about the technology. His vision of the future is about Asperger's.

Who Are These Aspies, Anyway?

Asperger's is essentially a state in which a person with a differently wired mind, often characterized as having higher than average intelligence and poor social skills, possesses intense interest and focus on specific topics and activities, such as trains, meteorology, or history, just to name a few. In the past, it was considered a developmental disorder, similar to autism. Many people with Asperger's refer to themselves as Aspie, and they are nothing short of amazing.[5] Many Aspies have exceptional memories, intense ability to hyper-focus, and obsessive interest in pattern recognition. In fact, the Danish-based company, LEGO, has created an assessment system specifically designed to identify people with Asperger's who could contribute in meaningful ways to their company, given their specific gifts in design and pattern recognition.[6]

The Aspie mind reaches from LEGO designs to the infinite expanse of relativity and faster-than-light travel. Sir Isaac Newton and Albert Einstein, both historically identified as having signs of Asperger's,[7] respectively gave us the theory of gravity and the theory of relativity, which together allow for a theoretical model of warp speed.[8] The Aspie mind has given the world an unimaginably long list of innovations, and as the world throws financial incentives toward the mind, innovative ideas and creations will continue at an ever-increasing rate.

Aspie individuals tend to be highly intelligent and possess an obsessive interest or focus that they can hold for hours and hours upon end. Aspies tend to be literal and are also justice-oriented. Their biggest difficulty is how to process and respond appropriately to social communication, which is primarily nonverbal in nature. Many people consider Asperger's to be a disorder or they hold a stereotype of these individuals as being introverted or as individuals to be feared, due to unfair media stereotypes. The stereotype could not be further from the truth and in my opinion is repeatedly confronted in Star Trek. Many of the individuals whom I would consider to be on the autism spectrum in the Star Trek universe are those desiring a closer relationship with humanity and a greater understanding of social nuances and connection. The Aspie-like characters of Star Trek strive to connect more deeply with humanity and are an important accelerant to humanity's efforts toward a greater future—most notably the Vulcans as they relate to Star Trek's human characters.

I describe the autism spectrum as the *lemon continuum*, ranging from having no lemon (no signs of autism) to plenty of lemons (abundant signs of autism).[9] Imagine a glass of water, a glass of water with a slice of lemon, lemon-flavored water, lemonade, a lemon, and a lemon farm. The lemon continuum is a representation of the degrees of lemon content, but regardless of the amount of lemon, it is never considered to be bad. How much lemon is in the water helps one understand where an Aspie may fall on the continuum. An example of a "lemon farm" individual (with many indicators on the autism spectrum) would be Sir Isaac Newton,[10] while lemonade (with some indicators but not as many) is actress Daryl Hannah[11] or pro surfer Clay Marzo.[12] In Star Trek, Vulcans are lemonade; however, I consider Spock to be lemon-flavored water. He certainly has his lemon moments, but due to being half-human, he is more in tune with social circumstances than most Aspies.

Exploring One's Own New Universe

I strive to help all my Aspies understand the world they live in using an analogy: They have been dropped off on Earth by a spacecraft and they have lost contact with their home world. This concept of comparing themselves to an exploring alien unwillingly dropped off on a highly socialized Earth resonates well with my Aspies. A Vulcan woman named T'Mir finds herself very much in the boat of the unwilling Aspie left among the humans when her ship, investigating the launch of *Sputnik* in 1957, crashes in Pennsylvania. She has to disguise her identity, concealing her habits and aspects of her own personality, in her efforts to live among the humans undetected until a rescue ship arrives.[13] Humans have a hard time understanding those who are different. *Different* often means bad as far as many people seem to feel. My Aspies have a hard time navigating the social world; and disguising themselves, just as T'Mir does, can be difficult and at times a necessity for existence. Being different most often means being bullied and hurt.

With this model of being different and feeling alone or unsafe in mind, my main job in life is to help find these young aliens, introduce them to other aliens, and assist them in building their own neurotribe.[14] The goal is to keep them safe from the humans and give them skills until they are able to live successfully in their world. Learning about the humans, understanding them, and celebrating the neurodiversity of our differences is the key. And is that not one of the greatest purposes of the Star Trek universe: to build an egalitarian, accepting, peaceful world of independent free thinkers? However, in reality Aspies are often taken advantage of, ignored, bullied, and mistreated.

But I Thought Asperger's Didn't Exist Anymore

The American Psychiatric Association first recognized Asperger's as a "syndrome" in the 4th edition of the *Diagnostic and Statistical Manual of Mental Disorders* (DSM-IV).[15] Asperger's was first clinically noted in 1944 by pediatrician Hans Asperger for whom this mind is named. While still hotly contested, the 5th edition of the *Diagnostic and Statistical Manual of Mental Disorders* (DSM-V) removed the term *Asperger's* and instituted the "Autism Spectrum"[16] with graded levels of severity. Most people who are "on the spectrum" identify with the term *Aspie*, and do not consider themselves as disordered or having a syndrome. Therefore, on some level, it is good news that Asperger's is no longer called a disorder, but unfortunately the DSM-V has made it much more difficult for people on the spectrum to get support.

Vulcan: An Aspie Planet

Everywhere you look, the Aspie mind is present in a variety of ways. Spock has a propensity to be literal and is curious about human nature. After discovering that the people of Earth have the capacity for deep space travel,[17] Vulcans provide guidance, along with the Vulcan's obsessive focus throughout humanity's first steps and bold adventures exploring beyond the solar system. Vulcans, in their quest for greater knowledge, peace, and self-control may represent the ultimate evolution of one kind of Aspie mind. Understand that there are a variety of Aspies, just as there are a variety of humans. If you have met one Aspie, then you have met one Aspie.[18] They are all different, but they do sync up along a few characteristics that tend to hang together.

Intelligent with Hyper-Focus

The most predominant stereotype of Vulcans may be their advanced intelligence, problem-solving, and tendency toward being highly focused in a particular area, such as religion, philosophy, technology, and the like. Their minds tend to operate in a very logical fashion, which is similar to how the Aspie mind works. Famously, Spock sacrifices himself to save the crew of the *Enterprise*.[19] Logic supersedes illogical, emotional connections. The Vulcan mind matches well with the Asperger's mind. Aspies tend to have great difficulty differentiating the justice of a situation from the social and emotional ramifications of that situation. It is difficult for them to recognize the gravity and importance of emotion in relationships, although they strive for understanding.

The emphasis on logic and intelligence seems to be a reactionary, balancing strategy in response to their deficiencies in understanding emotional relationships. In essence, if one is weak in one area, one will become strong in another. Spock's compensation for his lack of understanding emotions and social awareness has led toward a superior understanding of technology, logic, and the rule of law. Thus, the lack of or deficient understanding of social relationships has allowed for a brain that hyper-focuses on variables in society lacking an emotional component. The determined hyper-focus and high intelligence of the Vulcan mind allows for significant advancement across the entire Star Trek franchise. Similarly, the singular focus of an Aspie mind, stripped of the necessity of understanding and being swayed by social relationships, has allowed for the advancement of technology and invention across millennia of human history. Roddenberry seems to intuitively recognize the role of this mind and incorporates its intelligence and "freight-train brain" focus into his future-verse.

Socially Awkward

Aspies typically are socially awkward, and may obsess or hyper-focus for hours and hours on an activity or special interest while the rest of the world falls away. One theory as to why social communication becomes less valuable is that if one part of the brain becomes singularly specialized on a specific interest, such as science or technology, then the role of socialization becomes far less important. If one is to focus on astronomy, nuclear physics, or radiology for days on end, the brain's need to develop a social and emotional IQ becomes less important. This can be biologically manifested in the brain as reduced or lack of *othermindedness*.[20] Othermindedness is essentially the ability to take another person's perspective, allowing one to accurately and actively read nonverbal communication. This cognitive and social ability usually develops around the age of four or five, but some Aspies never fully develop this skill.

Author Steve Silberman made an astute observation about the tribal nature of Aspies.[21] Silberman recounted a sailing trip he took with the legendary coder, Larry Wall, who invented the Perl programming language. On the vessel were coders and hackers of all sorts and conversation surrounded geek life, including *Lord of the Rings*, theoretical physics, and puns of all sorts. Steve likened them to wizards who were among their own people, or "tribe," and were free to be themselves without fear of exclusion or bullying. He described Larry Wall's clothing as eccentric and flamboyant, with tuxedos in every color you could imagine. Such an appearance conjures *Star Trek: First Contact*'s Zefram Cochrane who also displays a flair for eccentric dress and obsession with scarves.[22]

Being within the realm of science fiction consistently exposed Gene Roddenberry to highly intelligent, creative, focused, and socially awkward people. It may be no coincidence that he gave the world the icon of Spock if the character was born out of Roddenberry's exposure to and experience with people on the spectrum. Spock seems like a full-fledged Aspie. During *Star Trek*'s original run, the term *Asperger's* had not become commonly known; however, the mind of the

Aspie has always been with us. This mind is not a disorder and has been an invaluable resource for humanity since the beginning of time.

Literal

> **Kirk:** "If we play our cards right, we may be able to find out when those whales are being released."
>
> **Spock:** "How will playing cards help?"[23]

The Aspie mind tends to be severely logical, which may interfere with the emotional nuance needed for social reciprocity. When asked on an IQ test, "Why do police officers wear uniforms?" the answer should be, "So that society will understand the difference between police officers and civilians." A common Aspie answer is "If they didn't wear uniforms, they would be naked." Spock epitomizes the concrete interpretation of language throughout his ongoing social and emotional conversations with the crew of the *Enterprise.*

> **Kirk:** "How close will we come to the nearest Klingon outpost if we continue on our present course?"
>
> **Chekov:** "One parsec, sir. Close enough to smell them."
>
> **Spock:** "That is illogical, Ensign. Odors cannot travel through the vacuum of space."[24]

Spock is endearing to society, as we have all known and loved individuals very smart but excessively literal, just like him. On a macro scale, society has known and loved the Aspie mind for thousands of years.

First Contact

First contact refers to the first encounter between humans and extraterrestrial aliens. In Star Trek, one of the first extraterrestrial Aspies to visit Earth may be Spock, when he journeys to 1930s New York City via time travel.[25] Without his superior intelligence, focus, and technical skills, time would be altered irreparably. Kirk can only succeed with the help of Spock's Aspie abilities.

Star Trek's official first contact between an Aspie-like alien and a human resembles a greeting between an Aspie and another Aspie. The inventor of warp technology is Zefram Cochrane, an eccentric, moody scientist who works tirelessly (when he's not drunk) to achieve faster-than-light travel. His special interest is science, and he tends to be blunt and highly opinionated. He often wears flamboyant outfits, possesses superior intelligence, and can hyper-focus on his special interests, one of which is late-twentieth-century rock music. When he is unable to listen to his music, he becomes very irritated. Similarly, Aspies can get very frustrated when they are unable to engage in or access their special interests. In Zefram's case, music is his soothing variable. I find it exceedingly fitting that an Aspie might be the first to meet a member of a species from another planet.

Damnit, Jim, It's Asperger's!

Humanity needs heterogeneity in order to continue its existence. We are explorers. And we are tinkerers. Asperger's has probably been with us since the beginning. The female or male Aspie could be the one who discovered how to make fire. Geology is a special interest of Aspies, and I would not be surprised if, while collecting rocks, an ancient Aspie stumbled upon flint. And upon striking the flint and creating a spark, this Aspie became invaluable to humanity. There is obviously no way of proving this, but my sentimental side believes an Aspie invented the arrow as well as the aqueduct system of the Roman Empire. The Aspie brain was and is needed for humanity's expansion and development. Without the hyper-focus of this mind, we would not know the world is round, nor would we have compasses or be able to understand the concept of gravity. Thank you, Isaac Newton and Albert Einstein. And thank you, Gene Roddenberry. You have created a universe that illustrates the necessity of the Aspie mind. What Roddenberry has not communicated is how likely it is that Asperger's is a more highly evolved version of humanity.

Human 2.0

A consistent pattern helps explain the explosion of the Asperger's mind upon Earth. Individuals with Aspie characteristics, perhaps highly intelligent but socially awkward, may be able to socialize and reproduce more easily as the world becomes more technologically advanced. Gene Roddenberry, consciously or unconsciously, may have introduced a love interest to Spock in the form of Nurse Chappell, a highly social and intelligent woman attracted to the less social but highly intelligent Spock. If so, Roddenberry may also have unconsciously shown us the future of humanity. Asperger's may be humanity's future. We might be seeing evolution occur right before our eyes. Gene Roddenberry seemingly described the future that is built on the minds and hyper-focus of the Aspies among us. Asperger's is definitely a different way of socializing, but it is not a wrong way of socializing.

References

American Psychiatric Association (2000). *Diagnostic and statistical manual of mental disorders* (4th ed., text rev.). Washington, DC: American Psychiatric Association.

American Psychiatric Association (2013). *Diagnostic and statistical manual of mental disorders* (5th ed.). Washington, DC: American Psychiatric Association.

Attwood, T. (2007/2015). *The complete guide to Asperger's syndrome.* London, UK: Jessica Kingsley.

Bornstein, D. (2011, June 30). *For some with autism, jobs to match their talents.* Opinionator: http://opinionator.blogs.nytimes.com/2011/06/30/putting-the-gifts-of-the-autistic-to-work/?_r=0.

Foresman, C. (2010, August 9). *How Star Trek artists imagined the iPad . . . 23 years ago.* Ars Technica: http://arstechnica.com/apple/2010/08/how-star-trek-artists-imagined-the-ipad-23-years-ago/.

Gaskill, F. (2012). *The world of Asperger's.* Southeast Psych: https://www.youtube.com/watch?v=Xg1Ngp1nGds.

Ledgin, N. (2002). *Asperger's and self-Esteem: Insight and hope through famous role models.* Arlington, TX: Future Horizons.

Maney, K. (2005, June 14). *Physics genius plans to make 'Star Trek' a reality.* USA Today: http://usatoday30.usatoday.com/money/industries/technology/maney/2005-06-14-replicator_x.htm.

Marzo, Clay. (n.d.). *About Clay.* Clay Marzo: http://www.claymarzo.com/about-clay.

Muir, H. (2003, April 30). *Einstein and Newton showed signs of autism.* New Scientist: https://www.newscientist.com/article/dn3676-einstein-and-newton-showed-signs-of-autism/.

Scanadu Scout (2014). *Scanadu Scout.* IndieGogo: https://www.indiegogo.com/projects/scanadu-scout#/story.

Silberman, S. (2015). *Neurotribes: The legacy of autism and the future of neurodiversity.* New York, NY: Penguin.

Steward, R. (2014, August 16). *Lesser-known things about Asperger's syndrome.* BBC: http://www.bbc.com/news/blogs-ouch-28746359.

Willingham, E. (2013, September 29). *'Wall Street' actress Daryl Hannah is an autistic woman.* Forbes: http://www.forbes.com/sites/emilywillingham/2013/09/29/wall-street-actress-daryl-hannah-also-autistic-woman/.

Zolfagharifard, D. (2015, August 19). *Warp speed could be a reality in the next 100 years: Star Trek-like travel between galaxies is possible, claims astrophysicist.* Daily Mail: http://www.dailymail.co.uk/sciencetech/article-3203772/Warp-speed-reality-100-years-Star-Trek-like-travel-galaxies-possible-claims-astrophysicist.html.

Notes

1. *Star Trek* episode 1–28, "The City on the Edge of Forever" (August 31, 1967).
2. Attwood (2007/2015), p. 357.
3. Foresman (2010); Scanadu Scout (2014).
4. e.g., Maney (2005).
5. Steward (2014).
6. Bornstein (2011).
7. Ledgin, (2002).
8. Zolfagharifard (2015).
9. Gaskill (2012).

10. Muir (2003).
11. Willingham (2013).
12. Marzo (n.d.).
13. *Enterprise* episode 2–2, "Carbon Creek" (September 25, 2002).
14. Silberman (2015).
15. American Psychiatric Association (2000).
16. American Psychiatric Association (2013).
17. *Star Trek: First Contact* (1996 motion picture).
18. Attwood (2007/2105).
19. *Star Trek II: The Wrath of Khan* (1982 motion picture).
20. Attwood (2007/2015).
21. Silberman (2015).
22. *Star Trek: First Contact* (1996 motion picture).
23. *Star Trek IV: The Voyage Home* (1986 motion picture).
24. *Star Trek* episode 2–15, "The Trouble with Tribbles" (December 29, 1967).
25. *Star Trek* episode 1–28, "The City on the Edge of Forever" (August 31, 1967).

Though the differences between the left and right sides of the brain have often been overstated, popular conceptions of "left-brained" and "right-brained" abilities open the door for discussion about those supposed differences and may help us recognize that intelligence is not one specific ability. "Smart" comes in many flavors.

•8•

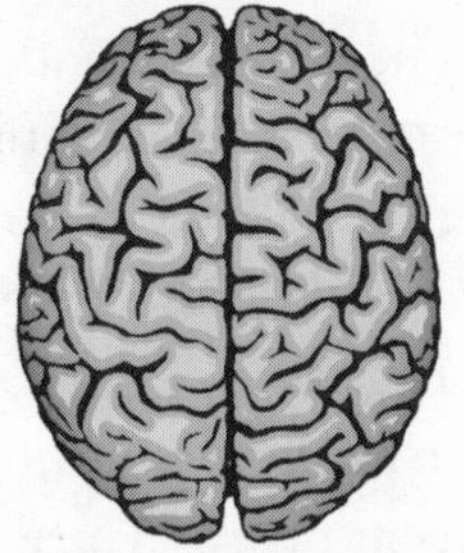

Right Brains, Left Brains, and Brains in the Middle: Star Trek's Exploration of Intellect

CRAIG POHLMAN

"Intellectual properties are not superposable, and therefore cannot be measured as linear surfaces are measured."

—intelligence test developer Alfred Binet[1]

"Brain. Brain. What is brain?"

—Kara the Eymorg[2]

Star Trek takes us to a lot of places: far-flung locations in the galaxy, alternate dimensions, and different time periods. Exploration is a motif that binds the canon together. Trek crews also have ventured into existential issues, including the nature of intellect. Humans need a varied set of mental abilities to solve problems, navigate life, and make progress (individually and collectively). Star Trek makes this point by depicting a range of characters, cultures, and civilizations that represent diverse forms of reasoning—namely, so-called right- and left-brained thinking.

Right Brains and Left Brains

Considerable research in the nineteenth and twentieth centuries (here, in Sector 001) indicated that the right and left halves of the brain are specialized to perform particular functions,[3] including speech abilities being localized in the left hemisphere.[4] The notion that certain types of thinking are limited to a particular hemisphere, though, has largely been debunked by more recent neuroscience research. Brain imaging has indicated relative levels of activation in the hemispheres in response to particular types of tasks, but thinking involves coordinated, cross-hemispheric connectivity and not separate left- and right-brained thinking.[5] Functionality is now known to be spread throughout healthy brains; for example, language areas tend to be located in the left hemisphere, but some aspects of language—such as interpretation of abstract language and humor—are typically found in the right hemisphere.[6]

Despite the fact that the terms oversimplify the distinction between the brain's hemispheres, "right-brained" and "left-brained" are now part of our vernacular, so much so that definitions for these terms can be found in dictionaries.[7] As commonly used, the term *right-brained* refers to thinking and behavior steered by emotion, creativity, intuition, nonverbal communication, and global reasoning rather than logic and analysis. On the other hand (or hemisphere), *left-brained* refers to thinking and behavior directed by logic, analytical thinking, and verbal communication, rather than emotion and creativity.[8] Star Trek is replete with so-called left-brained thinking, with its emphasis on science, analysis, exploration, and organized political structures, while other sci-fi canons are built much more on right-brained thinking, with references to spirituality and mystical forces. These two terms align with much more scientifically supported aspects of intelligence: fluid ("right-brained") and crystallized ("left-brained").

Fluid and Crystallized Intelligence

Psychologists have long since abandoned the notion that intelligence is a single ability. Rather, we now understand that intelligence comprises several abilities. Perhaps the most prominent theory of intelligence is *Cattell-Horn-Carroll* (CHC), which is grounded in an extensive body of research.[9] CHC is actually an amalgam of two bodies of work: Cattell-Horn theory and John Carroll's three-tier model of human cognitive abilities.

Research psychologist Raymond Cattell originally described a "fluid" ability that was thought to be able to flow into many mental activities; in other words, it was very adaptable to a multitude of experiences and tasks. He also defined "crystallized" ability that was considered an end product of experiences, such as education.[10] *Fluid* refers to solving new problems and using logic in novel situations, whereas *crystallized* refers to using previously acquired knowledge and experience. Cattell continued to refine these concepts, such as expanding the definition of *fluid intelligence* to include pattern recognition, abstract reasoning, and problem-solving.[11] A character like Deanna Troi, an extrasensory empath, exemplifies fluid intelligence with her holistic reading of emotional patterns and reliance on intuition. Chief Engineer Montgomery Scott relies on crystallized intelligence with his analysis of information related to the *Enterprise*'s operations. Certainly Scotty has to adapt and innovate with some of his problem-solving, but he really has to pull from his experience, established procedures, and specifications to get the job done.

In the 1960s, Cattell began a collaboration with cognitive psychologist John Horn, so his framework came to be known as Cattell-Horn. Their research looked at the relationship between fluid intelligence and crystallized intelligence. One study found that individuals with a high capacity for fluid intelligence tend to acquire more crystallized intelligence and at a faster rate.[12] It is as if fluid thinking primes the engine for the intake of facts and other information. This interplay between fluid and crystallized intelligence played out when *Enterprise-D*'s Lieutenant Reginald Barclay comes in contact with a Cytherian probe.[13] His fluid intelligence soars and he starts to soak up knowledge to the point that he interfaces his mind with the ship's computer. Fluid intelligence has paved the way for crystallized intelligence.

Yet another psychologist, John Carroll, later put forth his own framework on human cognitive abilities that bore several similarities to Cattell-Horn and also included fluid intelligence and crystallized intelligence.[14]

An important point about the CHC model is that each individual has a profile of abilities, as opposed to being a "fluid thinker" or having a "crystallized mind." Someone might be stronger in one area than the other, but even if that disparity is dramatic, he or she would still be capable of some degree of both. Again, Troi is great with fluid thinking and makes some use of crystallized thought, while Scotty is the opposite and can only operate using crystallized intelligence. Other Star Trek characters and civilizations illustrate both, helping to understand the distinctions between the two but also how they can be shared and balanced within an individual.

Trekking from the Right to the Left

So the lay definition of *right-brained thinking* lines up fairly well with fluid intelligence, which includes forming and recognizing logical relationships among patterns and transforming novel stimuli.[15] Seeing relationships in patterns and transforming new information sounds pretty close to creativity. The immortal Q are nearly omnipotent and can bring thoughts to reality in a blink, having mastered the cool trick of instantaneous matter-energy transformation.[16] High levels of fluid intelligence have been found to coincide with creativity; in fact, regression analyses suggested that fluid intelligence leads to creativity, as opposed to their merely being an unexplained correlation.[17] The Q lead a fluid existence—reasoning and problem-solving in novel ways—with the galaxy as their canvas.

Guinan represents a high level of fluid intelligence, but not as much as the Q. She has accrued a great deal of crystallized knowledge (facts and experiences) in her centuries-old existence, but she also employs fluid intelligence to facilitate problem-solving, such as when she helps Commander Riker to think outside the box to defeat the Borg and rescue Captain Picard.[18] As Guinan continues her march through the millennia, research suggests that she actually might lose some of her right-brained thinking over time. Fluid intelligence typically peaks in young adulthood and then steadily declines, possibly related to local atrophy of the brain in the right cerebellum.[19] On the other hand, crystallized intelligence typically increases gradually, stays relatively stable across most of adulthood, and then begins to decline.[20]

Vulcans are the nerds of the Trek universe. They would be the kids who always volunteer to answer teachers' questions, and they would repeatedly be correct, much to the chagrin of non-Vulcan peers. At first glance, they might seem very left-brained, primarily utilizing crystallized intelligence with their vast memory stores, but they actually combine right- and left-brained thinking to tackle challenges small and large. Anytime people solve math problems they utilize fluid intelligence, as research has shown that the stronger a person's fluid intelligence, the better his or her math reasoning.[21] This connection with math makes sense, given that fluid intelligence includes inductive, sequential, and quantitative reasoning.[22] Vulcans represent a balance of fluid and crystallized intelligence in other ways. Their use of logic is active and flows with the situation (fluid), whereas their rigorous education relies on considerable memorization (crystallized). To save their civilization from its own aggressive tendencies, ancient Vulcans adopt a philosophy based purely on logical principles that emphasize the repression and control of emotions.

Vulcan emotional self-control often leads to problematic peer relations (just ask Dr. McCoy). This socialization difficulty, combined with their high intelligence, is reminiscent of Asperger's syndrome. (See chapter 7, "Gene Roddenberry Saw the Future . . . and the Future is Asperger's.") Enhanced performance on fluid intelligence has been found among individuals in the autism population,[23] including Asperger's specifically.[24] So even though Vulcans may seem rather robotic, they balance right-brained thinking with their left-brained factual knowledge bases.

Speaking of robotic, Data's android brain allows for quite a bit of crystallized intelligence, but he is also equipped with a total linear computational speed, which enables him to mix in some fluid intelligence with all that knowledge.[25] On a number of occasions, Data uses his positronic neural network's equivalent of the human brain's right hemisphere, such as when he questions orders. A strictly left-brained, "by-the-book" thinker might obey the command of a superior officer without questioning the wisdom of it.

Lastly, all the way to the left side of the brain, are the Borg, who offer perhaps the best example of crystallized intelligence in Star Trek cannon. Their raison d'être is to achieve perfec-

The Jug Problem

You've got two empty jugs—one will hold exactly 3 gallons and the other 5 gallons. How can you measure precisely 1 gallon using only these two jugs, without wasting any water?

What would happen if Q, Guinan, a Vulcan (say, Tuvok), Data, and a Borg drone are tasked with solving this puzzle? Right-brained, fluid reasoning Q could snap his fingers to produce one gallon of water. Guinan might say that she is sure she's heard this puzzle before but doesn't remember the solution; instead, she'd pose prompting questions to the others to facilitate their reasoning. Tuvok would use both fluid and crystallized intelligence to nail it. Data also would nail it, but by downloading the response from his internal hard drive.

Incidentally, the solution is to fill the three-gallon jug and then empty the contents into the five-gallon jug. Then fill the three-gallon jug again and use it to fill the five-gallon jug to capacity. The remainder in the three-gallon jug is one gallon.

As for the Borg drone? It would tell everyone that "resistance is futile" and try to assimilate them. And the jugs. And the water.

tion through forcible assimilation of diverse species, civilizations, culture, and technology. As Q puts it, "The Borg is the ultimate user."[26] They accumulate vast amounts of knowledge, which they then utilize for decision-making and strategy use. Crystallized intelligence is about using acquired knowledge effectively.[27] The Borg show repeatedly how effective, even ruthless, they are at using co-opted knowledge. For example, rather than generating their own tactics for attacking the Federation, they instead kidnap Captain Picard to pirate his experience with Starfleet weaponry, capabilities, and maneuvers.[28] Just as the right-brained Q also have a degree of left-brained thinking, the Borg certainly use some fluid intelligence, but the Borg are primarily about acquiring and utilizing knowledge.

A Superior Intellect

Whether you use scientifically endorsed terminology—like *fluid intelligence* and *crystallized intelligence*—or lay terms like *right-* and *left-brained thinking*, intelligence comprises numerous components. A brain is kind of like a starship, with abilities related to the intake of information (sensors), memory (the holodeck or replicator), and planning (the bridge). The point is that intelligence isn't a single thing. And whether we're stronger with our left brains or our right brains, we need both to tackle challenges. Sometimes we need to make use of our knowledge, like Dr. Bones McCoy calling upon procedures he would have learned in medical school to save a patient or Geordi La Forge utilizing his experience with warp drive coils to avert disaster.[29] At other times, we need to think fluidly outside the box, like James Kirk reprogramming the simulator to solve the no-win scenario of the *Kobayashi Maru*.

References

Ackerman, P. L. (1996). A theory of adult intellectual development: Process, personality, interests, and knowledge. *Intelligence, 22*(2), 227–257.

American Heritage Dictionaries (2016). *American heritage dictionary of the English language* (5th ed.). Boston, MA: Houghton Mifflin.

Carroll, J. B. (1993). *Human cognitive abilities: A survey of factor analytic studies*. New York, NY: Cambridge University Press.

Cattell, R. B. (1943). *Abilities: Their structure, growth, and action*. New York, NY: Houghton Mifflin.

Cattell, R. B. (1963). Theory of fluid and crystallized intelligence: A critical experiment. *Journal of Educational Psychology, 54*(1), 1–22.

Cavanaugh, J. C., & Blanchard-Fields, F. (2006). *Adult development and aging* (5th ed.). Belmont, CA: Wadsworth.

Craig, J. D. (1979). Asymmetries in processing auditory nonverbal stimuli. *Psychological Bulletin, 86*(6), 1339–1349.

David, P. (1994). *Star Trek: The Next Generation—Q-squared*. New York, NY: Pocket.

Dawson, M., Soulières, I., Gernsbacher, M. A., & Mottron, L. (2007). The level and nature of autistic intelligence. *Psychological Science, 18*(8), 657–662.

Evans, J. J., Floyd, R. G., McGrew, K. S., & Leforgee, M. H. (2001). The relations between measures of Cattell-Horn-Carroll (CHC) cognitive abilities and reading achievement during childhood and adolescence. *School Psychology Review, 31*(2), 246–262.

Flanagan, D. P., McGrew, K. S., & Ortiz, S. (2000). *The Wechsler Intelligence Scales and Gf–Gc Theory: A contemporary approach to interpretation*. Needham Heights, MA: Allyn & Bacon.

Geake, J. (2008). Neuromythologies in education. *Educational Research, 50*(2), 123–133.

Gould, S. J. (1981). *The mismeasure of man*. New York, NY: W. W. Norton.

Hayashi, M., Kato, M., Igarashi, K., & Kashima, H. (2008). Superior fluid intelligence in children with Asperger's disorder. *Brain & Cognition, 66*(3), 306–310.

Lee, J-Y., Lyoo, I. K., Kim, S-U., Jang, H-S., Lee, D-W., Jeon, H-J., Park, S-C., & Cho, M. J. (2005). Intellect declines in healthy elderly subjects and cerebellum. *Psychiatry and Clinical Neurosciences, 59*(1), 45–51.

Proctor, B.E., Floyd, R.G., & Shaver, R.B. (2005). Cattell-Horn-Carroll broad cognitive ability profiles of low math achievers. *Psychology in the Schools, 42*(1), 1–12.

Roediger III, H. L., Rushton, J. P., Capaldi, E. D., & Paris, S. G. (1984). *Psychology*. Boston, MA: Little, Brown.

Roid, G. H., & Barram, R. A. (2004). *Essentials of Stanford-Binet Intelligence Scales (SB5) assessment*. Hoboken, NJ: Wiley.

Schneider, W. J., & McGrew, K. S. (2012). The Cattell-Horn-Carroll Model of Intelligence. In D. P. Flanagan & P. L. Harrison (Eds.), *Contemporary intellectual assessment: Theories, tests, and issues* (3rd ed., pp. 99–144). New York, NY: Guilford.

Sekuler, R., & Blake, R. (1998). *Star Trek on the brain: Alien minds, human minds*. London, UK: Freeman.

Sligh, A. C., Conners, F. A., & Roskos-Ewoldsen, B. (2005). Relation of creativity to fluid and crystallized intelligence. *Journal of Creative Behavior, 39*(2), 123–136.

Springer, S. P., & Deutsch, G. (2001). *Left brain, right brain: Perspectives from cognitive neuroscience*. London, UK: Freeman.

Stephens, R. (2016). *The left brain speaks, the right brain laughs: A look at the neuroscience of innovation & creativity in art, science, & life*. Jersey City, NJ: Viva.

Tokuhama-Espinosa, T. (2010). *The new science of teaching and learning: Using the best of mind, brain, and education science in the classroom*. New York, NY: Teachers College.

Notes

1. Binet, quoted by Gould (1981), p. 151.
2. *Star Trek* episode 3–1, "Spock's Brain" (September 20, 1968).
3. Roediger et al. (1984).
4. Craig (1979).
5. Geake (2008).
6. Tokuhama-Espinosa (2010).
7. e.g., *American Heritage Dictionaries* (2016).
8. Spring & Deutsch (2001); Stephens (2016).
9. Flanagan et al. (2000); Roid & Barram (2004).
10. Cattell (1943).
11. Cattell (1963).
12. Ackerman (1996).
13. *Star Trek: The Next Generation* episode 4–9, "The Nth Degree" (April 1, 1991).
14. Carroll (1993).
15. Evans et al. (2001).
16. First in *Star Trek: The Next Generation* episode 1–1, "Encounter at Farpoint," part 1 (September 28, 1987); arguably in *Star Trek* episode 1–17, "The Squire of Gothos" (January 12, 1967), according to David (1994).

17. Sligh et al. (2005).
18. *Star Trek: The Next Generation* episode 4–1, "The Best of Both Worlds," part 2 (September 24, 1990).
19. Lee et al. (2005).
20. Cavanaugh & Blanchard-Fields (2006).
21. Proctor et al. (2005).
22. Carroll (1993).
23. Dawson et al. (2007).
24. Hayashi et al. (2008).
25. Sekuler & Blake (1998).
26. *Star Trek: The Next Generation* episode 2–16, "Q Who?" (May 8, 1989).
27. Evans et al. (2001).
28. *Star Trek: The Next Generation* episodes 3–26 and 4–1, "The Best of Both Worlds," parts 1 (June 19, 1990) and 2 (September 24, 1990).
29. e.g., *Star Trek: The Next Generation* episode 6–25, "Timescape" (June 14, 1993).

Log File II

Star Trek: The Next Generation and the Need for Cognition

TRAVIS LANGLEY

Among the various theorists attempting to list human psychological needs, biologist-turned-psychologist Henry Murray may be the most influential.[1] Unlike previous personality theorists who developed their ideas from intuition, their own experience, or case studies of emotionally disturbed patients, Murray gathered data from normal individuals to develop his ideas about typical personality development.[2] From his findings, he compiled a list of twenty psychological needs that influence people to varying degrees. Needs vary in their power to influence us, and not everyone feels every need. One of the needs Murray identified, the *need for understanding* (valuing discussion, reason, and logic) manifests in *Star Trek: The Next Generation*'s leading characters more prominently than in other Trek series. Researchers tend to look at this more broadly as the *need for cognition* (the need to experience reality through *cognition*—all mental activities, including thought, reason, analysis, and understanding).[3]

When *Star Trek: The Next Generation* debuted, viewers immediately noted similarities to and differences from the original 1960s series. At the heart of all the comparisons and debates, one question kept coming up: Who would win in a fight—Kirk or Picard?[4] The original *Star Trek* regularly weighs the relative merits of logic and reasoning versus emotion and action, with Spock and McCoy acting as metaphorical devil and angel on Kirk's shoulders (swapping those roles at times, depending on the circumstances at hand). *The Next Generation*, while valuing emotion as a core aspect of human experience, places greater emphasis on finding logical, diplomatic solutions to problems. Picard needs to think.

People lower in need for cognition make decisions quickly and reach more conclusions based on *heuristics*, mental shortcuts. While Kirk might be more prone to forming judgments based on the *availability heuristic*, relying on whatever information is readily available and springs to his mind, Picard wants to gather as much information as possible. Each method has its advantages and disadvantages. The heuristic approach helps us take action when a quick decision is needed, but can also raise the possibility of making errors, such as when we make decisions based on *stereotypes* (beliefs that certain kinds of people act in specific ways). Picard is less prone to forming expectations about individuals based on *stereotypes*, assumptions about Klingons or any other individuals based solely on preconceptions about any group to which they might belong.[5] While Kirk might not score extremely low in need for cognition, Picard would score much higher.

Picard does not have Spock and McCoy arguing the merits and shortcomings of logic. Most characters in *The Next Generation* appreciate a reasoned line of problem-solving. Circumstances prove them right often, but not always. Whenever the more impulsive Worf recommends immediately raising shields, preparing weapons, or otherwise going into combat mode even in everyday interactions, other characters often take turns telling him, in effect, "No, thanks, you bull in a china shop."[6] Although they tend to be right, the *Enterprise* sometimes takes damage that Worf's warrior response might have prevented. People high in need for cognition make errors of their own.

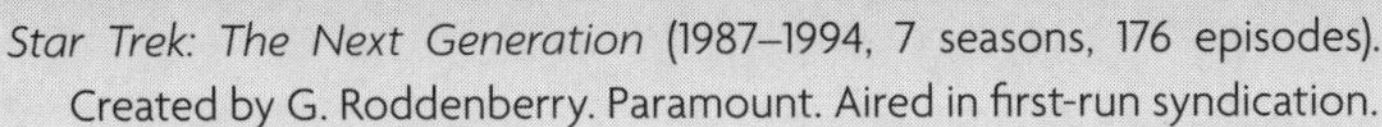

Star Trek: The Next Generation (1987–1994, 7 seasons, 176 episodes). Created by G. Roddenberry. Paramount. Aired in first-run syndication.

Each captain may be a product of his time. Kirk's cut-to-the-chase approach may be necessary more often at his point in the Federation's history. There is a time to act and a time to think.

References

Cohen, A. R., Stotland, E., & Wolfe, D. M. (1955). An experimental investigation of need for cognition. *Journal of Abnormal & Social Psychology, 51*(2), 291–294.

McDonnell, D. (2015, June 9). *Kirk vs. Picard: An enduring debate.* Star Trek: http://www.startrek.com/article/kirk-vs-picard-an-enduring-debate.

Murray, H. A. (1938). *Explorations in personality: A clinical and experimental study of fifty men of college age.* New York, NY: Oxford University Press.

Petty, R. E., Briñol, P., Loersch, C., & McCaslin, M. J. (2009). The need for cognition. In M. R. Leary & R. H. Hoyle (Eds.), *Handbook of individual differences in social behavior.* New York, NY: Guilford.

Schultz, D. P., & Schultz, S. E. (2013). *Theories of personality* (9th ed.) Belmont, CA: Wadsworth.

tarnationsauce2 (2011, April 5). *Worf gets DENIED again and again on Star Trek TNG.* YouTube: https://www.youtube.com/watch?v=edflm7Hh3hs.

Notes

1. Murray (1938).
2. Schultz & Schultz (2013).
3. Cohen et al. (1955).
4. McDonnell (2015).
5. Petty et al. (2009).
6. tarnationsauce2 (2011).

Mental disorder can warp a person's whole life or only certain pieces. It can inflict pain, distort personality, and waste human potential, but so can an emotional state such as terror. Whether a person suffers temporarily or for the long term, help may be available in surprising places and forms.

PART III

WARPED DRIVES

Science fiction can help us examine many kinds of human diversity with new perspective. Too often, though, it might treat superficially (or altogether overlook) variety in mental health.

•9•

What Happened to Mental Illness by the 23rd Century?

STEVEN SCHLOZMAN

"I'm a surgeon, not a psychiatrist."
—Dr. McCoy[1]

"Mental illness, the final frontier."
—journalist Tom Davis[2]

Things are pretty great on the Earth of twenty-third-century *Star Trek*. We've banished war, erased famine,[3] and probably even solved the vexing problems of occasionally bad pizza and accompanying lactose intolerance. Even San Francisco appears to have avoided (or perhaps even prevented) any kind of massive seismic event, and Starfleet Academy is a beacon of optimism and potential with the Golden Gate Bridge still proudly standing.[4] But, alas, there is still disease in this bright, shiny future. Each starship has a sick bay and a doctor. That doctor might be a virtual creation, such as the one aboard *Voyager*, or a simple country doctor as we see with Dr. McCoy, but it can never be said that humans and aliens don't get ill. Indeed, many of the show's episodes involve at least some version of sickness for which the presiding doctor must wring his hands. The final frontier, it seems, involves discovering strange new diseases as well.

Except when we talk about mental health.

Nearly one-fifth of U.S. adults suffer some form of mental illness in a given year.[5] Furthermore, the age of onset of many of these syndromes is early adulthood. Depression, bipolar disorder, schizophrenia, and panic disorder show up on average during late adolescence. On the sheer basis of that mental disorder prevalence, the *Enterprise*, if it were launched into space today, would quickly be teeming with psychiatric troubles. And yet, there is rarely a psychiatrist or a psychologist to be found.

Beaming Up Everything But Mental Illness

It is, in fact, not difficult to recall specific episodes in which various characters suffer ailments akin to psychosis or mania—for example, Sulu running around the *Enterprise* with a sword[6] or Lieutenant Barclay becoming grandiose in his newfound brilliance after he is assaulted by an energy surge.[7] People do indeed suffer psychiatrically on Star Trek, but the *reasons* they suffer differ markedly from most modern interpretations of psychopathology. Sulu's sword-wielding antics are caused by exposure to a contaminant on an Earth-like world that the *Enterprise* has been assigned to observe as that world effectively falls apart. Barclay does, in fact, become a super-genius, and to that end his grandiosity is at least grounded in his newly formidable intellect and not in his imagined grandeur.

Crew members may become *psychotic* (experiencing serious loss of contact with reality), but they are psychotic with clearly explicable *etiologies* (origins). This stands in stark contrast to what some have argued is the uncomfortable tautology of our current understanding of mental illness. If Sulu arrived in an emergency room today, his shirt off and his sword out and ready,[8] it is very likely that he would be seen as manic (in an abnormal, maladaptive energized state[9]) simply because he appears manic. We would without question do a toxicology screen and even perhaps an MRI of his brain if we could sedate him enough to hold him still, but we wouldn't be able to find a toxin that we're not looking for.[10] Whatever he was exposed to on the planet would evade our investigations and we would shrug our shoulders and call him manic. The irony of this presumed diagnosis is that our observation would be true. Our current *nosology* (classification of diseases) is based on observation and rule-outs only. If we could not rule out other causes of his behavior, then it would be entirely appropriate to call his behavior manic, and our treatments—probably a routine cocktail of antipsychotics and mood stabilizers—might also help.

People do not tend to fall psychiatrically ill aboard the *Enterprise* without a concrete, external reason unrelated to our world, such as alien infection[11] or time travel.[12] The central psychological message, therefore, would seem to be that if someone falls psychiatrically ill, there is little to no role for the mental health practitioner.[13] Those nebulous problems of the primitive twentieth and twenty-first centuries have been solved! (And, yes, Counselor Troi *is* a mental health practitioner of sorts, but we'll get to her in a few pages.)

All of this stands in stark contrast to current conceptualizations of psychiatric disease. Psychiatrists in recent decades have pushed back against the notion that psychiatric illness must have clear causes to be real. This is not to say that we are entirely comfortable with this stance. The famous psychiatric geneticist Ken Kendler notes that "many in our field want to move to a hard medical model," based on the disorders' causes.[14] Whereas Star Trek can, by the end of each episode or movie, explain exactly what has happened, modern-day psychiatrists cling to the more nebulous world of the *stress-diathesis model*.[15] We humans suffer some inborn or acquired biological *diathesis*—a predisposition, in other words—to mental illness, and an environmental stressor triggers the onset of the psychiatric disease. If we look again to the seemingly manic Sulu, we might be tempted to argue that the same model applies. Perhaps Sulu had an underlying tendency toward shirtless swashbuckling, but it took a clearly defined contaminant to bring this tendency to the forefront.

There are, however, fundamental differences between the eventual explanation for Sulu's manic break and our current understanding of something as descriptively clear-cut as mania. In the case of Sulu, viewers know exactly what the contaminant is, but there is no discussion of Sulu's existing predispositions.[16] Similarly, we know that Barclay's imbibed energy surge leads to his genuine brilliance, but the show fails to discuss what in Barclay's unique psychological makeup would lead to his grandiosity and subsequently dangerous behavior.[17] It is as if the "stress" aspect of the stress-diathesis model is the only aspect that matters in understanding aberrant behavior. Without this stress, crew members simply do not fall mentally ill. This conclusion, however, belies current epidemiological fact that approximately one in five people suffer some mental illness in a given year.[18]

Star Trek's Modernist View of Suffering

How do we understand this paradox? Is this a deliberate statement among the creators and writers of the show? Are we to believe that the almost 20 percent of the general population that used to develop psychiatric illness simply don't suffer anymore in the future? The answer to this query, like all answers that grapple with the messy world of mental health, most likely lies in the somewhat naive notion that if we cure the world of its social ills, we cure the world of its psychiatric suffering as well.

This is not a new idea. Critics of modern psychiatry have in the past argued forcefully that profound psychiatric suffering was instead a reasonable response to chaotic environments and the need for self-expression.[19] Even today, psychiatrists and psychologists are conflicted as to how much emphasis internal biology ought to play in the understanding of mental illness.[20]

If science is our guide and our savior in the Star Trek universe, then it would stand to reason that science has solved the mysteries of human existence, including the mysteries of mental illness. This means that what is left for the crew of the *Enterprise* when aberrant behavior strikes is to discover the scientific reason for the behavior. This approach goes beyond the modern-day rudimentary classification of psychiatric illness that characterizes current psychiatric nosology and explanation. To put it more simply, if the world of Star Trek has solved the problems of mental disease, then the remaining causes of apparent mental disease presentations can only be explicable and observable environmental phenomena.

Calling Counselor Troi a Therapist

People on the *Enterprise* do need to talk. That much is made clear implicitly by the many heart-to-heart discussions that Kirk, Spock, and McCoy share,[21] and then (and some might argue unfortunately[22]) through the explicit services of Counselor Troi.

While it is my argument that no formal psychiatric syndromes as we would define them today according to *DSM* criteria[23] appear on the *Enterprise*, it remains the case that the everyday neurotic suffering of humans persists and can easily be "counseled" away through a kind of psychotherapy that is at best a form of unsophisticated supportive psychotherapy. Modern mental health treatments come in a wide variety of forms, not simply talk therapy or medication.[24] Counselor Troi tells crew members over and over that what they feel is perfectly normal and this reassurance seems to "cure" them, and their suffering may be put at ease by relatively simple discussions with Counselor Troi.

Rehabilitating Instead of Intervening

When Kirk and Spock are dispatched to an actual psychiatric hospital to deliver a vital new medication that can cure the remaining criminally insane humans and aliens who have not been cured by the otherwise harmonious state of the Federation, Star Trek presents one of its few stories in which psychiatric illness is explicitly discussed.[25] A once-great military leader who is overcome with *grandiose delusions* (delusions of grandeur) fools Captain Kirk into thinking that he, the patient, is in fact the director of the hospital. We might look at this episode as an uneasy reconciliation in Star Trek's truce with modern conceptualizations of mental illness and the desire that mental illnesses will be erased when social injustices are eradicated. Criminal insanity, it would seem, is immune to the curing of the social ills that are put forth as reasons for other psychiatric diseases. For the criminally insane, medications are needed, restraints are often required, and patients at the asylum quite literally have lost touch with reality.

In this episode, we could arguably see the various philosophical forces that have characterized debates about psychiatry since the mid-twentieth century playing out in the typically overly dramatic fashion of Star Trek's genesis. Does the military genius become psychotic because of his ability to shapeshift into whatever he wants? Or does this even matter as long

Normal versus Abnormal Depression

Everyone feels down at times, some people more often or more severely than others, but without necessarily suffering mental illness. *Depressed mood*, a low mood with feelings such as sadness, emptiness, helplessness, or shame, can be a normal reaction to circumstances and fall within the range of common human responses. Though the deaths of his brother and nephew upset Picard and affect him deeply,[26] the distress is not a strange human reaction. Forms of abnormal depression as mental disorder involve greater severity, duration, and number of symptoms that the majority of people do not suffer (although *major depression* is the most frequently diagnosed specific mental illness). Miles O'Brien is one of the few main Star Trek characters whose depressed state may meet the criteria for major depressive disorder after *pseudomemories* (false memories[27]) of a twenty-year prison sentence are implanted in his head. He suffers over those memories to the point of turning suicidal until he at last accepts help in the form of medication and long-term counseling—but without immediate return to his previous level of emotional health.[28]

—T.L.

as he is treated with the proper medication? Should we call his treatment a medical intervention or, as the episode prefers, a *rehabilitation*? It is as if schools of psychiatric phenomenology were pitted against each other in this episode and, at the end of the day, the patients, whether dangerous or not, are treated with dignity and compassion.

Redemption

The sentiment—that psychiatric suffering deserves the benefit of dignity and the solace of compassion—may be how Star Trek redeems itself with regard to mental health. As with all treatments of life characteristic of the protagonists in Star Trek, things remain decent and civil. There might be what we would in today's world consider a naive view of how to perceive mental health problems and how best to treat them, but there is *no* ambiguity in terms of the fundamental humanity that unites our suffering—even if that suffering is itself in the form of a green-skinned alien or an android. At the end of the day, the unbridled optimism and goodwill of Star Trek prevail, even in the murky world of psychiatric epistemology.

References

Agius, M., & Goh, C. (2010). The stress-vulnerability model: How does stress impact on mental illness at the level of the brain and what are the consequences? *European Psychiatry, 251591* (10)71572–71578.

American Psychiatric Association. (2013). *Diagnostic and statistical manual of mental disorders* (5th ed.).Washington, DC: American Psychiatric Association.

Berent, S., & Albers, J. W. (2010). *Neurobehavioral toxicology: Neurological and neuropsychological perspectives* (vol. III). New York, NY: Taylor & Francis.

Berry, A., & Cirulli, F., (2016). Toward a diathesis-stress model of schizophrenia in neurodevelopmental perspective. In M. V. Pletnikov & J. Waddington (Eds.), *Modeling the psychological dimensions of schizophrenia: From molecules to behavior.* Amsterdam, Netherlands: Elsevier.

Culpepper, L. (2014). The diagnosis and treatment of bipolar disorder: Decision-making in primary care. *Primary Care Companion for CNS Disorders, 16*(3), PCC 12r01609.

Davis, T. (2008, May 29). *Mental illness, the final frontier.* Huffington Post: http://www.huffingtonpost.com/tom-davis/mental-illness-the-final_b_104067.html.

Duchak, J. (2016, September 18). *Star Trek's poor depiction of mental illness in a hopeful future.* Trek Movie: http://trekmovie.com/2016/09/18/star-treks-poor-depiction-of-mental-illness-in-a-hopeful-future/.

Green, J. P., Lyn, S. J., & Malinoski, P. (1998). Hypnotic pseudomemories, prehypnotic warnings, and malleability of suggested memories. *Applied Cognitive Psychology, 12*(5), 413–444.

Jongsma, A. E., Jr., Peterson, M., & Bruce, T. J. (2014). *The complete adult psychotherapy treatment planner* (5th ed.). New York, NY: Wiley.

Kendler, K. S. (2012). Levels of explanation in psychiatric and substance use disorders: Implications for the development of an etiologically based nosology. *Molecular Psychiatry, 17*(1), 11–21.

Lynn, S. J., Rhue, J. W., Myers, B. P., & Weekes, J. R. (1994). Pseudomemory in hypnotized and simulating subjects. *International Journal of Clinical & Experimental Hypnosis, 42*(2), 118–129.

National Institute of Mental Health (n.d.). *Any mental illness (AMI) among U.S. adults.* National Institute of Mental Health: http://www.nimh.nih.gov/health/statistics/prevalence/any-mental-illness-ami-among-us-adults.shtml.

Raeburn, P. (2006, January 23). *Finding bipolar disorder with MRI.* Technology Review: https://www.technologyreview.com/s/405200/finding-bipolar-disorder-with-mri/.

Sheehan, P. W., Green, V., & Truesdale, P. (1992). Influence of rapport on hypnotically induced pseudomemory. *Journal of Abnormal Psychology, 101*(4), 690–700.

Strakowski, S. M., Adler, C. M., Cerullo, M. A., Eliassen, J. C., Lamy, M., Fleck, D. E., Lee, J., & DelBello, M. P. (2008). MRI brain activation in first-episode mania during a response inhibition task. *Early Intervention Psychiatry, 2*(4), 225–233.

Szasz, T. (1960). The myth of mental illness. *American Psychologist, 15*(2), 113–118.

Szasz, T. (1994). Psychiatric diagnosis, psychiatric power, and psychiatric abuse. *Journal of Medical Ethics, 20*(3), 135–138.

Woo-kyoung, A., Proctor, C. C., & Flanagan, E. H. (2009). Mental health clinicians' beliefs about the biological, psychological, and environmental bases of mental disorders. *Cognitive Science, 33*(2), 147–182.

Notes

1. *Star Trek* episode 1–28, "The City of the Edge of Forever" (April 6, 1967).
2. Davis (2008).
3. *Star Trek: The Next Generation* episodes 7–25 and 7–26, "All Good Things . . ." parts 1 and 2 (May 23, 1994).
4. *Star Trek: The Motion Picture* (1979 motion picture); *Star Trek IV: The Voyage Home* (1986 motion picture).
5. National Institute of Mental Health (n.d.).
6. *Star Trek* episode 1–3, "The Naked Time" (September 29, 1966).
7. *Star Trek: The Next Generation* episode 4–19, "The Nth Degree" (April 1, 1991).
8. As in *Star Trek* episode 1–4, "The Naked Time" (September 29, 1966).
9. American Psychiatric Association (2013).
10. Berent & Albers (2010); Culpepper (2014); Raeburn (2006); Strakowski et al. (2008).
11. *Star Trek* episode 1–4, "The Naked Time" (September 29, 1966); *Star Trek: The Next Generation* episode 1–3, "The Naked Now" 1–3 (October 5, 1987).
12. *Star Trek: Voyager* episode 5–23, "Relativity" (May 12, 1999).
13. Duchak (2016).
14. Kendler (2012), p. 11.
15. e.g., Agius & Goh (2010); Berry & Cirulli (2016).
16. *Star Trek* episode 1–3, "The Naked Time" (September 29, 1966).
17. *Star Trek: The Next Generation* episode 4–19, "The Nth Degree" (April 1, 1991).
18. National Institute of Mental Health (n.d.).
19. e.g., Szasz (1960, 1994).
20. Woo-kyoung et al. (2009).
21. From the first episode aired through the last film to feature the three together—respectively, *Star Trek* episode 1–1, "The Man Trap" (September 6, 1966), and *Star Trek VI: The Undiscovered Country* (1991 motion picture).
22. e.g., Duchak (2016).
23. American Psychiatric Association (2013).
24. Jongsma et al. (2014).
25. *Star Trek* episode 3–14, "Whom Gods Destroy" (January 3, 1969).
26. *Star Trek: Generations* (1994 motion picture).
27. Green et al. (1998); Lynn et al. (1994); Sheehan et al. (1992).
28. Star Trek: Deep Space Nine episode 4–19, "Hard Time" (April 15, 1996).

Immersing oneself in the imaginary, despite its potential for keeping the person from facing reality, can also help someone face it more creatively. The holodeck in the 24th century holds therapeutic potential and promise akin to that of one of the most successful forms of therapy used in the 21st.

•10•

Holodeck Therapy: Psychological Healing in the 24th Century

PATRICK O'CONNOR AND CHRIS DAY

"It's been fun. Computer—end program. Erase all programs filed under 'Reginald Barclay.' Except program nine."
—Lieutenant Barclay[1]

"There are three musts that hold us back: 'I must do well.' 'You must treat me well.' 'And the world must be easy.'"
—clinical psychologist Albert Ellis[2]

People spend about half their waking hours in fantasy.[3] Whether we use our minds constructively to work on a problem before we can actually address it or we use it playfully to spin wild daydreams about the future, human imagination is boundless in its variety (and usefulness!) of fantasy. Imagine now if such dreams could be brought to everyday life. In Star Trek, technology has advanced to the point where fantasy can become virtual reality in the form of the holodeck.[4] Imagine the potential for fully immersive virtual reality, simulated experience indistinguishable from reality as far as the physical senses can detect. Therapists have already reported some success using virtual reality in therapeutic situations to treat or even prevent psychiatric problems, especially those involving anxiety over specific stimuli and situations.[5] *Meta-analysis* (analysis of other analyses) of studies assessing the success of virtual reality therapy shows that it can produce significant improvement in real-life situations.[6]

Psychological therapies often utilize fantasy in a myriad of ways. From the expressive arts (drama, visual art, music, dance and movement, poetry) to psychoanalysis to solution-focused approaches, working with fantasy is paramount to improving the well-being of an individual.[7] In fact, fantasizing about the concrete steps necessary to accomplish a goal or alleviate a stressor has been demonstrated to increase the likelihood of completing such a task.[8] We can see the power of thought processes in relieving stress and accomplishing goals. Because fantasy consists of a web of interconnected thoughts and emotions, focusing on *cognition* (a person's thinking patterns) seems obvious as an effective approach to addressing concerns within the individual. Change the thinking pattern, change the person. So how do we go about doing this? Perhaps the answer awaits on the holodeck.

The Holodeck

Simply put, the holodeck is a highly complex and immersive room of virtual reality that's utilized on twenty-fourth-century Federation starships.[9] Within its walls, this immersive virtual reality combines transportation, replication, and holographic technology to create nearly any possible environment, character, or scenario with an extreme sense of realism. Equipped with standard safety protocols, the technology typically prevents any serious harm from coming to its users. For non-starships, such as in Quark's bar in Deep Space 9, where there is no deck, this technology is often referred to as a *holosuite*.[10]

When Commander Riker is charged with murder by an alien species,[11] the holodeck is used to re-create detailed depictions of the events leading up to the crime. This is similar to therapy, in that a person involved with the event is given a chance to reconsider his or her thoughts on the matter. By revisiting a scene and challenging existing thought patterns, a person can gain new perspective and feel relief. The holodeck has even been used as a holding ground to transport a group of primitive people to a new planet without their knowledge of being aboard a starship.[12] With such capabilities to create people, scenes, or literal worlds out of nothing, it can easily bring up questions of "What is real?" and how to interpret reality.

Cognitive Behavior Therapies

Several forms of therapy exist that target personal interpretation of internal and external events, such as feeling an emotion (*internal event*, within themselves) or wondering why a friend or starship crew member is behaving a certain way (*external event*, outside themselves). By focusing on cognition, many psychologists believe a person can overcome troubles by changing the way a situation is understood, whether that means counteracting destructive thoughts or increasing awareness of the link between thoughts and behaviors that result in beneficial outcomes.

Cognitive Restructuring

Cognitive behavior therapy (CBT), an approach to therapy that focuses on changing thought patterns as well as behaviors, has been used in developing assertiveness or communicating opinions in an honest and appropriate way.[13] A major component to improving assertiveness involves *cognitive restructuring*, which changes the thinking patterns of the client. A therapist taking a CBT approach while using virtual reality simulations potentially could, among other things, offer clients a means to directly face worrisome situations without the fear of physical danger and therefore build confidence in their decision-making abilities.[14] By pointing out catastrophic thoughts, such as endless what-if's, the therapist can illuminate how unhelpful these fantasies can be when they are not acted upon.

As the first major holographic crew member in the Star Trek universe, *Voyager*'s Emergency Medical Holographic Program, otherwise known as "the Doctor," provides an example of the negative effects of absolutistic thinking and the challenging nature of altering ingrained patterns of thought.[15] As a highly complex and ambitious holographic program, the Doctor continually upgrades and adapts his programming to develop his personality throughout *Voyager*'s journey home.[16] Having the desires to expand his empathy for human relationships (*interpersonal effectiveness*) and to relate better to his fellow crew members, the Doctor creates a homelife simulation.[17] B'Elanna Torres points out that his experiment, by involving a perfect family and immaculate home, has little to no basis in reality and will provide him no insight into familial relationships. This illustrates how crucial it is to ground fantasy in reality.

In an effort to give the Doctor a more realistic family experience, Chief Engineer B'Elanna Torres updates his holodeck program to allow for the random, everyday conflicts and chaos that we encounter in life. Confident that he can handle any situation, the Doctor is quickly overwhelmed by his now sullen and willful children, an assertive on-the-go wife, and a messy home. A therapeutic approach similar to CBT would address these challenging situations by examining potential scenarios

Enter the Holodeck Yourself!

When not serving as an ambassador to the Federation, Counselor Troi's mother, Lwaxana, can be found on a holodeck lounging in a simulated mud bath in the Parallax Colony program.[18] You, too, can experience the benefits of relaxation via simulation by practicing visualization!

- Begin by ensuring that you are in a quiet, distraction-free environment.
- Close your eyes and scan your body for signs of tenseness.
- Relax those muscles.
- Visualize a step you can take to reach your goal.
- What are you wearing in this setting? Is anyone with you?
- Build this mental scene with sensory details. Imagine the sights, sounds, smells, tastes, and touch sensations that accompany your accomplishment of this step.
- Tell yourself positive affirmations that support you in achieving this step, such as "I am [making the phone call]" or "I am [practicing that song on guitar]," replacing the bracketed statements with the step you are visualizing.
- Watch yourself enact the step, noting what you are doing in order to achieve it.
- Dedicate one minute to visualization three times per day until the step is completed.

Use fantasy to your benefit to enjoy a holodeck in your head through the use of established relaxation exercises![19]

when things go wrong and how the client plans to respond. Despite these new challenges, the Doctor holds fast to his deeply held belief that he can foster a perfect, pristine home life. He finds himself getting increasingly frustrated when his attempts are met with resistance and anger by his holographic family. In order to achieve his goal of simulating a perfect family, he must test his adaptability to imperfection. Without a challenge to practice with in a predictable virtual world, he would be unable to adapt to problems that arise in the unpredictable real world.

Behavioral Rehearsal

While cognitive restructuring can change thinking patterns, it can also be helpful to practice these new cognitions in simulated scenarios. *Behavioral rehearsal* can help individuals practice their newly developed thinking patterns, much as athletes run drills to practice their skills in anticipation of the real competitions for which they are preparing. By asking a person to respond to rejection with a belief of "Things did not work out now, but maybe they will in another situation," instead of "Things never work out for me," the therapist encourages that person to experience the improvement personally in the moment.

On Deep Space Nine, Ensign Nog experiences such an example of behavioral reversal. After suffering injuries from a casualty-heavy war zone, Nog finds himself deeply depressed and retreats to the fictional, holographic casino of 1960s Las Vegas crooner Vic Fontaine.[20]

Nog's counselor Ezri Dax sees the potential that therapeutic opportunity for utilizing the holosuite to rebuild Nog's confidence. Nog assists Vic in developing his casino, effectively giving Nog meaningful work. To succeed at this goal, Nog is forced to interact with other characters and to contribute to Vic's holographic society.

CBT methods can help us change the thoughts we experience, and follow up with a change in behavior through practice. The holodeck provides an excellent avenue for members of Starfleet to challenge their thoughts and behaviors in a safer environment by providing fantastical experiences that do not necessarily involve real people and real reactions. However, to people experiencing immersive virtual reality, those experiences are real enough to see how they might feel if those experiences were brought into the real world, much like a client asking a group member to role-play as a mother and practicing assertiveness skills in that moment.

Rational-Emotive Behavior Therapy

Rational-Emotive Behavior Therapy (REBT), founded by Albert Ellis, is an approach that acts upon the notion that a person's belief system influences one's behaviors following an event.[21] That is, (A) an *activating* event occurs, (B) a person applies a *belief* to it, and (C) a *consequence* results. This A-B-C framework is best illustrated in the example of the *U.S.S. Enterprise*'s Lieutenant Reginald Barclay. Shy and anxiety ridden, Lieutenant Barclay is a brilliant yet troubled engineer. He is often ridiculed by other crew members (stage A—the activating event) for his awkward, withdrawn demeanor. These events serve to reinforce his belief system (stage B) that he is a social misfit and a failure. The consequence (stage C) is that his career and social life suffer.

The consequence at stage C does not simply derive from the activating event at A; rather, it is because A passes through the belief filter at stage B that one arrives at C.[22] By focusing on discovering, understanding, and changing the belief system, undesirable consequences no longer present themselves, and a person can respond more effectively to activating events and experience fewer emotional disturbances.

Falling victim to the A-B-C framework, Lieutenant Barclay finds himself becoming even more detached from his peers and superior officers. He retreats to an environment where he can feel empowered and in complete control of his actions, emotions, and social outcomes: the holodeck.[23] Barclay creates wildly outlandish scenarios, loosely based on reality. He aggressively acts out his frustrations or pursues romantic wish fulfillment with holographic representations of *Enterprise* crew members. However, as these virtual reality programs have little to no basis in actual reality, Barclay does not achieve any real therapeutic benefit from them in terms of untangling his faulty belief system.

The key, according to Ellis, to making this change is by teaching a client to develop three insights. The first insight involves realizing that something causes undesirable behaviors. Barclay finds himself so entrenched in his fantasies that he neglects his responsibilities and fails to report for duty, resulting in him acknowledging his overuse of the holodeck.

Ellis states that the second change "takes place when the clients come to understand that the reason why the original causes of their disturbance still upset and disorganize them is because they still believe in, and endlessly keep repeating to themselves, the irrational beliefs that they previously acquired."[24] By re-creating recent work conflicts in the holodeck and restructuring himself as the clever and brave, yet victimized hero, Barclay doesn't look for the source of these issues and only reinforces his patterns of negative thinking.

Ellis's third insight leads a client to admit to him- or herself that psychological problems can only be resolved by "observing, questioning, and challenging" one's own beliefs.[25] This occurs during in-the-moment observations voiced by the therapist to highlight a client's irrational beliefs and make it the focus of treatment. Counselor Troi and Commander Riker confront Barclay while he's in an event simulation to discover exaggerated, demeaning representations of the *Enterprise*'s crew, all of whom are idolizing or fawning over Barclay. To the great offense of Riker and Troi, Barclay ultimately acknowledges that the people he creates in virtual reality feel more real to him than those he meets in real life. In a later therapy session with Counselor Troi, Barclay accepts that this is an irrational belief in need of challenging, thereby reaching Ellis's third insight.

Ellis's approach to therapy has been described as controversial, and his abrasive nature even resulted in his removal from the Board of Trustees at the Albert Ellis Institute.[26] However, Ellis believed this was all in the name of being a more authentic person by separating the person from the action. Actions are essentially an expression of our beliefs, and by holding a person accountable for his or her beliefs by holding up a figurative mirror whenever an unhealthy belief is expressed, a person can discover new ways of thinking, and thus new ways of behaving. Albert Ellis was unapologetic in his approach, and so is the holodeck. By presenting experiences in a very real way, members of Starfleet learn quickly how their beliefs, and therefore their actions, serve them well or serve them poorly.

CBT and REBT: Bridging Fantasy and Reality

The holodeck exemplifies how to improve mental health by utilizing many CBT and REBT standards. Giving someone the opportunity to practice new ways of thinking and behaving in a relatively safe environment reflects both the holodeck's virtual reality experience and the therapeutic experience. Whether asking a group member to role-play as the client's intimidating friend or being able to speak to a lifelike virtual representation in a realistic setting, an individual can challenge his or her way of thinking and experience the effects in the moment, learning how he or she brings about desirable or undesirable outcomes. It is not enough to simply fantasize and suppose how things will go in a given situation; one must boldly go and learn in the process.

References

Albin, J. (2009). *Treating fear of flying using biofeedback and virtual reality.* Saarbrücken, Germany: VDM Verlag.

Anderson, C. A. (1983). Imagination and expectation: The effect of imagining behavioral scripts on personal influences. *Journal of Personality & Social Psychology, 45*(2), 293–305.

Bandura, A. (1986). *Social foundations of thought and action: A social cognitive theory.* Englewood Cliffs, NJ: Prentice-Hall.

Damer, D. E., Latimer, K. M., & Porter, S. H. (2010). "Build your confidence": A social anxiety group for college students. *Journal for Specialists in Group Work, 35*(1), 7–22.

Dobkin, M. (n.d.). *Behaviorists behaving badly.* New York Magazine: http://nymag.com/nymetro/news/people/features/14947/

Epstein, R. (2001, January 1). *The prince of reason.* Psychology Today: https://www.psychologytoday.com/articles/200101/the-prince-reason

Ellis, A., & Grieger, R. (1977). *Handbook of rational-emotive therapy.* New York, NY: Springer.

Ellis, A., & Dryden, W. (1990). *The essential Albert Ellis: seminal writings on psychotherapy.* New York, NY: Springer.

Eva, K. W., Armson, H., Holmboe, E., Lockyer, J., Loney, E., Mann, K., & Sargeant, J. (2012). Factors influencing responsiveness to feedback: On the interplay between fear, confidence, and reasoning processes. *Advances in Health Sciences Education, 17*(1), 15–16.

Freeman, D., Pugh, K., Dunn, G., Evans, N., Sheaves, B., Waite, F., Cernis, E., Lister, R., & Fowler, D. (2014). An early phase II randomized controlled trial testing the effect on persecutory delusions using CBT to reduce negative cognitions about the self: The potential benefits of enhancing self-confidence. *Schizophrenia Research, 160*(1–3), 186-192.

Gottschall, J. (2012). *The storytelling animal: How stories make us human.* Boston, MA: Houghton Mifflin Harcourt.

Hyman, R. B., Feldman, H. R., Harris, R. B., Levin, R. F., & Malloy, G. B. (1989). The effects of relaxation training on clinical symptoms: A meta-analysis. *Nursing Research, 38*(4), 216–220.

Kavak, F., Ünai, S., & Yilmaz, E. (2016). Effects of relaxation exercises and music therapy on the psychological symptoms and depression levels of patients with schizophrenia. *Archives of Psychiatric Nursing, 30*(5), 508–512.

Kim, B H., Newton, R. A., Sachs, M. L., Giacobbi, P. R., Jr., & Glutting, J. J. (2011). The effect of guided relaxation and exercise imagery on self-reported leisure-time exercise behaviors in older adults. *Journal of Aging & Physical Activity, 19*(2), 137–146.

Lange, A. J., & Jakubowski, P. (1976). *Responsible assertive behavior: Cognitive/behavioral procedures for trainers.* Champaign, IL: Research Press.

McLay, R. N. (2012). *At war with PTSD: Battling post traumatic stress disorder with virtual reality.* Baltimore, MD: Johns Hopkins University Press.

Morina, N., Ijntema, H., Meyerbröker, K., & Emmelkamp, P. M. G. (2015). Can virtual reality exposure therapy gains be generalized to real-life? A meta-analysis of studies applying behavioral assessments. *Behaviour Research & Therapy, 74*(1), 18–24.

Ngai, I., Tully, E. C., & Anderson, P. L. (2015). The course of the working alliance during virtual reality and exposure group therapy for social anxiety disorder. *Behavioural & Cognitive Psychotherapy, 43*(2), 167–181.

Ross-Stewart, L., & Short, S. E. (2009). The frequency and perceived effectiveness of images to build, maintain, and regain confidence. *Journal of Applied Sport Psychology, 21*(1), S34–S47.

Singer, J. L. (2006). *Imagery in psychotherapy.* Washington, DC: American Psychological Association.

Sternbach, R., & Okuda, M. (1991). *Star Trek: The Next Generation—Technical manual.* New York, NY: Pocket.

Taylor, S. E., Pham, L. B., Rivkin, I. D., & Armor, D. A. (1998). Harnessing the imagination: Mental simulation, self-regulation, and coping. *American Psychologist, 53*(4), 429–439.

Wiederhold, B. K., & Wiederhold, M. D. (2004). *Virtual reality therapy for anxiety disorders: Advances in education and treatment.* Washington, DC: American Psychological Association.

Willis, S. L. (1976). Structured fantasy as an adjunctive technique for the treatment of depression. *Psychotherapy: Theory, Research, & Practice, 13*(3), 249–252.

Zimmerman, H., Sternbach, R., & Drexlet, D. (1998). *Star Trek: Deep Space Nine—Technical manual.* New York, NY: Pocket.

Notes

1. *Star Trek: The Next Generation* episode 3–21, "Hollow Pursuits" (April 30, 1990).
2. Quoted by Epstein (2001).
3. Gottschall (2012).
4. Sternbach & Okuda (1991); Zimmerman et al. (1998).
5. Albin (2009); McLay (2012); Ngai et al. (2015); Wiederhold & Wiederhold (2004).
6. Morina et al. (2015).
7. Anderson (1983); Bandura (1986); Singer (2006); Willis (1976).
8. Taylor et al. (1998).
9. First appearing in *Star Trek: The Animated Series* episode 2–3, "The Practical Joker" (September 21, 1974), set in the twenty-third century; in live action in *Star Trek: The Next Generation* episode 1–1, "Encounter at Farpoint," part 1 (September 28, 1987), set in the twenty-fourth century.
10. *Star Trek: Deep Space Nine* episode 2–12, "The Alternate" (January 9, 1994); Zimmerman et al. (1998).
11. *Star Trek: The Next Generation* episode 3–14, "A Matter of Perspective" (February 12, 1990).
12. *Star Trek: The Next Generation* episode 7–13, "Homeward" (January 17, 1994).
13. Lange & Jakubowski (1976).
14. For more on building confidence by facing worries and fears or through the use of imagery, rather than direct experience, see Damer et al. (2010); Eva et al. (2012); Freeman et al. (2014); Ross-Stewart & Short (2009).
15. *Star Trek: Voyager* episodes 1–1 and 1–2, "Caretaker," parts 1 and 2 (January 16, 1995).
16. *Star Trek: Voyager* episodes 3–18, "Darkling" (February 19, 1997); 6–4, "Tinker, Tailor, Doctor, Spy" (October 13, 1999); 7–7, "Body and Soul" (November 15, 2000); 7–16, "Workforce," part 1 (February 21, 2001).
17. *Star Trek: Voyager* episode 3–2, "Real Life" (April 23, 1997).
18. *Star Trek: The Next Generation* episode 5–20, "Cost of Living" (April 20, 1992).
19. Hyman et al. (1989); Kavak et al. (2016); Kim et al. (2011).
20. *Star Trek: Deep Space Nine* episode 7–10, "It's Only a Paper Moon" (December 30, 1998).
21. Ellis (1977).
22. Ellis & Dryden (1990).
23. *Star Trek: The Next Generation* episode 3–21, "Hollow Pursuits" (April 30, 1990).
24. Ellis & Grieger (1977), p. 190.
25. Ellis & Grieger (1977), p. 191.
26. Dobkin (n.d.).

Military psychologists work to keep personnel fit for duty and help them function during their post-duty years. Military life carries risks even in times of peace because disasters and conflicts can arise at any time. Those who live through combat and other crises can carry the stress and trauma without end. How, then, might mental health treatment make life better for them and those around them?

•11•

Starfleet and Military Psychology

JENNA BUSCH
AND JANINA SCARLET

"The leader who harnesses the power of real empathy fosters better communication, tighter cohesion, stronger discipline, and greater morale throughout his or her organization."
—psychologist Henry C. Garner[1]

"My parents had told me about the dangers of Starfleet missions. I knew it could happen. . . . No, I wasn't prepared at all. How can anyone be prepared to hear that a parent is never coming home again?"
—Wesley Crusher[2]

Active-duty service members and veterans face many struggles, including excruciating losses,[3] traumatic experiences,[4] family struggles,[5] and addiction,[6] as well as having to make difficult decisions and struggle with self-forgiveness.[7]

These struggles often call for mental health counseling. Similarly, Star Trek represents many of the struggles that service members and veterans face, including the need for counseling. Specifically, the *U.S.S. Enterprise* has the counselor Deanna Troi just as Deep Space 9 has Ezri Dax to provide counseling services to the military personnel on board

The Struggles

Though crew members aboard the *U.S.S. Enterprise* and Deep Space 9 are advised to turn to counselors for help, Troi and Dax often seek out those who seem to be suffering. For example, Troi seeks out Captain Picard and offers her support when he loses his closest living relatives.[8] Unfortunately, the stigma attached to seeking help with a mental health issue leads too many individuals to refuse to seek the help they need.[9] How might the difficulties encountered in the military affect an individual's family, work, or academic performance, and what are some helpful tools for recovery?

Grief

Perhaps one of the most common struggles that service members experience is grief. Particularly during wartime, the number of service members who are negatively affected by grief can be as high as 20 percent.[10] When Captain Picard gets the message that his brother and his nephew, René, have been killed in a fire, he quickly shuts Counselor Troi out without accepting her help.[11] As is the case with many military personnel who have experienced loss, his initial impulse is to push his emotions away and focus on his job.

Untreated grief can lead an individual to shut down, withdraw from others, and potentially develop physical or mental health disorders, most of which may not be obvious for a long time.[12] People who have a hard time coping with grief may develop sleep problems, physical pain, and fatigue and have a hard time fulfilling their obligations at work.[13] For example, Deanna Troi's mother, Lwaxana, deals with her first daughter's death as a child by *repressing* the memory, completely burying her memory of Deanna's older sister. Lwaxana doesn't discuss the child's existence with Deanna, going so far as to physically erase seven years of journal entries to keep her grief at bay. This eventually comes to a head, making her physically ill and almost killing her.[14]

Making Difficult Decisions

Military personnel sometimes have to make difficult decisions in cases in which there may not be a clearly "right" answer.[15] Such decisions often conflict with the individual's moral code. This is called *moral injury*.[16] Service members often witness extreme violence and suffering,[17] which puts them at risk for developing a mental health disorder such as posttraumatic stress disorder (PTSD), anxiety, depression, or chronic pain.[18] When Riker is forced to argue in court that his friend Data is nothing but a machine, even shutting off Data's power in a courtroom demonstration, Riker feels so affected by his part in the trial that he cannot bring himself to face his friends after the trial is over despite the fact that Data has won.[19]

Experiencing moral injury may put servicemen and women at greater risk for developing mental health disorders[20] because of the guilt produced by a transgression. When Captain Kirk learns that a woman he loves will die in an accident, he also learns that if he saves her, she will begin a peace movement that will give the Nazis time to take over the world. He therefore makes the difficult decision to let her die in order to save millions of others and suffers immense grief as a result.[21]

Trauma

Another reason some service members may experience guilt is the *freeze response.* During times of extreme stress, the human body typically releases certain hormones, such as adrenaline and cortisol, that allow the individual to fight against the enemy or run away (the *fight-or-flight response*). In some instances, the individuals may not be able to move or react to extreme stress (the *freeze response*).[22] Even though the freeze response may be involuntary under extreme stress, it may produce feelings of guilt, putting the individual at a higher risk for developing post-traumatic stress disorder or a related mental health disorder.[23] Shortly after receiving his emotion chip, for instance, Data deals with a strong sense of guilt over freezing during an attack.[24]

Addiction Disorders

Many people who have experienced traumatic events may turn to substances such as alcohol as a way to escape their suffering. Addiction disorders are common among trauma survivors, including the military population.[25] In fact, psychological disorders such as PTSD increase survivors' risk for developing addiction disorders.[26] For example, Riker introduces the *Enterprise* crew to an addictive game that stimulates the pleasure centers of the brain. It spreads through the crew members, leaving them vulnerable to attacks.[27]

In the short term, addictions might help an individual become distracted and might alleviate some of the undesirable symptoms. However, in the long term, addictions tend to make the symptoms worse, potentially increasing the person's struggles.[28] We see this when Lieutenant Reginald Barclay creates a fantasy life in the holodeck, imagining himself battling against the officers he feels are giving him a hard time. After running through these scenarios time and again, Barclay neglects his duties on the ship and grows insubordinate toward both Lieutenant Commander La Forge and Commander Riker.[29]

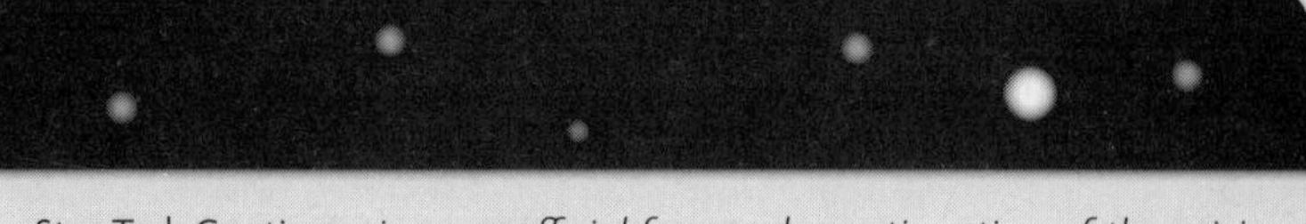

Star Trek Continues is an unofficial fan-made continuation of the original series as seasons 4 and 5.[30] *One of the few changes while re-creating the style of the 1960s program is the addition of a ship's counselor, Dr. Elise McKennah, played by Michele Specht.*

Busch: Why add a therapist to Kirk's *Enterprise*?

Specht: You saw the seed that was planted by Gene Roddenberry in the very first episode,[31] what he kind of had in mind for strong female characters. That tree blossomed in *TNG* (*Star Trek: The Next Generation*) with Doctor Crusher and Deanna Troi. I was thinking about McKennah as a bridge [between series]. It makes perfect sense to me to have a counselor on a five-year mission on a ship when you're trapped on board with this many people. I want her to have the perspective I think a psychologist would have, which is to take a step back and to see the bigger picture. Not just what is happening in the moment, action-wise, but trying to see more of a pulled back perspective of what the long-term ramifications are for the people involved and in the long term. For me, I kind of think of her as a bit like a universal equalizer.

What's still so fundamentally beautiful about the whole *Star Trek* universe is that it shows a future in which humanity makes good, a vision of the future in which we turn out to be the best versions of ourselves.

Family Problems

The military lifestyle does not affect only the service members; it also affects their families.[32] Some children of service members may struggle with behavioral and mental health problems that potentially affect their academic and social performance.[33] After Worf is reunited with his son, Alexander, whom he had sent away after Alexander's mother was killed, Alexander starts stealing and acting out in class, bullying other students, and lying about it.[34] This is not an uncommon response, as many children of frequently absent parents may struggle with feelings of abandonment and may act out.[35] Worf initially demands that Alexander follow his orders to avoid dishonoring him. When he is unsuccessful, Worf considers sending Alexander away to a Klingon school. It is not until Worf realizes that his son has been struggling with fears of abandonment that the two are able to communicate and reestablish their relationship.[36] In fact, such communication can greatly reduce the child's distress, whereas continued abandonment or failure to address such issues can lead to the development of psychiatric disorders, including depression and PTSD.[37]

Mental Health Treatment

Because of all the struggles that military personnel go through, it is important that doctors and mental health professionals as well as military leaders be empathetic and compassionate.[38] Teaching service members to be compassionate to themselves and others is also helpful at reducing the symptoms of stress and PTSD in the military population.[39] Both *self-compassion*[40] (being kind to oneself when going through a hard time) and *self-forgiveness*[41] (not condemning oneself for a specific act) can help people reduce their symptoms of PTSD, anxiety, and depression.[42] When Deep Space 9's Counselor Ezri Dax attempts to help Elim Garak overcome his *claustrophobia* (extreme fear of closed spaces), over time Garak discovers that his panic attacks are due to his actions to help the Federation that resulted in the deaths of his own people.[43] Through Dax's support, Garak is able to overcome his anxiety.

In many ways Star Trek depicts life in the military, a regimented profession, and the issues that go along with it from dealing with loss, grief, and trauma to treating those conditions. It also shows that though these things are universal, there are specific circumstances military personnel go through that require a special brand of compassion and empathy. Through counselors such as Deanna Troi and Ezri Dax, with a supportive environment such as the one maintained on these ships, the crew members are able to find the conditions necessary for overcoming these struggles.

References

Bovin, M. J., Dodson, T. S., Smith, B. N., Gregor, K., Marx, B. P., & Pineles, S. L. (2014). Does guilt mediate the association between tonic immobility and posttraumatic stress disorder symptoms in female trauma survivors? *Journal of Traumatic Stress, 27*(6), 721–724.

Bracha, H. S. (2004). Freeze, fight, flight, fright, faint: Adaptationist perspectives on the acute stress response spectrum. *CNS Spectrums, 9*(9), 679–685.

Cohen, J. A., Deblinger, E., Mannarino, A. P., & Steer, R. A. (2004). A multisite, randomized controlled trial for children with sexual abuse–related PTSD symptoms. *Journal of the American Academy of Child & Adolescent Psychiatry, 43*(4), 393–402.

Cohen, J. A., & Mannarino, A. P. (2011). Trauma-focused CBT for traumatic grief in military children. *Journal of Contemporary Psychotherapy, 41*(4), 219–227.

Drescher, K. D., & Foy, D. W. (2008). When they come home: Posttraumatic stress, moral injury, and spiritual consequences for veterans. *Reflective Practice: Formation & Supervision in Ministry, 28,* 85–102.

Garner, H. C. (2009). Empathy: A true leader skill. *Military Review, 89*(6), 84–92.

Gewirtz, A. H., Erbes, C. R., Polusny, M. A., Forgatch, M. S., & DeGarmo, D. S. (2011). Helping military families through the deployment process: Strategies to support parenting. *Professional Psychology: Research & Practice, 42(1),* 56–62.

Greene-Shortridge, T. M., Britt, T. W., & Castro, C. A. (2007). The stigma of mental health problems in the military. *Military Medicine, 172*(2), 157–161.

Jacobson, I. G., Ryan, M. K., Hooper, T. J., Smith, T. C., Amoroso, P. J., Boyko, E. J., Gackstetter, G. D., Wells, T. S., & Bell, N. S. (2008). Alcohol use and alcohol-related problems before and after military combat deployment. *JAMA: Journal of the American Medical Association, 300*(6), 663–675.

Kaplow, J. B., Layne, C. M., Saltzman, W. R., Cozza, S. J., & Pynoos, R. S. (2013). Using multidimensional grief theory to explore the effects of deployment, reintegration, and death on military youth and families. *Clinical Child & Family Psychology Review, 16*(3), 322–340.

Kearney, D. J., Malte, C. A., McManus, C., Martinez, M. E., Felleman, B., & Simpson, T. L. (2013). Loving kindness meditation for posttraumatic stress disorder: A pilot study. *Journal of Traumatic Stress, 26*(4), 426–434.

Leach, J. (2004). Why people “freeze” in an emergency: Temporal and cognitive constraints on survival responses. *Aviation, Space, & Environmental Medicine, 75*(6), 539–542.

Litz, B. T., Stein, N., Delaney, E., Lebowitz, L., Nash, W. P., Silva, C., & Maguen, S. (2009). Moral injury and moral repair in war veterans: A preliminary model and intervention strategy. *Clinical Psychology Review, 29*(8), 695–706.

Maguen, S., & Litz, B. (2012). Moral injury in veterans of war. *PTSD Research Quarterly, 23*(1), 1–6.

Mantzios, M., Wilson, J. C., Linnell, M., & Morris, P. (2015). The role of negative cognition, intolerance of uncertainty, mindfulness, and self-compassion in weight regulation among male army recruits. *Mindfulness, 6*(3), 545–552.

Nash, W. P., Carper, T. M., Mills, M. A., Au, T., Goldsmith, A., & Litz, B. T. (2013). Psychometric evaluation of the Moral Injury Events Scale. *Military Medicine, 178*(6), 646–652.

Nash, W. P., & Litz, B. T. (2013). Moral injury: A mechanism for war-related psychological trauma in military family members. *Clinical Child & Family Psychology Review, 16*(4), 365–375.

Park, N. (2011). Military children and families: Strengths and challenges during peace and war. *American Psychologist, 66*(1), 65–72.

Resick, P. A., Monson, C. M., & Chard, K. M. (2008) *Cognitive processing therapy veteran/military version: therapist's manual.* Washington, DC: Department of Veterans Affairs.

Rizvi, S. L., Kaysen, D., Gutner, C. A., Griffin, M. G., & Resick, P. A. (2008). Beyond fear: The role of peritraumatic responses in posttraumatic stress and depressive symptoms among female crime victims. *Journal of Interpersonal Violence, 23*(6), 853–868.

Romero, D. H., Riggs, S. A., & Ruggero, C. (2015). Coping, family social support, and psychological symptoms among student veterans. *Journal of Counseling Psychology, 62*(2), 242–252.

Roopa, C. G., & Joseph, C. (2007). A preliminary study on empathy and personality in military medical officers. *Indian Journal of Aerospace Medicine, 51*(2), 28–39.

Shatan, C. F. (1973). The grief of soldiers: Vietnam combat veterans' self-help movement. *American Journal of Orthopsychiatry, 43*(4), 640–653.

Stahre, M. A., Brewer, R. D., Fonseca, V. P., & Naimi, T. S. (2009). Binge drinking among U.S. active-duty military personnel. *American Journal of Preventive Medicine, 36*(3), 208–217.

Taft, C. T., Kaloupek, D. G., Schumm, J. A., Marshall, A. D., Panuzio, J., King, D. W., & Keane, T. M. (2007). Posttraumatic stress disorder symptoms, physiological reactivity, alcohol problems, and aggression among military veterans. *Journal of Abnormal Psychology, 116*(3), 498–507.

Toblin, R. L., Riviere, L. A., Thomas, J. L., Adler, A. B., Kok, B. C., & Hoge, C. W. (2012). Grief and physical health outcomes in U.S. soldiers returning from combat. *Journal of Affective Disorders, 136*(3), 469–475.

Van der Kolk, B. A. (2005). Developmental trauma disorder. *Psychiatric Annals, 35*(5), 401–408.

Witvliet, C. O., Phipps, K. A., Feldman, M. E., & Beckham, J. C. (2004). Posttraumatic mental and physical health correlates of forgiveness and religious coping in military veterans. *Journal of Traumatic Stress, 17*(3), 269–273.

Worthington, E. J., & Langberg, D. (2012). Religious considerations and self-forgiveness in treating complex trauma and moral injury in present and former soldiers. *Journal of Psychology & Theology, 40*(4), 274–288.

Wyman, P. A., Cowen, E. L., Hightower, A. D., & Pedro-Carroll, J. L. (1985). Perceived competence, self-esteem, and anxiety in latency-aged children of divorce. *Journal of Clinical Child Psychology, 14*(1), 20–26.

Notes

1. Garner (2009).
2. *Star Trek: The Next Generation* episode 3–5, "The Bonding" (October 23, 1989).
3. *Star Trek: The Next Generation* episodes 1–23, "Skin of Evil" (April 25, 1988); 2–9,

"The Measure of a Man" (February 13, 1989); *Star Trek Generations* (1994 motion picture).

4. *Star Trek Generations* (1994 motion picture).
5. *Star Trek: The Next Generation* episodes 5–10, "New Ground" (January 6, 1992); 4–2, "Family" (October 1, 1990).
6. *Star Trek: The Next Generation* episodes 3–21, "Hollow Pursuits" (April 30, 1990); 5–6, "The Game" (October 28, 1991).
7. *Star Trek: The Next Generation* episode 7–7, "Dark Page" (November 1, 1993); *Star Trek Generations* (1994 motion picture).
8. *Star Trek Generations* (1994 motion picture).
9. Greene-Shortridge et al. (2007).
10. Toblin et al. (2012).
11. *Star Trek Generations* (1994 motion picture).
12. Romero et al. (2015); Shatan (1973); Toblin et al. (2012).
13. Toblin et al. (2012).
14. *Star Trek: The Next Generation* episode 7–7, "Dark Page" (November 1, 1993).
15. *Star Trek: The Next Generation* episodes 7–16, "Thine Own Self" (February 14, 1994); 2–9, "The Measure of a Man" (February 13, 1989).
16. Litz et al. (2009); Maguen & Litz (2012); Nash et al. (2013).
17. Litz et al. (2009).
18. Romero et al. (2015).
19. *Star Trek: The Next Generation* episode 2–9, "The Measure of a Man" (February 13, 1989).
20. Drescher & Foy (2008); Litz et al. (2009).
21. *Star Trek* episode 1–28, "The City on the Edge of Forever" (April 6, 1967).
22. Bracha (2004); Leach (2004).
23. Bovin et al. (2014); Rizvi et al. (2008).
24. *Star Trek Generations* (1994 motion picture).
25. Jacobson et al. (2008); Stahre et al. (2009); Taft et al. (2007).
26. Jacobson et al. (2008).
27. *Star Trek: The Next Generation* episode 5–6, "The Game" (October 26, 1991).
28. Resick et al. (2008).
29. *Star Trek: The Next Generation* episode 3–21, "Hollow Pursuits" (April 30, 1990).
30. *Star Trek Continues* (beginning 2013). *Star Trek Continues.* https://www.youtube.com/user/StarTrekContinues.
31. *Star Trek* unaired pilot, "The Cage" (n.d.), presented as flashbacks in episodes 1–11 and 1–12, "The Menagerie" parts 1 and 2 (November 17 and 24, 1966).
32. Cohen & Mannarino (2011); Gewirtz et al. (2011); Kaplow et al. (2013); Nash & Litz (2013).
33. Park (2011).
34. *Star Trek: The Next Generation* episode 5–10, "New Ground" (January 6, 1992).
35. Wyman et al. (1985).
36. *Star Trek: The Next Generation* episode 5–10, "New Ground" (January 6, 1992).
37. Van der Kolk (2005).
38. Garner (2009); Roopa & Joseph (2007).
39. Kearney et al. (2013).
40. Mantzios et al. (2015).
41. Witvliet et al. (2004); Worthington & Langberg (2012).
42. Witvliet et al. (2004).
43. *Star Trek: Deep Space Nine* episode 7–3, "Afterimage" (October 14, 1998).

Life leads to death, and knowledge of that fact can terrify us. In a war-torn outpost far from any other life a person has known, mortality is salient and death cannot be ignored. Although some reactions entail unhealthy mismanagement of the terror, other methods can be used to celebrate life and manage the terror in healthy ways.

•12•

Terror Management: Mortality Salience on Deep Space 9

WIND GOODFRIEND

"And so, mad beneath the beam of hatred in those eyes, lurks the certain knowledge of its impending death, and it begins to know fear."

—Silaren, a Cardassian[1]

". . . through our meaning-providing worldview, we keep at bay the potential for terror engendered by the possibility that we are mere material animals clinging to a clump of dirt . . . for a brief period of time that ends with our complete obliteration upon death."

—social psychologist Jeff Greenberg[2]

We are all dying. What does psychology offer as a way to deal with this inevitable and terrifying truth? An irrefutable fact about life is that it must end sooner or later, and despite the most devout faith in religion or science, none of us is absolutely sure what happens next. Human culture has responded to our mortality in a wide variety of fascinating ways. We have elaborate death rituals ranging from burning corpses and sending the ashes down sacred rivers to preserving the bodies and safekeeping them in expensive boxes. Whereas religion and culture attempt to explain death and offer methods to assuage our grief, psychology has produced one of the more controversial theories of the last 50 years in the form of *terror management theory.* This theory proposes that all of religion, culture, and even pop culture—including television and movies—is produced specifically to deal with the fear of death.

At times, we shrink from death, avoiding the inevitable by desperately grabbing at whatever form of distraction is available. At other times, the human race seems to embrace death as entertaining. We put ourselves into fearful situations for recreation. We include death and war in popular culture.

In Star Trek, mortality is a common theme. Across the various television series and films, wars and genocide occur, beloved characters die, and sometimes they even come back to life. The critically acclaimed series *Star Trek: Deep Space Nine* confronted death and war directly in its story line from beginning to end as viewers watched the confrontation between the Federation and the Dominion, a collaboration of enemies led by a ruthless, murdering, shape-shifting alien species. Grappling with death is perhaps the most fundamental challenge of life. How do psychology and terror management theory explain this existential irony, and how can we link it to Star Trek?

Terror Management Theory

Terror management theory (TMT)[3] may be the most relevant and comprehensive paradigm from psychology to explain the human reaction to mortality. The theory contains several central premises that can be summed up in these ideas:

- Living beings all want to keep living.
- Humans (perhaps uniquely) are existentially aware of our own mortality both for the species in general and for ourselves as individuals.
- The thought of our own eventual death is terrifying.
- We "manage" that terror by embracing a variety of customs, beliefs, and behaviors that are designed to accomplish the goal of (1) avoiding thinking about death or (2) trying to make our short lives meaningful.

The theory further suggests that our personal focus on death will come and go depending on the circumstances. When thoughts of death become temporarily unavoidable or more central to our mental focus, this state is called *mortality salience.* Mortality salience is common in the entire Star Trek universe, but death is a salient and central theme in *Deep Space Nine.* Research on TMT shows that mortality salience can occur on a national or even global level after events such as the terrorist attacks on the United States on September 11, 2001; for months and even years, international culture grew highly focused on security and on protecting ourselves from possible harm.[4] The unexpected and hateful nature of the 9/11 attacks made mortality even more salient as we were forced to confront the fact that death is sometimes unpredictable and sudden.

Mortality salience can also occur on a personal, individual level when someone in our family dies, when we get bad news from the doctor, or even when we walk past a funeral home.[5] On the dangerous and war-torn outpost of Deep Space 9, death is ubiquitous and cannot be ignored. For example, during the latter seasons, which focus on the war between the Federation and the Dominion, characters write letters to be delivered to their loved ones in the event of their death.[6] How do soldiers and civilians psychologically react to constant fear and threats of death?

The creators of their theory sum up TMT like this: "It is essentially a theory about the effect of death on life. . . . Human beings attempt to fulfill culturally sanctioned dreams forged to escape the encompassing nightmare, not just of human history but also of human existence itself."[7] At its foundation, TMT says that when we are forced to think about death, we search for the meaning of life. What are some of the specific ways in which the characters on *Deep Space Nine* react to mortality salience? Among *Deep Space Nine*'s diverse examples, the character Nog experiences posttraumatic stress disorder (PTSD), Jadzia Dax and Worf fall in love, and Captain Sisko's word-views become galvanized as the war progresses.

Posttraumatic Stress Disorder: Nog

There are relatively healthy ways to react to mortality salience, and there are unhealthy ways. One path toward mismanagement of terror, or an unhealthy reaction, is the one leading to psychopathology or mental illness. Schizophrenic hallucinations and delusions often focus on horrible fears, personality disorders can include paranoia and consuming conspiracy theories, and anxiety disorders by definition come from deep-seated worry and pessimism about the future. Viewers see management of terror fail when the character Nog experiences posttraumatic stress disorder (PTSD) after he is confronted with the war head-on and is severely injured.[8]

As the name implies, PTSD is a mental illness caused by exposure to an extremely traumatic event, such as long-term relationship abuse, a natural disaster, or being the victim of a violent crime. One context in which PTSD is particularly relevant is that of soldiers or veterans of combat, such as the crew of DS9, who live with the war between the Federation and the Dominion for several years. They directly experience mortality salience as they consistently watch ships exploding, their friends being injured and killed, and their own lives and livelihoods being threatened.[9] The war has a direct impact on one of the youngest characters on the show, Nog, who is a sweetly eager Ferengi. Nog is unique in that his ambition does not lie in the traditional Ferengi context of acquisition and profit; instead, he becomes the first person from his species to join the Federation, fully committed to its ostensible goals of exploration, goodwill, and peace.[10] Nog's world is turned upside down when he is assigned to the front lines of the war and must trade his naive platitudes about morality and righteousness for getting shot and losing his leg.[11] Understandably, he does not respond well.

According to the American Psychiatric Association, typical PTSD symptoms focus on four groups of behaviors: (1) intrusion, (2) avoidance, (3) "negative alterations in cognitions and mood," and (4) "alterations in arousal and reactivity."[12] *Intrusion* includes symptoms that disrupt daily functioning, such as nightmares or traumatic memory flashbacks. *Avoidance* occurs when someone persistently avoids thinking about the trauma or actively avoids anyone or anything that serves as a reminder. The third cluster, *negative alterations in cognitions and mood*, includes persistent pessimism or low self-esteem, diminished interest in former activities, and feelings of alienation or isolation from other people. *Alterations in arousal and reactivity* can refer to aggressive or self-destructive behavior, sleep disturbances, hypervigilance, and more.

After Nog's accident on the front lines of battle and the loss of his leg, he experiences all these symptoms.[13] He hides in his room, refusing to spend time with his friends or family. When friends do try to interact with Nog, he has sudden bursts of anger and aggression.[14] He experiences phantom limb pain, has flashbacks, and obsessively listens to the same song over and over. Nog's emotional range has become limited to alternating swings of anger and apathy, and eventually he retreats fully by living full-time in a holosuite fantasy world in which nothing truly matters because nothing is truly real. When he eventually gains some perspective, he condenses the experience of PTSD by explaining that he was able to handle war until it became truly personal for him. With the damage to his leg came the realization that he, too, could die.[15]

Nog is insightful enough to realize that it's his fear of death and anxiety about the unpredictability of the future that have exacerbated his PTSD symptoms. Mortality salience made his experience traumatic in a manner that is extremely common in real-life soldiers as they suffer the mental aftershocks of combat. Nog's struggle displays one relatively unhealthy response to fears of death that are predicted and explained by TMT.

Falling in Love: Worf and Dax

PTSD is one example of mismanagement of terror; on the other end of the spectrum we can see reactions to mortality salience that instead embrace all the best parts of life. One of these relatively healthy and even wonderful reactions is to fall in love or engage in sexual intimacy. After the 9/11 terrorist attacks, both marriage rates and birthrates throughout the United States significantly increased.[16] TMT explains that increased desire for sexual or otherwise intimate relationships should increase under conditions of mortality salience for two general reasons. First, being in love provides a happy distraction from thoughts of death and makes us feel that we have at least made life as worthwhile as possible. Second, if the relationship leads to sex and children, we can die knowing that we have left an enduring legacy, something that provides immense comfort.

The central romantic story arc in *Deep Space Nine* is between Jadzia Dax and Worf. At first, they don't seem well suited for each other, and it's possible that if they had not been under conditions of mortality salience as a result of the war, they would never have fallen in love. Their initial attraction only appears when they physically battle each other in a holosuite exercise program.[17] In short, their sexual desire seems directly correlated with bat'leth battles. Jadzia seems to expect this reaction in Worf; she uses morality salience to her advantage, combining a dangerous battle with sexual flirtation.[18]

Although a holographic battle simulation can increase sexual interest, their relationship does not turn into love until the mortality salience becomes real. As the war progresses, things stay status quo until either or both of them might die; then things progress quickly (for example, Jadzia promises to marry Worf).[19] The actual wedding preparations stall again until Jadzia is wounded,[20] after which Worf's commitment increases. When Jadzia tragically dies only two months later, her last words to Worf are "Our baby would have been so beautiful."[21] The last thing on her mind, on her deathbed, is her love and her missing legacy—just as TMT predicts.

Validation of Worldviews: Captain Sisko

Worldviews are perceptions or beliefs about reality that provide structure and meaning to life. Examples include religion, political ideology, and culturally constructed goals such as "the American dream." Psychologists have produced scores of studies supporting TMT's prediction that these worldviews will be dramatically solidified under conditions of mortality salience, because worldviews provide comforting meaning and stability in times of anxiety and fear. A central theme throughout *DS9* may be that Captain Sisko's worldviews become galvanized as the war progresses and as mortality becomes increasingly salient.

Sisko's story arc begins by showing him personally lost and without many strong beliefs,[22] but as the war intensifies, so do his worldviews.[23] He is even aware that this galvanization comes from viewing multiple casualty lists of Federation officers; as he reads the list of the dead, he decides that an alliance with the Romulans (long his enemy) is worthwhile to maintain the larger goal of ending the bloodshed.[24] Sisko makes decisions he never would have made in times of peace.[25]

Sisko acknowledges that in the face of death he ignores doubt and embraces his worldview without regret. He lies, trades in biological weapons, deals with criminals, and bribes officials.[26] Although Sisko would probably never condone such actions under normal circumstances, under mortality salience they become justified. They further the cause and validate the worldview—the ends suddenly justify the means. Terror has been managed by blind belief in something that makes death seem worthwhile, and the Federation wins the war.

Experimental Manipulations of Terror

Dozens, if not hundreds, of studies have been done to test the predictions made by terror management theory. Although some of these studies occur in natural settings, such as waiting for people to walk past a funeral home, most studies are conducted in labs on university campuses.

How do research psychologists experimentally manipulate mortality salience? One of the most common methods is to split all participants randomly into two groups.[27] Then each group is asked to write answers to essay questions. The "mortality salience" participants first write about the emotions that arise when they think about their own deaths, then write about what will happen to their bodies once they are physically dead. As a comparison or *control group*, the other half of the participants instead write about the emotions and physical experiences they would have under extreme dental pain. In other words, both groups are thinking about something extremely unpleasant, but the difference is that one is thinking specifically about death. Only this group—the mortality salience group—should therefore show the signs described by terror management theory. These results do not come just from thinking about a negative experience or even intense pain; they come only when thinking about our own demise.

Death Comes for Us All

According to the psychologists who proposed TMT, "All the evils that people perpetuate can be viewed as products of terror management errors stemming from fear and weakness. This is not to say that we should not hold people responsible for these errors; we should, because if we do not, we will most likely all end up victimized by them."[28] Are the moral compromises Sisko makes worth it because they stop the Dominion from killing everyone on "our side"? Or is the hero of the story falling victim to what we all tell ourselves—that our hard choices are worth it because they support our nation, our culture, our god? Perhaps the most intriguing question that arises from terror management theory is this: How will I react when death comes for me?

References

American Psychiatric Association. (2013). *Diagnostic and statistical manual of mental disorders* (DSM-5). Washington, DC: American Psychiatric Association.

Greenberg, J. (2008). Understanding the vital human quest for self-esteem. *Perspectives on Psychological Science, 3*(1), 48–55.

Hirschberger, G., Florian, V., & Mikulincer, M. (2002). The anxiety buffering function of close relationships: Mortality salience effects on the readiness to compromise mate selection standards. *European Journal of Social Psychology, 32*(5), 609–625.

Pyszczynski, T., Solomon, S., & Greenberg, J. (2003). *In the wake of 9/11: The psychology of terror.* Washington, DC: American Psychological Association.

Pyszczynski, T., Wicklund, R. A., Floresku, S., Koch, H., Gauch, G., Solomon, S., & Greenberg, J. (1996). Whistling in the dark: Exaggerated consensus estimates in response to incidental reminders of mortality. *Psychological Science,* 7(6), 332–336.

Wisman, A., & Goldenberg, J. L. (2005). From the grave to the cradle: Evidence that mortality salience engenders a desire for offspring. *Journal of Personality & Social Psychology, 89*(1), 46–61.

Notes

1. *Star Trek: Deep Space Nine* episode 5–11, "The Darkness and the Light" (January 6, 1997).
2. Greenberg (2008), p. 48.
3. Pyszczynski et al. (2003).
4. Pyszczynski et al. (2003).
5. Pyszczynski et al. (1996).
6. e.g., *Star Trek: Deep Space Nine* episode 4–23, "To the Death" (May 13, 1996).
7. Pyszczynski et al. (2003), p. 8.
8. *Star Trek: Deep Space Nine* episode 7–10, "It's Only a Paper Moon" (December 30, 1998).
9. e.g., *Star Trek: Deep Space Nine* episode 5–26, "Call to Arms" (June 16, 1997).
10. *Star Trek: Deep Space Nine* episode 3–25, "Facets" (June 12, 1995).
11. *Star Trek: Deep Space Nine* episode 7–8, "The Siege of AR-558" (November 18, 1998).
12. American Psychological Association (2013).
13. *Star Trek: Deep Space Nine* episode 7–10, "It's Only a Paper Moon" (December 30, 1998).
14. *Star Trek: Deep Space Nine* episode 7–10, "It's Only a Paper Moon" (December 30, 1998).
15. *Star Trek: Deep Space Nine* episode 7–10, "It's Only a Paper Moon" (December 30, 1998).
16. CNN (2002), as cited in Wisman & Goldenberg (2005).
17. *Star Trek: Deep Space Nine* episode 4–15, "Sons of Mogh" (February 12, 1996).

18. *Star Trek: Deep Space Nine* episode 5–3, "Looking for par'Mach in All the Wrong Places" (October 14, 1996).
19. *Star Trek: Deep Space Nine* episode 5–26, "Call to Arms" (June 16, 1997).
20. *Star Trek: Deep Space Nine* episode 6–16, "Change of Heart" (March 4, 1998).
21. *Star Trek: Deep Space Nine* episode 6–26, "Tears of the Prophets" (June 17, 1998).
22. *Star Trek: Deep Space Nine* episodes 1–1 and 1–2, "Emissary" (January 3, 1993).
23. *Star Trek: Deep Space Nine* episode 6–11, "Waltz" (January 8, 1998).
24. *Star Trek: Deep Space Nine* episode 6–19, "In the Pale Moonlight" (April 15, 1998).
25. *Star Trek: Deep Space Nine* episode 6–19, "In the Pale Moonlight" (April 15, 1998).
26. *Star Trek: Deep Space Nine* episode 6–19, "In the Pale Moonlight" (April 15, 1998).
27. e.g., Hirschberger et al. (2002).
28. Pyszczynski et al. (2003), p. 196.

Log File III

Star Trek: Deep Space Nine and the Need for Power

TRAVIS LANGLEY

Of the twenty psychological needs that Henry Murray identified,[1] Harvard psychologist David McClelland considered three to exert the greatest influence on people's actions and personality growth: the needs for power (nPow), affiliation (nAffil), and achievement (nAch).[2] Two of those three (high nPow and low nAffil) may play a greater role in determining leadership styles[3]—especially the need for power.[4] *Star Trek: Deep Space Nine*, from beginning to end, is about power struggles on many levels. Characters overtly and covertly seek social influence (power over others) and control over their own lives (freedom from others).[5]

Unlike previous series, in which lead characters were all Starfleet officers who work together and cooperate, the majority of integral characters aboard space station Deep Space 9 are not in Starfleet and frequently find themselves at odds with one another. According to co-creator Rick Berman, "the ones that are Starfleet officers aren't crazy about where they are, so we have a lot of frustration and conflict."[6] Some individuals who feel a lack of control in their own lives overcompensate and go too far in trying to take control not only over their own lives but also over the lives of other people.

Neo-Freudian psychologist Karen Horney saw the needs to exploit and to wield power over others as neurotic, irrational solutions to life's difficulties.[7] While most people want to feel strong, Horney believed that certain kinds of neurotic individuals would desperately, aggressively try to gain control over others and get the better of them in order to make themselves feel stronger and more capable in life.

When *Star Trek: Deep Space Nine* begins, occupants of the planet Bajor have only recently been released from enslavement by Cardassians and are working to maintain control over their own lives. The discovery of a stable wormhole nearby, a passage to another quadrant of the galaxy, turns Bajor into a location of strategic importance—which leads Cardassians, Klingons, Romulans, Changelings, the Federation, and many others into conflict and even wars during the course of the series. Some fight to control the wormhole, some fight to control everyone else, and some fight simply to control their own lives.

Not all pursuit of power is unhealthy, not even power over others. Parents, employers, government officials, pet owners, and many others must exert authority over others in the natural course of fulfilling their duties. Authority figures bear responsibility to those under their control. Not everyone in authority accepts such responsibility, though. Some use the responsibility as an excuse to abuse power. Gul Dukat, the principal antagonist in *Star Trek: Deep Space Nine*, often speaks of Bajorans as if they were children who needed their enslavement under grown-up Cardassians.

DS9's Commander (later Captain) Benjamin Sisko seems more *Machiavellian* (pragmatically manipulative) than other series' captains,[8] but then again, he is dealing with different circumstances. We can easily make the mistake of attributing someone's actions to ingrained traits while underestimating the power of the situation to shape behavior—the *fundamental attribution error.*[9] Nevertheless, he is the one series captain who openly wants to become an admiral, indicating that he does hold aspirations for power and status beyond what is necessary to cope with conflicts from *DS9*. Motives for pursuing power

Star Trek: Deep Space Nine (1993–1999, 7 seasons, 176 episodes). Created by R. Berman, M. Piller. Paramount Domestic Television. Aired in first-run syndication.

can range from benevolent to malignant, from other-serving to self-serving.[10]

The series *Deep Space Nine* ends with Gul Dukat gaining godlike powers and Sisko making the greatest sacrifice of any series captain, plunging himself and Dukat into a fiery chasm in order to protect everyone from the Gul's power. The villain dies. The hero's old life ends as Sisko becomes a different kind of being with new powers of his own, able to appear to his wife in an angelic vision, now existing outside linear time and promising one day to return from the other side.[11]

References

Fodor, E. M., & Farrow, D. L. (1979). The power motive as an influence on use of power. *Journal of Personality & Social Psychology, 37*(11), 2091–2097.

Gross, E., & Altman, M. A. (1995). *Captains' logs: The unauthorized complete Trek voyages.* New York, NY: Little, Brown.

Horney, K. (1937). *The neurotic personality of our time.* New York, NY: Norton.

Horney, K. (1945). *Our inner conflicts.* New York, NY: Norton.

Howard, E. S., Gardner, W. L., & Thompson, L. (2007). The role of self-concept and the social context in determining the behavior of power holders: Self-construal in intergroup versus dyadic dispute resolution negotiations. *Journal of Personality & Social Psychology, 93*(4), 614–631.

Jacobs, R. L., & McClelland, D. C. (1994). Moving up the corporate ladder: A longitudinal study of the leadership motive pattern and managerial success in women and men. *Consulting Psychology Journal: Practice & Research, 46*(1), 32–41.

Lammers, J., Stoker, J. I., & Stapel, D. A. (2009). Differentiating social and personal power: Opposite effects on stereotyping, but parallel effects on behavioral approach tendencies. *Psychological Science, 20*(12), 1543–1549.

McClelland, D. C. (1961). *The achieving society.* Princeton, NJ: Van Nostrand.

McClelland, D. C. (1975). *Power: The inner experience.* New York, NY: Irvington-Wiley.

McClelland, D. C., & Boyatzis (1982). Leadership motive pattern and long-term success in management. *Journal of Applied Psychology, 67*(6), 737–743.

McClelland, D. C., & Burnham, D. (1976). Power as the great motivator. *Harvard Business Review, 25*, 159–166.

Murray, H. A. (1938). *Explorations in personality: A clinical and experimental study of fifty men of college age.* New York, NY: Oxford University Press.

Ross, L. D. (1977). The intuitive psychologist and his shortcomings: Distortions in the attribution process. In L. Berkowitz (Ed.), *Advances in experimental social psychology,* vol. 10 (pp. 173–220). New York, NY: Academic Press.

Suessenbach, F., & Moore, A. B. (2015). Individual differences in the explicit power motive predict 'utilitarian' choices in moral dilemmas, especially when this choice is self-beneficial. *Personality & Individual Differences, 86*(2), 297–302.

Notes

1. Murray (1938).
2. McClelland (1961).
3. Jacobs & McClelland (1994); McClelland & Boyatzis (1982).
4. McClelland (1975); McClelland & Burnham (1976).
5. Lammers et al. (2009).
6. Gross & Altman (1995), p. 328.
7. Horney (1937, 1945).
8. e.g., *Star Trek: Deep Space Nine* episodes 5–13, "For the Uniform" (February 3, 1997); 6–19 "In the Pale Moonlight" (April 15, 1998).
9. Ross (1977).
10. Fodor & Farrow (1979); Howard et al. (2007); Suessenbach & Moore (2015).
11. *Star Trek: Deep Space Nine* episode 7–26, "What You Leave Behind" part 2 (June 2, 1999).

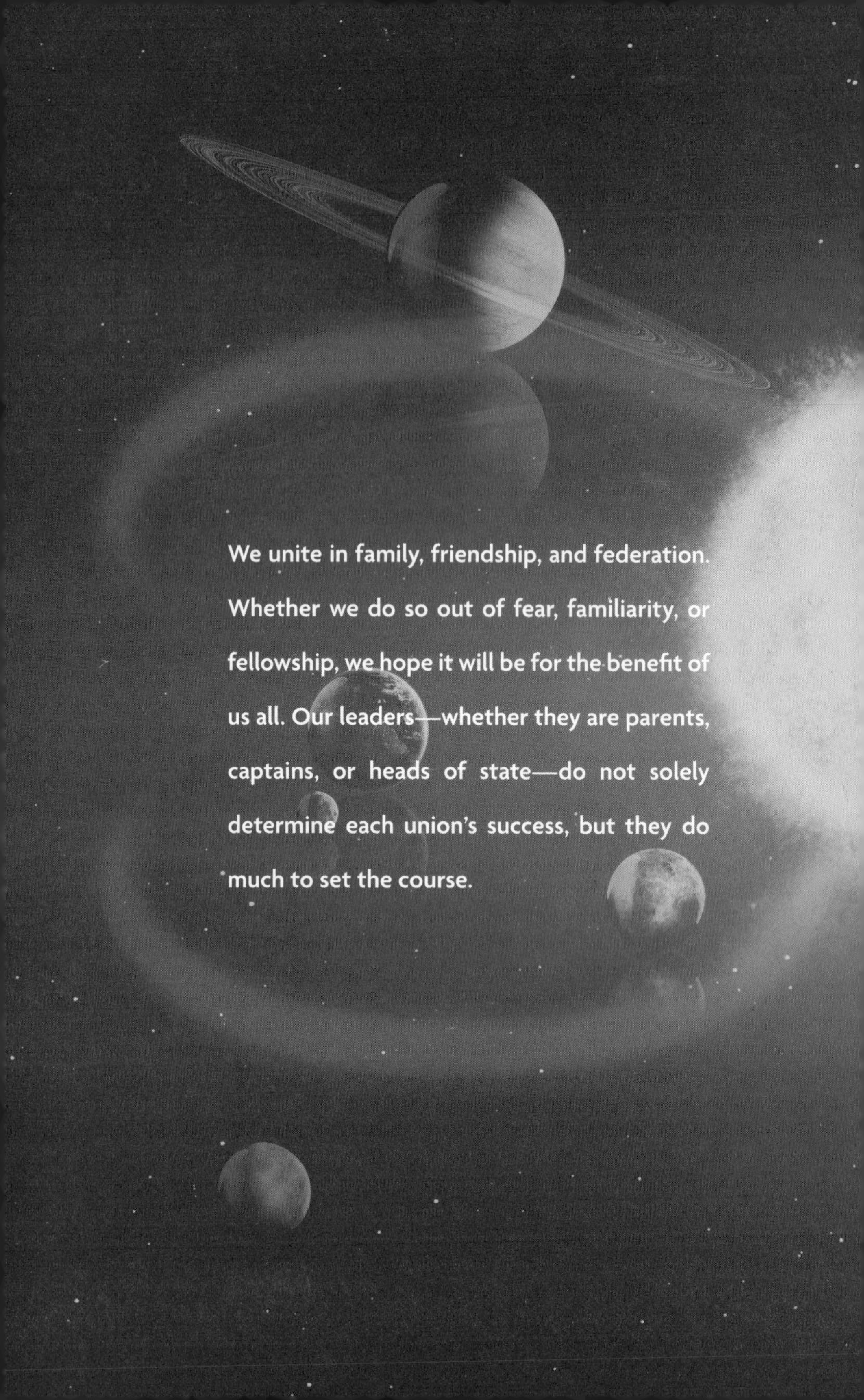

We unite in family, friendship, and federation. Whether we do so out of fear, familiarity, or fellowship, we hope it will be for the benefit of us all. Our leaders—whether they are parents, captains, or heads of state—do not solely determine each union's success, but they do much to set the course.

PART IV

FEDERATION

While one leads by inspiring loyalty, another prefers to instill fear. A leader can share authority, responsibility, and power or cling greedily to them all. Different kinds of leaders have their own advantages, with no one kind clearly looking best for every situation. Who should lead may depend on where, when, and why a group needs a leader.

•13•

The Captain's Seat: Leadership in Starfleet

BILLY SAN JUAN AND TRAVIS LANGLEY

"You're the captain of this ship. You haven't the right to be vulnerable in the eyes of the crew. You can't afford the luxury of being anything less than perfect. If you do, they lose faith, and you lose command."

—Spock[1]

"The success of our leadership is dependent upon respect for our mission. . . ."

—U.S. President John F. Kennedy[2]

What is a leader? A person can inherit power or be assigned a position of authority without possessing any ability to lead. A leader gets individuals to conform to group goals and coordinates them in the pursuit of those goals, pulling a team together and guiding it to victory.[3] Leadership requires a range of skills but not the same skills for every leader, group, or situation.

Masses of individuals acting independently with no guidance, no coordination of efforts, and no individual responsibility to each other cannot build a starship and fly it to the stars, much less pull together and build the kind of civilization that can attempt that feat in the first place.[4] Leaders must emerge. Someone must hold authority. Leaders can emerge in any situation involving more than one person,[5] and leadership is by no means proprietary to a specific species.[6] Every ship requires a captain, and every Star Trek series cast list from *Star Trek* through *Star Trek: Enterprise* opens with whoever plays the commanding officer because that is who, more than any other character, shapes the direction that each mission will take and in many cases chooses which adventures the crew will have.

Who should sit in the captain's chair?

Who Shall Lead?

Why do leaders matter? What exactly do they do, and what do their followers need from them? The person in charge needs to serve a number of functions:[7]

- A leader must provide *strategic direction and vision* for followers and sometimes to entire organizations.[8]
- A leader must provide followers with *motivation and coaching*.[9]
- A leader enforces and interprets organizational policies.[10]
- A leader obtains resources for the group.[11]

Not every leader will serve each need to the fullest, but not every leader needs to be best at accomplishing them all. A strong first officer, chief engineer, head of security, or ship's physician can help supplement and fill in for areas in which the captain is not as strong. When the captain's stern words fail to motivate a crew member in the way that is needed, the ship's counselor may be able to provide what that person requires.

Leader Types

Kurt Lewin, known as the founder of social psychology,[12] studied leadership styles in an early examination of how leaders differ in effectiveness. At a time when Hitler's approach looked successful in pulling Germany out of the Great Depression, when people such as Lewin's family had to flee from persecution under the Third Reich, Lewin wanted to know how a totalitarian approach might compare with a democratic approach overall. In his original experiment on leadership styles, Lewin divided a group of boys into three groups whose leaders differed in how strictly they controlled their respective groups.[13] An *autocratic* leader, who followed an *authoritarian* approach by exerting rigid control over the group and making decisions without consulting others, got the most work out of the group but only when that dictatorial leader was present. When the autocratic leader was not present, group organization fell apart and the members barely worked. A *democratic* leader, whose approach was to seek input and involve group members in decision-making, got the best work overall, with work continuing even when the leader left the room. A *laissez-faire* leader wielded no control, made no decisions, and left group members to form their own goals and solve problems. The essentially unled group members produced the least and poorest work, strayed from task, and were more likely to fall into aggression and chaos.

No laissez-faire leader will captain a starship, at least not for long. Commanding officers range in the degree to which they lead autocratically or democratically. Although each makes it clear that he or she is the one with the power and responsibility to make the final decisions, those who lead the crew in each series solicit input from others, involve them in the decision-making process, and make them feel like partners in the process overall. Not every commanding officer behaves this way, however, and not everyone wants a democratic leader. People with unstable personalities or low self-esteem are more likely to prefer an autocratic leader who will help them feel that someone in charge will keep things under control.[14] Star Trek repeatedly depicts reasons to distrust dictators. Kirk is especially likely to encourage the locals to overthrow tyrants.[15]

Autocratic and democratic leaders each have advantages, with neither being more productive than the other *on average*.[16] Each does better sometimes. Some problems require immediate, one-sided decisions, for example, without the leader first taking time to hold a conversation. When Kirk refers to the villain Khan as "the best of tyrants," acknowledging Khan's success in achieving stability under his totalitarian rule, the captain must clarify to Spock that they can recognize the man's achievements and even admire qualities in him while still opposing his goals and methods.[17]

Fiedler's Contingency Theory

Fiedler's *contingency theory* proposes two main kinds of leadership whose value and success will be contingent on situational factors.[18] *Task-motivated leaders*, those focused on performance, are best suited to chaotic events and extreme situations, which Star

Neutralizers and Substitutes

Leadership may be contingent on situational factors known as neutralizers and substitutes.[19]

Neutralizers of leadership detrimentally affect leadership behaviors, reducing their effectiveness. These are obstacles that may decrease the effectiveness or influence of a leader on his or her followers. Examples include spatial distance, which can make a leader lack ability to provide rewards. The United Federation of Planets cannot provide direct leadership aside from communications that may take a long time to reach Starfleet and therefore must rely on its high-ranking officers as its proxy.

Substitutes for leadership decrease, if not eliminate, the need for a leader by replacing that need. For example, menial tasks or self-managed teams do not necessarily need a high-ranking, charismatic leader. Officers on the bridge of the *Enterprise* may require the captain's direct attention, whereas crew members performing routine maintenance do not.

Trek depicts on a regular basis. In moderate situations requiring creativity, however, a task-motivated leader may undermine creativity by focusing on the task at hand. *Relationship-motivated leaders*, those characterized by their concern for followers, excel more often in stable circumstances that are free from chaos and turmoil. During times of crisis, however, they may be overwhelmed by their followers' needs. Khan Noonien Singh's relationship-based leadership over Starfleet historian Marla McGivers is stable until Khan's attempted takeover of the *Enterprise* conflicts with her values, leading to a reduction of devotion in their leader-follower dynamic.[20]

Path-Goal Leadership Theory

Path-goal leadership theory posits that a leader's role is to align the goals of the followers with the goals of the organization. Upon alignment of goals, the leader must assist in the achievement of the goals by enabling the followers to realize their ability to meet them. In this theory, there are four categories of behavior that leaders exhibit to motivate their followers[21]:

- *Participative leadership behaviors* involve decision-making. The leader fosters the correspondence between follower and organizational goal by involving the followers in the decision-making process. Likewise, the leader solicits feedback from the followers. When he is concerned about how his romantic relationship with a lieutenant might compromise his objectivity, for example, Picard consults with Counselor Troi and asks for her feedback.[22]
- *Directive path-goal clarifying leadership behaviors* motivate followers to achieve their goals by reducing ambiguity in a follower's role. Tasks are structured, feedback is given, and rewards are iterated on the basis of performance. At the end of Jonathan Archer's first mission as captain of his *Enterprise*, he debriefs Commander Tucker and T'Pol by relaying an admiral's orders, commending their work, and offering T'Pol a position on the *Enterprise.*[23]
- *Supportive leadership behaviors* include demonstrations of attention toward the needs and best interests of the followers. These behaviors also allow for the removal of obstacles that prevent the followers from achieving the goal. For example, when Kes asks that *Voyager*'s holographic doctor be treated with greater respect, Janeway grants him partial control over his own computer program and activation.[24]

- *Achievement-oriented leadership behavior* creates performance goals consistent with high standards. The leader not only creates these goals but also expresses confidence in the followers' ability to meet the goals. Captain Archer provides this kind of motivation to his crew in the aftermath of a battle in which they sustained heavy damage and losses. "We're going to succeed," he tells them, "to accomplish our mission for everyone on Earth who's relying on us. . . ."[25]

Charismatic and Transformational Leadership

In *charismatic and transformational leadership,* certain behaviors and traits exhibited by a leader can both influence and inspire his or her followers.[26] These leaders accomplish certain tasks and exhibit certain traits.

- These leaders provide a *vision,* or a generalized ideal state representing the shared values and morals of the organization. Once it becomes clear that members of Starfleet and the Maquis, recently at odds with one another, must work together to survive and get home, Captain Janeway shares a vision with them all and tells them that they will unite as a single crew.[27]
- These leaders not only provide a vision but also *implement* it. The leader must articulate the vision well and motivate others to follow it. In many episodes, Star Trek captains inspire others with impromptu speeches about following the principles of the Federation, Starfleet, or, in one case, the U.S. Constitution.[28]

- Leaders implement the vision by demonstrating a *charismatic communication style.* The person who shows *charisma* displays a captivating tone, confidence, and a variety of related traits that allows a leader to create a superior impact on his or her followers. Khan's charisma is undeniable. His dramatic flair and self-assurance attract people to him, captivate his followers, make him a major player in the Eugenics Wars, and turn him into the most formidable of Kirk's foes.[29]

A Leadership Quality

Leaders follow a variety of styles, not only those we've addressed here. Two leaders can differ greatly while achieving similar levels of success that depend on the task, setting, skills, and people involved. They can fail for the same kinds of reasons. Success appears to be contingent on the group's needs, and the most successful leaders vary their approaches with different circumstances. Democratic dialogue may work well in the ready room but not as well when people are under attack and immediate decisions must be made. Even then, though, the captains in Star Trek work with people they trust and sometimes defer to them without discussion.

Great leaders have focus (vision, principles, priorities) and legitimacy based on trust and personal credibility.[30] These qualities are both *intrapersonal* (within that individual) and *interpersonal* (between that individual and others). A great captain needs a great crew, whether the crew starts out great or the captain brings out the best in it. Starships and space stations such as Deep Space 9 are captained by a select, elite few whose knowledge, talents, charisma, and leadership ability blend together into the right combination for their situations, and Star Trek's leading characters emerge to become the best of Starfleet's commanding officers. Why else would they keep becoming admirals[31] or, in Sisko's case,[32] something godlike?

References

Barker, B. (2001). Do leaders matter? *Educational Review*, 53(1), 65–76.

Barling, B., Christie, A., & Hoption, C. (2011). Leadership. In S. Zedeck (Ed.), A*PA handbook of industrial and organizational psychology* (vol. 1, pp. 183–228). Washington, DC: American Psychological Association.

Bass, B. M. (1998). *Transformational leadership: Industry, military, and educational impact.* Mahwah, NJ: Erlbaum.

Bednarz, T. F. (2011). *Great! What makes leaders great.* Stevens Point, WI: Majorium Business Press.

Bonanni, R., Cafazzo, S., Valsecchi, P., & Natoli, E. (2010). Effect of affiliative and agonistic relationships of leadership behaviour in free-ranging dogs. *Animal Behaviour, 79*(5), 981–991.

Couzin, I. D., Krause, J., Franks, N. R., & Levin, S. A. (2005). Effective leadership and decision-making in animal groups on the move. *Nature, 434*, 513–516.

Foley, R. A. (1997). The adaptive legacy of human evolution: A search for the environment of evolutionary adaptedness. *Evolutionary Anthropology, 4*(2), 194–203.

Gastil, J. (1994). A meta-analytic review of the productivity and satisfaction of democratic and autocratic leadership. *Small Group Behavior, 25*(3), 384–410.

Hakimi, N., van Knippenberg, D., & Giessner, S. (2010). Leader empowering behavior: The leader's perspective. *British Journal of Management, 21*(3), 701–716.

Howell, J. P., Bowen, D. E., Dorfman, P. W., Kerr, S., & Podsakoff, P. M. (1990). Substitutes for leadership: Effective alternatives to ineffective leadership. *Organizational Dynamics, 19*(1), 21–38.

Jahoda, G. (2007). *A history of social psychology: From the eighteenth-century enlightenment to the Second World War.* Cambridge, UK: Cambridge University Press.

Jex, S. M., & Britt, T. W. (2008). Organizational psychology: A scientist-practitioner approach (2nd edition). New York, NY: Wiley.

Kennedy, J. F. (1963). *Trade mart speech, 1963.* PBS: http://www.pbs.org/wgbh/americanexperience/features/primary-resources/jfk-trademart/.

Kenrick, D., Li, N. P., & Butner, J. (2003). Dynamical evolutionary psychology: Individual decision rules and emergency social norms. *Psychological Review, 110*(1), 3–28.

Langley, T. (2017, January 29). *Kurt Lewin, the refugee who founded social psychology.* Psychology Today: https://www.psychologytoday.com/blog/beyond-heroes-and-villains/201701/kurt-lewin-the-refugee-who-founded-social-psychology.

Lewin, K., Lippitt, R., & White, R. K. (1939). Patterns of aggressive behavior in experimentally created social climates. *Journal of Social Psychology, 10*(2), 271–301.

Lunenberg, F. C. (2010) Leader-member exchange theory: Another perspective on the leadership process. *International Journal of Management, Business, & Administration, 13*(1), 1–5.

Mitman, G. (1990). Dominance, leadership, and aggression: Animal behavior studies during the Second World War. *Journal of the History of the Behavioral Sciences, 26*(1), 3–16.

Ortiz-Plata, C., De Lucas-Tron, J., & Miranda-de la Lama, G. C. (2012). Breed identity and leadership in a mixed flock of sheep. *Journal of Veterinary Behavior: Clinical Applications & Research, 72*(2), 94–98.

Pless, N. M., Maak, T., & Waldman, D. A. (2012). Different approaches toward doing the right thing: Mapping the responsibility orientations of leaders. *Academy of Management Perspectives, 26*(4), 51–65.

Schoel, C., Bluemke, M., Mueller, P., & Stehlberg, D. (2011). When autocratic leaders become an option: Uncertainty and self-esteem predict implicit leadership preference. *Journal of Personality & Social Psychology, 101*(3), 521–540.

Van Vugt, M. V., & De Cremer, D. (1999). Leadership in social dilemmas: The effects of group identification on collective actions to provide public goods. *Journal of Personality & Social Psychology, 76*(4), 587–599.

Van Vugt, M. V., Hogan, R., & Kaiser, R. B. (2008). Leadership, followership, and evolution: Some lessons from the past. *American Psychologist, 63*(3), 182–196.

Wilson, K. S., Sin, H., & Conlon, D. (2010). What about the leader in leader-member exchange? The impact of resource exchanges and substitutability on the leader. *Academy of Management Review, 35*(3), 358–372.

Notes

1. *Star Trek* episode 1–5, "The Enemy Within" (October 6, 1966).
2. Kennedy's final speech, written but not delivered (1963).
3. Van Vugt et al. (2008).
4. Couzin et al. (2005); Foley (1997); Kenrick et al. (2003).
5. e.g., Van Vugt & De Cremer (1999).
6. Bonanni et al. (2010); Mitman (1990); Ortiz-Plata et al. (2012).
7. Jex & Britt (2008).
8. Bass (1998).
9. Barker (2001); Hakimi et al. (2010).
10. Pless et al. (2012).
11. Wilson et al. (2010).
12. Jahoda (2007); Langley (2017).
13. Lewin et al. (1939).
14. Schoel et al. (2011).
15. e.g., *Star Trek* episode 2–21, "Patterns of Force" (February 16, 1968).
16. Gastil (1994).
17. *Star Trek* episode 1–22, "Space Seed" (February 16, 1967).
18. Barling et al. (2011).
19. *Star Trek* episode 1–22, "Space Seed" (February 16, 1967).
20. Howell et al. (1990).
21. Barling et al. (2011).
22. *Star Trek: The Next Generation* episode 6–19, "Lessons" (April 3, 1993).
23. *Enterprise* episode 1–2, "Broken Bow" (September 26, 2001).
24. *Star Trek: Voyager* episode 1–7, "Eye of the Needle" (February 20, 1995).
25. *Star Trek: Enterprise* episode 3–20, "The Forgotten" (April 28, 2004).
26. Jex & Britt (2008).
27. *Star Trek: Voyager* episode 1–1, "Caretaker" (January 16, 1995).

28. *Star Trek* episode 2–23, "The Omega Glory" (March 1, 1968).
29. *Star Trek* episode 1–22, "Space Seed" (February 16, 1967); *Star Trek II: The Wrath of Khan* (1982 motion picture); and maybe *Star Trek into Darkness* (2013).
30. Bednarz (2011).
31. Kirk, admiral in *Star Trek: The Motion Picture* (1979 motion picture); Janeway, vice admiral in *Star Trek: Nemesis* (2002 motion picture); Archer, revealed in *Star Trek: Enterprise* episode 4–19, "In a Mirror, Darkly," part II (April 29, 2005) to have retired as admiral. Picard turned down admiralty in *Star Trek: The Next Generation* episode 1–19, "Coming of Age" (March 14, 1988).
32. *Star Trek: Deep Space Nine* episode 7–26, "What You Leave Behind," part II (June 2, 1999).

How do groups come together and what keeps them going? When different groups encounter each other, is conflict between them inevitable? Is conflict within each group inevitable as well?

•14•

Four Quadrants, Many Life Forms: Group Dynamics Inside and Outside the Federation

W. Blake Erickson
and John C. Blanchar

"Once formed, categories are the basis for normal prejudgment. We cannot possibly avoid this process."
—personality psychologist Gordon Allport[1]

"We have reason to mistrust one another but even better reason to set those differences aside. Of course, the question is who will take the initiative?"
—Captain Jean-Luc Picard to Romulan Commander Tolumak[2]

Humans have inherited a social structure that offers an array of intergroup behaviors. These include aggressive tendencies resulting from competition but also prosocial behaviors, such as charity, that might eliminate the need for competition.[3] Each facilitates survival in different ways, but the progress of human history has steadily moved toward more peaceful coexistence, based on shared values.[4] After making first contact with Vulcans,[5] Earth's inhabitants move further in this direction after finding that they are part of an even more complex mosaic of sentient life forms in the Milky Way.

However, this new paradigm brings unique challenges, unfolding from their group alliances and dynamics in the larger galactic community. How these problems emerge is closely tied to how groups form in the first place, and the ways the great powers of the four quadrants resolve conflicts is not so different from the ways we resolve our own real-life intergroup struggles.

How and Why Do Groups Form?

Humans naturally divide ourselves into groups of similar individuals. These groups range from biological relatives to professional colleagues to multinational coalitions. Star Trek takes the next logical step: uniting worlds and exotic far-flung races in such coalitions as the United Federation of Planets, the Dominion, and even the Borg Collective. But why do groups form in the first place?

Adaptive Advantages

People form groups because groups help individuals survive. To this end, they engage in "constant commerce"[6] with the environment to satisfy basic physical needs and to ensure safety. This environment, of course, includes other intelligent beings. Providing for oneself is cumbersome when there is competition over resources, such as food and mates, but a group can establish norms where resources are shared among members. At the root of this is *reciprocal altruism*, which is a way of saying that people help others while expecting help in return in the future.[7] Moreover, as a group grows more complex, members take on specialized *roles* that influence how others interact with them and what they can contribute to the rest of the group.[8] To us, this means that college professors are met with different expectations than car mechanics, and so on.

Onboard the original series' *Enterprise*, organization is not so different: Leonard McCoy provides medical treatment, Montgomery Scott ensures that the ship runs smoothly, and Uhura's xenolinguistic expertise makes her an excellent communications officer.[9] McCoy, in particular, relishes reminding others that he's a doctor, not a bricklayer,[10] mechanic,[11] coal miner,[12] or many other professions that do not match his role.

Similar Values

Groups do not merely form out of the need to share or reinforce categories. A driving force behind group formation is a general attraction to life forms whose values are similar to our own.[13] In fact, very different individuals may unite under a common thread of values that holds the larger group together. Shared values are at the core of the founding of the United Federation of Planets,[14] whose charter states that member worlds all believe in the ". . . dignity and worth of all life forms, in the equal rights of members of planetary systems large and small . . . and to promote social progress and better standards of living on all worlds."[15]

Not all groups come together willingly, however. Sometimes, one group unites less powerful groups by force under its banner and preserves its place at the top through social dominance.[16] Other powers in the Alpha and Beta Quadrants, such as the Klingon and Romulan Empires, colonize and conquer by brute force, at the peril of native races, with social dominance as their motivation.[17]

A Need for Hierarchy

Once groups form, they often also establish a *hierarchy* within the group, which stratifies the group based on who holds power.[18] Although Klingons and Romulans display the dark side of this group structure, hierarchies do aid group survival because concentrated leadership can produce quick decisions when survival is at stake.[19] A group without a clear hierarchy is less stable and operates less efficiently, potentially continuing to debate solutions up to the point of annihilation.[20]

Ships in the Federation and elsewhere show the success of hierarchical structure, as all crew members ultimately answer to the commanding officer. Consider when Picard takes control of the hostage situation with the malevolent entity Armus on Vagra II, which the away team has failed to resolve as a group.[21] Once he arrives and gives his crew orders, Picard saves the captured crew members by outsmarting Armus. The Borg Collective also runs smoothly but by adhering to its extreme hierarchy: Drones do the grunt work, exploring space and assimilating new races, and Queens serve as data hubs of the consciousness coordinating all Borg.[22]

What Keeps Groups Together?

Living in groups is essential for survival for many species on Earth and for those spread across the four quadrants, but what psychologically bonds members in ways that keeps groups together? Several factors seem important in maintaining cohesion among members of social groups and Star Trek characters provide great examples of such factors which are encountered while hurling through space at warp speed on the *U.S.S. Enterprise.* These factors include group cohesion, similarity between members in appearance, behavior, culture, etc., the sharing of a common fate, and favoritism toward members of their in-group. Each is described below.

Group Cohesion

The feeling of closeness that bonds groups together and perception of the group as the perfect unit is what social psychologists call *entitativity.*[23] It stresses unity, coherence, and structure within a social group, allowing cooperation and improved performance.[24] A great example of this "groupness" comes from the Borg Collective, which assimilates individuals of many species in service of attaining perfect entitativity—to the point where there is no "I," only "we." This disturbs something that other groups' members tend to strive for, which is a sense of individuality within the confines of a group called *optimal distinctiveness.*[25] Such a quest for perfect unity and cohesion can result in dark consequences, stemming from the loss of individual identity—just ask Captain Jean-Luc Picard, who suffers nightmares from his brief stint among the collective.[26]

Similarity

Similarity can draw groups together in the first place, but the bonds maintaining them tend to be stronger when members are highly similar to one another.[27] This similarity may be in appearance, behavior, culture, and interests or goals. Most discernibly, social groups in Star Trek are organized by species membership—human, Vulcan, Romulan, Klingon, and so forth. Indeed, it is rare to see social groups composed of diverse species. Subgroups within larger groups also form and are maintained through similarities, such as the tight bond shared by Kirk, Spock, and McCoy, all of whom have high-ranking officer positions on the *U.S.S. Enterprise*. At the opposite extreme, Klingon culture draws sharp and deep lines separating their *in-group* from members of *out-groups*.

Common Fate

Group bonds also grow stronger when members share a common fate with one another.[28] For instance, the crew of the *Enterprise* collectively faces the prospect of doom, and the success of victory should enhance group cohesiveness.[29] Group successes then allow for members to bask in the reflected glory of the group and improve their self-esteem.[30] In particular, a group such as the Klingon Empire has a culture that stresses the belief that each member is bonded by a common fate in which an individual's failure reflects on their group as a whole. Worf, for example, refuses to discuss Klingons' failed attempts at genetic enhancement with "outsiders," due to embarrassment felt collectively among all Klingons.[31]

In-Group Favoritism

A funny thing happens when social beings are placed into groups, even when these groups are completely arbitrary or meaningless (e.g., arranged by the toss of a coin)—they show favoritism toward members of their *in-group* over members of *out-groups*.[32] Membership in a group, even when it stems from minor characteristics, is sufficient to create a sense of loyalty to those like oneself, a phenomenon called *in-group favoritism*. Curiously, Vulcans exhibit in-group favoritism that borders on

Out-Groups: Do They All Look Alike?

After Wesley Crusher mistakes one Benzite for another, he asks how members of their species can tell each other apart, and the Benzite answers, "We just do."[33] Wesley makes this false alarm because of the *own-race bias*, which makes people better at recognizing faces of their own race or ethnicity than faces of other races.[34] Seeing "race" and "bias" in the same phrase might sound politically loaded, but the real culprit for the effect is basic perceptual learning dating to birth. An infant usually first learns to recognize members of his or her own race before going out into the world to see other-race faces.[35] The basic structure of faces reliably varies among ethnicities and races, offering people many opportunities to make a mistake, as Wesley does, if they are not experienced with members of other groups. Do all Benzites look alike? That depends on who's looking.

xenophobia, the fear of out-groups. They discriminate against minorities (particularly those with limited ability to mind-meld[36]), quell dissidents by exiling the Romulans' ancestors,[37] and value Vulcan purity to the point that Spock's own father begrudged his son's human heritage.[38] Despite how unsavory this sounds, through such behavior the group manages to remain intact for centuries of peaceful prosperity.

Intergroup Conflict

With so many distinct social groups in our planet's history, some intergroup conflict is inevitable, just as it is with the groups that inhabit Star Trek's Milky Way. Warp travel makes their intergroup conflict possible. Opportunity for behavior such as conflict is not its cause, though. What causes conflict, and how might it be avoided or abated? Here we discuss three causes of intergroup conflict: competition for resources, perceptions of threat, and prejudice.

Competition for Resources

The most obvious cause for conflict arises when a shared resource is rare, creating competition. Moreover, a strongly bonded group will see members take personal risks that might seem irrational at the individual level but make sense for the group's survival.[39] In Star Trek, while many resources appear to be plentiful by the twenty-second century, a few do remain limited. Consider dilithium crystals, which power warp cores that propel starships capable of faster-than-light interstellar travel. Like present-day oil, this energy resource is coveted by many different groups, which consequently drives hostility and conflict between them.[40] Although conflict over dilithium is rarely portrayed in the prime universe, the mirror universe's Terran Empire extorts the mineral from worlds with a very sincere threat of destruction.[41] To multiplanetary civilizations, territory in the form of life-sustaining planets is another limited resource worth fighting for. Crossing into the Romulan Neutral Zone, for example, is considered an act of war by both the Federation and the Romulan Empire.[42]

Perceptions of Threat

Another cause of intergroup conflict centers on *perceptions of threat* that can be symbolic as well as physical.[43] The Borg Collective is perceived as threatening to every group across the four quadrants, and predictably is met with aggression and hostility. In fact, no diplomacy is sought with the Borg; they are seen as a menace that must be eradicated. Of course, this position seems reasonable, given statements like the following: "Strength is irrelevant. Resistance is futile. We wish to improve ourselves. We will add your biological and technological distinctiveness to our own. Your culture will adapt to service ours."[44] The Borg not only remove someone's individuality; they erase that individual's symbolic existence as well.

Prejudice

Prejudice is the negative attitude toward another person based on his or her group membership. Not surprisingly, prejudiced attitudes have the potential to ignite aggression toward out-groups,[45] and lifeforms in the twenty-second century are not immune to their influence. Even Dr. McCoy, in moments of frustration, calls Mr. Spock such epithets as "green-blooded hobgoblin,"[46] but his outbursts do not predict his behavior toward the half-Vulcan, with whom he develops a close bond. The best example of actual conflict stemming from prejudice comes from the planet Cheron, in which two warring peoples—both with half-black and half-white faces but on opposite sides—engage in a struggle to enslave each other.[47] Their hatred may literally only be skin deep but nonetheless fuels this civilization-destroying conflict.

How to Heal Rifts and Prevent Conflict

Once divided, are groups doomed to hate and antagonize one another? Fortunately for us all, the answer is no. Achieving cooperation and peace requires the reapplication of group formation and preservation principles. Groups form because together they can preserve health and safety better than their members can alone.

Members of different groups may be different from one another, as the Allies of Earth's Second World War were, but they come together when necessary to preserve their own existence. Although the Federation, the Klingon Empire, and the Romulan Star Empire engage in hot and cold conflicts through the centuries, the threat posed by the Dominion's invasion of the Alpha Quadrant is enough to convince them to join forces under the banner of the Federation Alliance.[48] Whatever these groups' cultural differences may be, they share a *superordinate* (higher-order) goal when they agree that autonomy is better than subjugation to the Founders, who wish to dominate the galaxy.

Preventing conflict is possible with careful execution of *intergroup contact*, which can reduce prejudice as well as aggressive tendencies by allowing individual group members to see members of other groups also as individuals.[49] What sets the United Federation of Planets apart from many other galactic civilizations is the Prime Directive, which codifies noninterference with less developed civilizations and affords protocols for first contact because previous attempts at interfering with less developed civilizations have typically proven to be disastrous.[50] The principle directs space travelers to wait until a civilization has already developed warp capability before making contact. This minimizes the power difference between the groups, as they are both at a similar level of technology and see each other as equals. In this way, the Prime Directive is also an investment: Not interfering with other civilizations makes them less likely to see the more powerful group as conquerors, a perception that might threaten in-group cohesion in the future. This may be the best lesson that Star Trek can teach us about how to live our lives in an increasingly globalized world.

References

Allport, G. W. (1954). *The nature of prejudice.* Reading, MA: Addison-Wesley.

Asch, S. E. (1952). *Social psychology.* New York, NY: Prentice-Hall.

Ashton, M. C., Paunonen, S. V., Helmes, E., & Jackson, D. N. (1998). Kin altruism, reciprocal altruism, and the Big Five personality factors. *Evolution & Human Behavior, 19*(4), 243–255.

Bar-Haim, Y., Ziv, T., Lamy, D., & Hodes, R. M. (2006). Nature and nurture in own-race face processing. *Psychological Science, 17*(2), 159–163.

Bornstein, G. (2003). Intergroup conflict: Individual, group, and collective interests. *Personality & Social Psychology Review, 7*(2), 129–145.

Brewer, M.B. (1991). The social self: On being the same and different at the same time. *Personality and Social Psychology Bulletin, 17*(5), 475–482.

Cialdini, R. B., Borden, R. J., Thorne, A., Walker, M. R., Freeman, S., & Sloan, L. R. (1974). "Basking in reflected glory: Three (football) field studies." *Journal of Personality & Social Psychology 34*(3), 366–375.

Campbell, D. T. (1958). Common fate, similarity, and other indices of the status of aggregates of persons as social entities. *Behavioral Science, 3*(1), 14–25.

Fiske, S. T. (2002). What we know now about bias and intergroup conflict, the problem of the century. *Current Directions in Psychological Science, 11*(4), 123–128.

Fiske, S. T., & Taylor, S. E. (1984). *Social cognition.* Reading, MA: Addison-Wesley.

Greene, J. (2014). *Moral tribes: Emotion, reason and the gap between us and them.* London, UK: Atlantic.

Hibbing, J. R., Smith, K. B., & Alford, J. R. (2014). Differences in negativity bias underlie variations in political ideology. *Behavioral & Brain Sciences, 37*(3), 297–307.

Meissner, C. A., & Brigham, J. C. (2001). Thirty years of investigating the own-race bias in memory for faces: A meta-analytic review. *Psychology, Public Policy, & Law, 7*(1), 3–35.

Mullen, B., & Copper, C. (1994). The relation between group cohesiveness and performance: An integration. *Psychological Bulletin, 22*(2), 210–227.

Pinker, S. (2007). A history of violence. *The New Republic, 236*, 18.

Piper, W., Marrache, M., Lacroix, R., Richardson, A., & Jones, B. (1983). Cohesion as a basic bond in groups. *Human Relations, 36*(2), 93–108.

Pratto, F., Sidanius, J., Stallworth, L. M., & Malle, B. F. (1994). Social dominance orientation: A personality variable predicting social and political attitudes. *Journal of Personality & Social Psychology, 67*(4), 741–763.

Al Ramiah, A., & Hewstone, M. (2013). Intergroup contact as a tool for reducing, resolving, and preventing intergroup conflict: evidence, limitations, and potential. *American Psychologist, 68*(7), 527–542.

Riek, B. M., Mania, E. W., & Gaertner, S. L. (2006). Intergroup threat and outgroup attitudes: A meta-analytic review. *Personality & Social Psychology Review, 10*(4), 336–353.

Sherif, M. (1966). *In common predicament: Social psychology of intergroup conflict and cooperation.* Boston, MA: Houghton Mifflin.

Sidanius, J., & Pratto, F. (2001). *Social dominance: An intergroup theory of social hierarchy and oppression.* Cambridge, UK: Cambridge University Press.

Stephan, W. G., & Renfro, C. L. (2002). The role of threats in intergroup relations. In D. Mackie & E. R. Smith (Eds.), *From prejudice to intergroup emotions* (pp. 191–208). New York, NY: Psychology Press.

Tajfel, H. (1970). Experiments in intergroup discrimination. *Scientific American, 223*(5), 96–102.

Terrizzi, J. A., Shook, N. J., & McDaniel, M. A. (2013). The behavioral immune system and social conservatism: A meta-analysis. *Evolution & Human Behavior, 34*(2), 99–108.

Wilson, D. S. & Wilson, E. O. (2007). Rethinking the theoretical foundation of sociobiology. *Quarterly Review of Biology, 82*, 327–348.

Notes

1. Allport (1954), p. 20.
2. *Star Trek: The Next Generation* episode 3–07, "The Enemy" (November 6, 1989).
3. Wilson & Wilson (2007).
4. Pinker (2007).
5. *Star Trek: First Contact* (1996 motion picture).
6. Asch (1952).
7. e.g., Ashton et al. (1998).
8. Fiske & Taylor (1984).
9. *Star Trek* episode 1–01, "Where No Man Has Gone Before" (September 22, 1966).
10. *Star Trek* episode 1–26, "The Devil in the Dark" (March 9, 1967).
11. *Star Trek* episode 2–06, "The Doomsday Machine" (October 20, 1967).
12. *Star Trek* episode 3–08, "The Empath" (December 6, 1968).
13. Greene (2014).
14. *Star Trek: Enterprise* episode 4–22, "These Are the Voyages" (May 13, 2005).
15. *Star Trek: Voyager* episode 7–15, "The Void" (February 14, 2001).
16. Sidanius & Pratto (2001).
17. e.g., *Star Trek: The Next Generation* episode 7–04, "Gambit" (October 11, 1993); *Enterprise* episode 2–19 "Judgment" (April 9, 2003).
18. e.g., Pratto et al. (1994).
19. Terrizzi et al. (2013).
20. Hibbing et al. (2014).
21. *Star Trek: The Next Generation* episode 1–23, "Skin of Evil" (April 25, 1988).
22. *Star Trek: First Contact* (1996 motion picture).
23. Campbell (1958).
24. Mullen & Copper (1994).
25. Brewer (1991).
26. *Star Trek: The Next Generation* episode 4–02, "Family" (October 1, 1990).
27. Campbell (1958).
28. Campbell (1958).
29. Mullen & Copper (1994).
30. Cialdini et al. (1974).
31. *Star Trek: Deep Space Nine* episode 5–06, "Trials and Tribble-ations" (November 4, 1996).
32. Tajfel (1970).
33. *Star Trek: The Next Generation* episode 2–08, "A Matter of Honor" (February 6, 1989).
34. Meissner & Brigham (2001).
35. Bar-Haim et al. (2006).
36. *Enterprise* episode 2–14, "Stigma" (February 5, 2003).
37. *Star Trek: Nemesis* (2002 motion picture).
38. *Star Trek V: The Final Frontier* (1989 motion picture).

39. Bornstein (2003).
40. Sherif (1966).
41. *Star Trek* episode 2–10, "Mirror, Mirror" (October 6, 1967).
42. *Star Trek* episode 1–14, "Balance of Terror" (December 15, 1966).
43. Stephan & Renfro (2002).
44. *Star Trek: The Next Generation* episode 3–26, "The Best of Both Worlds" (June 18, 1990).
45. Fiske (2002).
46. *Star Trek* (2009 motion picture).
47. *Star Trek* episode 3–15, "Let That Be Your Last Battlefield" (January 10, 1969).
48. *Star Trek: Deep Space Nine* episodes 5–15, "By Inferno's Light" (February 17, 1997); 6–19, "In the Pale Moonlight" (April 15, 1998).
49. Ramiah & Hewstone (2013).
50. *Star Trek: The Next Generation* episode 1–22, "Symbiosis" (April 18, 1988).

Children are explorers. Those who grow into confident, self-reliant, secure travelers through the universe they inhabit tend to be those whose parents treat them with both nurturance and authority. While these can be difficult to balance in the midst of other duties in life, one captain and son make it work well with warmth, respect, and style.

•15•

The Authoritative Captain: Parenting Style and Successful Child Development

SCOTT ALLISON
AND JIM BEGGAN

"It takes courage to look inside yourself and even more courage to write it for other people to see. I'm proud of you, son."

—Captain Benjamin Sisko[1]

"[Authoritative parents] are assertive, but not intrusive and restrictive. Their disciplinary methods are supportive, rather than punitive. They want their children to be assertive as well as socially responsible, and self-regulated as well as cooperative."

—developmental psychologist Diana Baumrind[2]

Studying changes in family dynamics after World War II, psychologists began to examine differences in *parenting styles.*[3] These patterns of child rearing vary in what the parent requires from the child in terms of obedience and initiative (*demandingness*) and what the parent can offer the child in terms of rewards, such as time, attention, and positive reinforcement (*responsiveness*). In what is considered the optimal child-rearing strategy, the *authoritative* parenting style is both demanding and responsive. The authoritative parent raises the child to act in a mature (although age-appropriate) fashion, but at the same time forgives shortcomings and provides rewards. Although protective, the authoritative parent allows children autonomy and personal growth. The reward for this style of parenting is a child who grows up to be a healthy, well-adjusted adult.

Where does Star Trek get matters of family most right? Without a doubt, the award for best parent would go to *Star Trek: Deep Space Nine*'s Benjamin Sisko, the first leading Star Trek character to be recognized as both a great commanding officer and one of the best fathers in TV history.[4]

The Authoritative Sisko

Benjamin Sisko clearly demonstrates the authoritative parenting style, which has been shown to produce children with happier dispositions, better emotional control, more positive social skills, and greater confidence in their ability to learn.[5] Sisko communicates high expectations for Jake, sets firm boundaries, and gives directive feedback. Spending significant time with a child and remaining emotionally connected at all times helps a parent avoid being neglectful, no matter how many other duties and responsibilities a parent must meet.

Sisko is a responsible male with the highly prestigious job of captain of the entire Deep Space 9 station. Despite this responsibility, he capably balances his two roles as captain and father and gladly accepts the responsibility to raise his son. Author-

Other Parenting Styles

Other parenting styles reflect different levels of demandingness and responsiveness. Like the authoritative parents, *authoritarian* parents exert authority and are demanding, but unlike the authoritative parents, they are not very responsive. They tell children what to do but do not allow children to explore the world on their own or develop their own unique interests and style. Children raised by authoritarian parents tend to be shy, less socially skilled, and less happy.

Permissive parents are responsive but not demanding. They are indulgent and give in to the child's desires, but do not foster the child's ability to exercise self-control. *Neglectful* parents are neither demanding nor responsive. Ignored by their parents, neglected children often develop behavior problems that can manifest themselves in an attempt to seek out love from sources other than a parent.

itative parents such as Sisko eagerly embrace their parenting roles and serve as healthy, high-functioning adult role models for their children.

As an authoritative parent, Sisko is consistently loving, affectionate, and nurturing in his approach to raising Jake. At the same time, Sisko is not overprotective or smothering. He demonstrates and encourages autonomy and independence, giving Jake the freedom to engage in his own individual pursuits and learn from his mistakes. When disagreements occur, Sisko displays strong conflict-resolution skills and disciplines Jake in a fair and consistent manner.

The sidebar, "Other Parenting Styles," describes some styles that do not fit Sisko's parental behavior because they are less responsive (authoritarian), less demanding (permissive), or both (neglectful).

Being a Good Father in the Face of Trauma

A child who loses a parent has a 25 percent chance of developing mental health problems. Possible negative psychological and emotional consequences include emotional regression, lower self-esteem, and anxiety through fear of annihilation.[6] A parent's violent death is more likely to produce symptoms of posttraumatic stress disorder (PTSD), such as hostility, fear, and anxiety, or self-destructive behaviors that can manifest as aggression or substance abuse.[7]

The pilot episode of *Deep Space Nine* introduces the father-son tandem of Sisko and Jake in dramatic fashion by showing flashbacks of the military attack that killed Sisko's wife Jennifer three years earlier.[8] Because Jennifer died unexpectedly during a Borg attack, Jake probably feels even more strongly affected by her loss, given that he had no time prior to the loss to prepare for it psychologically (as he might have if she had instead died after a long illness). In the aftermath, adjustment to life without Jennifer is difficult, but Sisko resolves to maintain a close connection with his fourteen-year-old son and involve him in decisions that affect both of them.

An important factor in helping children cope with loss is when the surviving parent or caregiver provides an anchor of security that includes a feeling of being noticed and attended to and a sense of having structure and order.[9] Sisko's behavior toward Jake is a positive model for how to help a child cope with such a devastating loss. Sisko's commitment to parenthood while commanding the space station represents a marked difference from the original *Star Trek* and *Star Trek: The Next Generation* series, where the ships' captains show indifference to or even disdain for families and children.[10] For Sisko, there is no *diffusion of responsibility* (people's tendency to feel less responsibility on the assumption that others will do the work).[11]

On this space station, Sisko seizes responsibility and takes command of parenthood, demonstrating his commitment to being emotionally and physically available to Jake as much as possible. This willingness to become appropriately involved in the life of one's child is a hallmark of the authoritative parent.

Balancing the Role of Captain with the Role of Father

Work-family conflict can be a serious problem for those in demanding occupations.[12] Possible interference can occur in both directions. A tumultuous home life can adversely affect occupational success. The stress of work can hurt family dynamics. Sisko's professional obligations as commanding officer of the space station are daunting, but he includes Jake in his life in meaningful ways. When Sisko and Jake spend days in close quarters aboard a small craft,[13] they use the opportunity to enjoy many meaningful discussions that strengthen the bonds between them. One way to increase cooperation and sociability is to work on joint tasks.[14]

Although it could be assumed that the demands of being a single father would hinder workplace productivity, in some cases the desire to be a good parent can increase performance because it provides an additional motivation for success while at the same time forcing someone to work more efficiently.[15] *Deep Space Nine* characters often face conflicts between doing what is best for family members and doing what is best for their careers. The ideal to strive for with regard to work-family conflict is to achieve a work-family balance.[16] Almost without fail, the show's characters balance the two priorities of work and family to the best of their ability, with the welfare of the family usually trumping professional advancement. The tendency of *Deep Space Nine*'s characters to accord family and children equal (or greater) importance in relation to career distinguishes the series from other Star Trek series. Sisko's willingness to view Jake as equally important or more important than his career demonstrates a *work-life balance*.[17]

Effective Parenting Skills

Characteristic strengths that psychologists identify as qualities of an effective parent include social intelligence, fairness, perspective, and humility, and these qualities may be interdependent.[18] An authoritative parent needs *social intelligence* (the type of intelligence that includes the capacity for interacting well with others—"people smarts") in order to act in a respectful manner and show *fairness* toward a child.

One important element of social intelligence with regard to parenting is to use the emotional and physiological benefits of *interpersonal touch* as mechanisms for loving, healing, and nurturing others.[19] In many an episode featuring the two characters, Sisko wraps his arm around Jake or puts his hand on Jake's shoulder.[20]

The loving bond between father and son may be best exemplified when Jake believes his father has died.[21] In this alternative future, Jake becomes an astrophysicist to develop the skills to save his father. This devotion can be seen as a consequence of Sisko's authoritative parenting style, which creates in Jake both a loyalty to his father and the confidence to take on such a daunting challenge.

In addition to showing affection, Sisko displays sensitivity to his son's needs by using an open and effective communication style and *perspective* in appreciating Jake's point of view. Among other things, *humility* helps because the humble parent may revise an opinion where a prideful one might not. When Jake dates a Bajoran girl who works as a scantily clad cocktail waitress at the station's bar, Sisko has dinner with them, hoping to reveal her unsuitability as a girlfriend.[22] To his surprise, he learns that she has many intellectual gifts and impressive ambitions that reflect very well on her. Being willing to change his opinion demonstrates all those character strengths.

When Sisko eventually marries cargo ship commander Kasidy Yates,[23] she becomes Jake's stepmother.[24] Psychologists have realized that a stepmother has a better chance of being an effective parent if she or he can come to terms with the role in a positive light.[25] The long-term presence of Yates comes close to creating the feeling of an intact nuclear family.

To use an authoritative style effectively, parents have to stay connected to their children's lives. Psychologists have emphasized the importance of the family meal in promoting interpersonal bonds and healthy emotional expression in families.[26] Dinner conversations between Sisko and Jake (and later Kasidy) often provide opportunities for sharing feelings or making announcements.

Authoritative Parenting to Transcend Trauma

When a child loses a parent, that may mean the other parent has lost a spouse. Just as the loss of a parent can harm the development of a child, the loss of a spouse can adversely affect the surviving parent. When dealing with his or her own loss, a surviving parent may engage in self-destructive behaviors, such as drug use or alcohol abuse, as part of the grieving process.[27] One consequence of losing a spouse is even an increase in the likelihood that the surviving spouse will die.[28]

In the face of the death of a parent, the remaining members of a nuclear family must strike a delicate balance. It might be tempting for the surviving spouse to become a more permissive parent, reasoning that children have lost so much already it might be helpful to give in to their desires. Alternatively, the demands of being a single parent might act as such an additional stress that the parent might go to one of two extremes and either become neglectful, distracted by other problems, or too strict, in hope of exerting greater control at home. Likewise, as part of the grieving process, a child might act out defiantly, working against, rather than with, the surviving parent, a course of action that might be exacerbated by the choices made by the surviving parent.

Given all the demands placed on him by his role as captain of a space station at the center of a galactic war, it would be easy for Benjamin Sisko to adopt a poor parenting style by becoming either too permissive or too restrictive. Instead, he chooses what is the most nurturing but difficult parental strategy: authoritative. In doing so, he illustrates one of the most positive examples of parenting in any Star Trek series. Sisko assumes the role of single father with grace, humor, courage, and love. Unlike lead characters in previous Star Trek shows, Sisko embraces his role as father and gladly raises his child, rather than abandoning him. Balancing his work life with his home life takes skill and patience, and clearly challenges him, but Sisko is able to create a safe and loving environment for Jake amid a backdrop of persistent violent conflicts that beset the space station. His achievement is even more impressive given that he has to grieve over the loss of his wife even as he helps Jake cope with the loss of his mother.

Although time-consuming and psychologically costly in the short term, a parent who adopts an authoritative style lays a foundation to nurture a child who matures into a successful adult, well-liked by those around them and capable of self-determination. Jake grows up to become a talented, mature, successful young man who trusts and adores his father, but at the same time has his own identity and exhibits self-determination. Rather than following in his father's footsteps to become a Starfleet officer, he walks his own path as a writer. Jake's success, both personally and professionally, offers the ultimate evidence of Sisko's effective use of the authoritative parenting style.

References

Argyle, M. (1991). *Cooperation: The basis of sociability.* New York, NY: Routledge.

Baumrind, D. (1967). Child care practices anteceding three patterns of preschool behavior. *Genetic Psychology Monographs, 75*(1), 43–88.

Baumrind, D. (1991). The influence of parenting style on adolescent competence and substance use. *Journal of Early Adolescence, 11*(1), 56-95.

Boushey, H. (2016). *Finding time: The economics of work-life conflict.* Cambridge, MA: Harvard University Press.

Cleve, E. (2008). *A big and a little one is gone: Crisis therapy with a two-year-old boy.* London, UK: Carnac.

Darley, J. M., & Latané, B. (1968). Bystander intervention in emergencies: Diffusion of responsibility. *Journal of Personality & Social Psychology, 8*(4, pt. 1), 377–383.

Fulkerson, J. A., Story, M., Mellin, A., Leffert, N., Neumark-Sztainer, D., & French, S. A. (2006). Family dinner meal frequency and adolescent development: Relationships with developmental assets and high-risk behaviors. *Journal of Adolescent Health, 39*(3), 337–345.

Gallace, A., & Spence, C. (2010). The science of interpersonal touch: An overview. *Neuroscience & Biobehavioral Reviews, 34*(2), 246–259.

Kaltman, S., & Bonanno, G. A. (2003). Trauma and bereavement: Examining the impact of sudden and violent deaths. *Journal of Anxiety Disorders, 17*(2), 131–147.

Knoester, C., Petts, R. J., & Eggebeen, D. J. (2007). Commitments to fathering and the well-being and social participation of new, disadvantaged fathers. *Journal of Marriage & Family, 69*(4), 991–1004.

Larzelere, R. E., Morris, A. S. E., & Harrist, A. W. (Eds.) (2013). *Authoritative parenting: Synthesizing nurturance and discipline for optimal child development.* Washington, DC: American Psychological Association.

Maccoby, E. E., & Martin, J. A. (1983). Socialization in the context of the family: Parent-child interaction. In P. Mussen and E. M. Hetherington (Eds.), *Handbook of child psychology, volume IV: Socialization, personality, and social development* (pp. 1–101). New York: Wiley.

Nilsson, D., & Ängarne-Lindberg, T. (2016). *Children who lose a parent suddenly: What kind of assistance do they feel provides relief? A content analysis study of children and their parents.* Child Care in Practice: http://www.tandfonline.com/doi/full/10.1080/13575279.2015.1118014.

Peterson, C., & Seligman, M. E. P. (2004). *Character strengths and virtues: A handbook and classification.* New York, NY: Oxford University Press.

Reddick, R. J., Rochlen, A. B., Grasso, J. R., Reilly, E. D., & Spikes, D. D. (2012). Academic fathers pursuing tenure: A qualitative study of work-family conflict, coping strategies, and departmental culture. *Psychology of Men & Masculinity, 13*(1), 1–15.

Riness, L. S., & Sailor, J. L. (2015). An exploration of the lived experience of stepmotherhood. *Journal of Divorce & Remarriage, 56*(3), 171–179.

Sossin, K. M., Bromberg, Y., & Haddad, D. (2014). Loss of a parent during childhood and adolescence: A prismatic look at the literature (pp. 1–28). In P. Cohen, K. M. Sossin, & R. Ruth (Eds.), *Healing after parent loss in childhood and adolescence: Therapeutic interventions and theoretical considerations.* New York, NY: Rowman & Littlefield.

Stikkelbroek, Y., Bodden, D. H., Reitz, E., Vollebergh, W. A., & van Baar, A. L. (2016). Mental health of adolescents before and after the death of a parent or sibling. *European Child & Adolescent Psychiatry, 25*(1), 49–59.

TV Week (2014, January 3). *TV Guide's '50 greatest TV dads of all time.'* TV Week: http://www.tvweek.com/in-depth/2014/01/tv-guides-50-greatest-tv-dads/.

What Culture (n.d.). *Star Trek: 10 reasons why Benjamin Sisko is the greatest Starfleet captain.* What Culture: http://whatculture.com/tv/star-trek-10-reasons-why-benjamin-sisko-is-the-greatest-starfleet-captain.

Ytterstad, E., & Brenn, T. (2015). Mortality after the death of a spouse in Norway. *Epidemiology, 26*(3), 289–294.

Zuckoff, A., Shear, K., Frank, E., Daley, D. C., Seligman, K., & Silowash, R. (2006). Treating complicated grief and substance use disorders: A pilot study. *Journal of substance abuse treatment, 30*(3), 205–211.

Notes

1. *Star Trek: Deep Space Nine* episode 5-4, ". . . Nor the Battle to the Strong" (October 21, 1996).
2. Baumrind (1991), p. 62).
3. Baumrind (1967); Maccoby & Martin (1983).
4. TV Week (2014); What Culture (n.d.).
5. Larzelere et al. (2013).
6. Sossin et al. (2014); Stikkelbroek et al. (2016).
7. Kaltman & Bonanno (2003).
8. *Star Trek: Deep Space Nine* episodes 1–1 and 1–2, "Emissary" parts 1 and 2 (January 3, 1993).
9. Cleve (2008); Nilsson & Ängarne-Lindberg (2016); Sossin et al. (2014).
10. *Star Trek II: The Wrath of Kahn* (1982); *Star Trek: The Next Generation* episodes 1–1 & 1–2, "Encounter at Farpoint" parts 1 and 2 (September 28, 1987).
11. Darley & Latané (1968).
12. Reddick et al. (2012).
13. *Star Trek: Deep Space Nine* episode 3–22, "Explorers" (May 8, 1995).
14. Argyle (1991).
15. Knoester et al. (2007).
16. *Star Trek: Deep Space Nine* episodes 6–16, "Change of Heart" (March 4, 1998); 5–5 "The Assignment" (October 28, 1996).
17. Boushey (2016).
18. Peterson & Seligman (2004).
19. Gallace & Spence (2010).

20. *Star Trek: Deep Space Nine* episode 2–9, "Second Sight" (November 21, 1993).
21. *Star Trek: Deep Space Nine* episode 4–2, "The Visitor" (October 9, 1995).
22. *Star Trek: Deep Space Nine* episode 3–6, "The Abandoned" (October 31, 1994).
23. *Star Trek: Deep Space Nine* episode 3–23, "Family Business" (May 15, 1995).
24. *Star Trek: Deep Space Nine* episode 7–18, "'Til Death Do Us Part" (April 14, 1999).
25. Riness & Sailor (2015).
26. Fulkerson et al. (2006).
27. Zuckoff et al. (2006).
28. Ytterstad & Brenn (2015).

Through bonds forged by shared experience rather than affiliation by birth, friendship connects some people together more strongly than family does. Like living things, friend relationships grow in stages. Maturing and changing through circumstances and over time while varying in intimacy and intensity along the way, they serve many needs—some more of emotion and some more of logic.

•16•

The Logic of Friendship

JAY SCARLET

"I have been, and always shall be, your friend."
—Spock[1]

"[I]n the everyday working of friendships, it is not the particular behaviors that matter most, but rather the meanings they convey and the intentions presumed to underlie them."
—social scientist Daniel J. Hruschka[2]

Even Vulcans have friends. This may seem counterintuitive, as most human cultures think of friendship as a type of social relationship with an emotional component. Nevertheless, a classic episode in which Spock states that according to Vulcan tradition the groom may ask his friends to accompany him to a bonding ritual akin to marriage makes it clear that this type of relationship exists even in Vulcan society, and it is not just some weird thing that Spock does as an unfortunate side effect of being half human.[3]

The fact that this is the case may raise a number of questions: What exactly do we mean when we use the words *friend* or *friendship*? How do these relationships come about in the first place, and how do they play out over the course of an individual's life? Why would such a relationship not only exist but be esteemed even among a people like the Vulcans, whose highest ideals call for the rejection of all things related to emotion?

What?

Friendships may bear certain similarities to other types of social relationships, such as those shared between family members or romantic partners, yet are clearly distinct from those other relationship types.[4] Friends spend downtime together, as Kirk, Spock, and McCoy do when the three of them take shore leave together,[5] and they may remain friends for a lifetime or more, as with Benjamin Sisko and "Old Man" Dax, whose relationship spans multiple symbiotic hosts.[6] Some distinguishing characteristics of friendship include the voluntary nature of the relationship, the nonexclusivity of it (as opposed to exclusive romantic love such as that which develops between Worf and Jadzia Dax[7]), and the relative lack of specific rituals that mark changes in friendship status.[8] However, it is important to note that many of these features may be more applicable to modern Western (or even specifically American) cultural norms without reflecting the full diversity of societies on planet Earth,[9] much less the even wider range of cultures reflected in the universe of Star Trek. A broader view of practices here on Earth reveals examples of cultures in which choice of friends is more constrained, even inherited, or in which varying levels of friendship are marked by ceremonial traditions (for example, blood brotherhood,[10] which is somewhat paralleled by the

Klingon R'uustai, or bonding, ceremony[11]). At its most basic level, friendship seems to be a social relationship, "involving support in times of need that is regulated by mutual affection between friends."[12]

Although much of the research on friendships focuses on the relationship between two people, or *dyads* (for example, Kirk and Spock or Kirk and McCoy), circles and networks of friends are also important structural factors that may impact how these relationships are viewed and support is provided. Researchers often break the relationship down into distinct phases, including formation, maintenance, and deterioration or dissolution. All these factors may influence the way the friends think of, feel about, or act toward the friend and the friendship.[13]

How?

Formation: First Contact

A necessary first step in any social relationship is that the two individuals must come into contact, whether meeting face to face or through another mode of communication. Unfortunately, the original *Star Trek* television series does not disclose to viewers these early stages of the relationships between Kirk, Spock, and McCoy, but subsequent series generally do depict other characters meeting for the first time. Once they have met, for a friendship to begin, the individuals must decide that they like each other well enough to continue meeting, or there must be some degree of mutual *social attraction* influencing the desire to spend time interacting. This attraction is influenced by information conveyed both verbally and nonverbally that may include physical appearance and personal attitudes.[14]

Many researchers have reported the importance of perceived similarity in terms of *demographic factors* (e.g., gender, race, social class, age), attitudes, experiences, and behaviors in the formation of friendships from an early age and persisting throughout the life span. For example, Jake Sisko is initially interested in befriending Nog primarily because of their similar ages.[15] Psychologists have speculated that greater interpersonal similarity allows people to feel better able to predict a friend's actions and therefore feel more secure.[16] Interestingly, research suggests that shared experience can be one of the most powerful forms of similarity, setting the stage for a future friendship, even if at the time of the original experience the two individuals were scarcely acquainted and were not yet interested in becoming friends with each other, more so than proximity, demographic variables, or attitudes.[17]

Even though Jake and Nog are age peers, their friendship could also be viewed as one between members of very different groups. These *cross-category friendships*, although less common than friendships with people who share more similarities, can help individuals reduce stereotyping and improve their ability to take on different perspectives.[18] For example, men who have female friends may gain additional emotional insight.[19] Research suggests that these types of friendships come about when the individuals involved place less emphasis on the importance of similarity between friends rather than attempting to downplay the differences that exist between them.[20]

Despite the need for two people to share an interest in becoming friends with each other in order for the relationship to work, this does not necessarily mean that both are motivated by the same thing.[21] For example, although Geordi and Data clearly think of one another as friends, it is possible that Geordi entered the relationship seeking companionship, whereas Data may have been acting more out of curiosity about human behavior.

Maintenance: Steady as She Goes

Developmental psychologists sometimes refer to social relationships as progressing through three stages: acquaintance to friend, friend to close friend, close friend to best friend.[22] The first of these stages is essentially the process of initial contact and learning about ways in which another person's friendship may be attractive, whereas the latter stages are marked by providing more and more support for each other and feeling less guarded in communications, leading to an increased sense of closeness or *intimacy*.[23] When Spock first admits to Kirk that he has any feelings, he is sharing intimate information.[24] Intimacy has generally been regarded as having to do with talking about one's feelings and is closely linked with *self-disclosure*, though more recently psychologists have increasingly sought to distinguish between different types of intimacy, as it has been found that this definition tends to favor relationships between women over those between men.[25] Even though some psychologists have attempted to demonstrate that male friendships can be characterized as having a type of intimacy that is based more on doing things together than on talking about one's emotional issues,[26] others have reported that some people, particularly men, are simply less likely to regard self-disclosure as a prerequisite for intimacy or even friendship.[27]

Men may be reluctant to describe their friendships as intimate regardless of their actual behavior precisely because the traditional sense of the term is seen as being associated with femininity.[28] Instead, men are more likely to report having behaved in ways that are seen as being more traditionally masculine, such as being stoic (not unlike a certain half-Vulcan science officer).[29] Interestingly, there is evidence to indicate that men who fulfill traditionally masculine roles in other aspects of life, such as serving in the military, may be more willing to report having engaged in behaviors with their male friends, such as being empathetic, that are not commonly associated with the masculine ideal.[30]

In fact, behaviors can be interpreted in a variety of ways, and among friends, the perceived underlying intention seems to be more important than the behavior itself.[31] Thus, for example, it is not uncommon to see friends who are working on solving a problem offering criticism and even getting into conflicts with each other—a dynamic frequently displayed by Spock and McCoy—without harming the friendship.[32] Friends may also call each other names or engage in mock violence in a joking manner that may appear to avoid intimacy but may actually serve as a more socially acceptable means of expressing intimacy, reminiscent of Odo and Quark's complex relationship.[33]

Dissolution: All Good Things Must End

Some people manage to remain friends for life, but it is more common for a friendship to end at some point. There are many reasons this happens, including developing new interests, moving away, attending a new school or getting a new job, and becoming involved in a new relationship either with another friend or with a romantic partner.[34] Alternatively, there may be a more specific reason why one friend calls an end to the relationship, such as physical aggression (as Kirk suffers at the hands of his old friend Gary Mitchell, who develops telekinetic powers[35]) or perceived disloyalty or rumor spreading.[36] Similarly, there are certain behaviors that are expected of a friend, such as helping when one is in need or asking for help if it is needed, the failure of which may cause the friendship to end.[37]

Naturally, most people are reluctant to dissolve a long-standing friendship, as time and effort have been put in over the course of the relationship to learn to be able predict the friend's thoughts and actions and forge common bonds. These invest-

Friendship and Technology

There has been significant debate since the inventions of the telegraph and telephone regarding the impact of emerging technologies on social relationships. It is easy to imagine similar arguments arising around the use of subspace communications. On the one hand, some complain that people spend too much time interacting with devices rather than with human beings. On the other hand, some researchers point out that technologies such as the Internet and social networking sites reduce the impact of distance and may enable more cross-category friendships by limiting certain constraints of social class, race, and gender.[39]

Social networking sites such as Facebook have already made the word *friend* into a verb, and some researchers believe that those sites may lead to a more fundamental change in society's understanding of friendship[40] even though most users employ them as one means to maintain relationships formed offline.[41] In a similar way, Data communicates information about his daily routines to Bruce Maddox via his personal log.[42]

ments are lost if the friendship is ended. This reluctance to accept the change in his relationship with Gary Mitchell nearly costs Kirk his life.[38]

Why?

The support received from social relationships, including friendships, has been found to have numerous benefits to health, both physical and psychological. Among these benefits are reduced susceptibility to infection, cardiovascular disease, and cancer; increased longevity (though perhaps not enough to account entirely for Dr. McCoy's incredibly long life[43]); better sleep; reduced impact of stress; enhanced self-esteem; and better adjustment to developmental challenges.[44] Researchers hypothesize that social and emotional experiences are linked by the hormones oxytocin and vasopressin, which are also involved in the body's stress response.[45]

Friendships can serve as substitutes for other types of relationships that may be lacking in an individual's life, such as familial connections (for example, when Data stands in as "father of the bride" at a wedding[46]), aiding in development and serving as buffers against daily stresses. Social relationships can be sources of security and well-being, especially during developmental transitions such as entering school, marriage, retirement, and more. Indeed, research indicates that adults who have friends have better outcomes when facing challenges such as the death of a spouse than do those who do not have friends.[47]

Logic Indicates . . .

Most people have friends, although the ways they experience friendship may differ. These differences may arise from personality factors such as a desire for many friends, having only a few close friends, or having friendly but not close relationships[48] or from cultural meanings assigned to the term *friend*. The experience of friendships may also vary with stage of life and phase of the relationship, whether it is still forming, being maintained (with or without increasing intimacy), or coming to an end. Friendships may provide multiple health benefits, both physical and psychological, providing ample reason for a Vulcan to conclude that the social support from friends may be for many people a key ingredient in a long life and prosperity.

References

Adams, R. G., & Blieszner, R. (1994). An integrative conceptual framework for friendship research. *Journal of Social & Personal Relationships, 11*(2), 163–184.

Becker, J. H., Johnson, A. J., Craig, E. A., Gilchrist, E. S., Haigh, M. M., & Lane, L. T. (2009). Friendships are flexible, not fragile: Turning points in geographically-close and long-distance friendships. *Journal of Social & Personal Relationships, 26*(4), 347–369.

Bryant, E. M., & Marmo, J. (2012). The rules of Facebook friendship: A two-stage examination of interaction rules in close, casual, and acquaintance friendships. *Journal of Social & Personal Relationships, 29*(8), 1013–1035.

Cacioppo, J. T., Ernst, J. M., Burleson, M. H., McClintock, M. K., Malarkey, W. B., Hawkley, L. C., Kowalewski, R. B., Paulsen, A., Hobson, J. A., Hugdahl, K., Spiegel, D., & Berntson, G. G. (2000). Lonely traits and concomitant physiological processes: The MacArthur social neuroscience studies. *International Journal of Psychophysiology, 35*(2–3), 143–154.

Charles, S. T., & Mavandadi, S. (2004). Social support and physical health across the life span: Socioemotional influences. In F. R. Lang & K. L. Fingerman (Eds.), *Growing together: Personal relationships across the lifespan* (pp. 240–267). New York, NY: Cambridge University Press.

Fehr, B. (2004). Intimacy expectations in same-sex friendships: A prototype interaction-pattern model. *Journal of Personality & Social Psychology, 86*(2), 265–284.

Galupo, M. P., & Gonzalez, K. A. (2013). Friendship values and cross-category friendships: Understanding adult friendship patterns across gender, sexual orientation and race. *Sex Roles, 68*(11–12), 779–790.

Hartup, W. W., & Stevens, N. (1997). Friendships and adaptation in the life course. *Psychological Bulletin, 121*(3), 355–370.

Hruschka, D. J. (2010). *Friendship: Development, ecology, and evolution of a relationship.* Berkeley, CA: University of California Press.

Kaplan, D., & Rosenmann, A. (2014). Toward an empirical model of male homosocial relatedness: An investigation of friendship in uniform and beyond. *Psychology of Men & Masculinity, 15*(1), 12–21.

Migliaccio, T. (2009). Men's friendships: Performances of masculinity. *Journal of Men's Studies, 17*(3), 226–241.

Niland, P., Lyons, A. C., Goodwin, I., & Hutton, F. (2015). Friendship work on Facebook: Young adults' understandings and practices of friendship. *Journal of Community & Applied Social Psychology, 25*(2), 123–137.

Roy, M. P., Steptoe, A., & Kirschbaum, C. (1998). Life events and social support as moderators of individual differences in cardiovascular and cortisol reactivity. *Journal of Personality & Social Psychology, 75*(5), 1273–1281.

Sherman, A. M., de Vries, B., & Lansford, J. E. (2000). Friendship in childhood and adulthood: Lessons across the life span. *International Journal of Aging & Human Development, 51*(1), 31–51.

Sias, P. M., & Cahill, D. J. (1998). From coworkers to friends: The development of peer friendships in the workplace. *Western Journal of Communication, 62*(3), 273–299.

Swain, S. O. (1992). Men's friendships with women: Intimacy, sexual boundaries, and the informant role. In P. M. Nardi, (Ed.), *Men's friendships* (pp. 153–171). Thousand Oaks, CA: Sage.

Sykes, R. E. (1983). Initial interaction between strangers and acquaintances: A multivariate analysis of factors affecting choice of communication partners. *Human Communication Research, 10*(1), 27–53.

Notes

1. *Star Trek II: The Wrath of Khan* (1982 motion picture).
2. Hruschka (2010), p. 43.
3. *Star Trek* episode 2–1, "Amok Time" (September 15, 1967).
4. e.g., Sias & Cahill (1998).

5. e.g., *Star Trek V: The Final Frontier* (1989 motion picture).
6. Established in *Star Trek: Deep Space Nine* episode 1–1, "Emissary" part 1 (January 3, 1993).
7. *Star Trek: Deep Space Nine* episode 5–3, "Looking for par'Mach in All the Wrong Places" (October 14, 1996).
8. e.g., Sias & Cahill (1998).
9. Hruschka (2010).
10. Hruschka (2010).
11. *Star Trek: The Next Generation* episode 3–5, "The Bonding" (October 23, 1989).
12. Hruschka (2010), p. 12.
13. Adams & Blieszner (1994).
14. Sykes (1983).
15. *Star Trek: Deep Space Nine* episode 1–1, "Emissary" (January 3, 1993).
16. Sykes (1983).
17. Sykes (1983).
18. Galupo & Gonzalez (2013).
19. Swain (1992).
20. Galupo & Gonzalez (2013).
21. Sias & Cahill (1998).
22. Sias & Cahill (1998).
23. Sias & Cahill (1998).
24. *Star Trek* episode 1–3, "Where No Man Has Gone Before" (September 22, 1966).
25. Kaplan & Rosenmann (2014); Migliaccio (2009).
26. Migliaccio (2009).
27. Fehr (2004); Hruschka (2010).
28. Kaplan & Rosenmann (2014).
29. Migliaccio (2009).
30. Migliaccio (2009).
31. Hruschka (2010).
32. Hartup & Stevens (1997).
33. Kaplan & Rosenmann (2014).
34. Sherman et al. (2000); Hruschka (2010).
35. *Star Trek* episode 1–3, "Where No Man Has Gone Before" (September 22, 1966).
36. Sherman et al. (2000).
37. Hruschka (2010).
38. *Star Trek* episode 1–3, "Where No Man Has Gone Before" (September 22, 1966).
39. Becker et al. (2009); Hruschka (2010).
40. Niland et al. (2015).
41. Bryant & Marmo (2012).
42. *Star Trek: The Next Generation episode* 4–11, "Data's Day" (January 7, 1991).
43. *Star Trek: The Next Generation* episode 1–1, "Encounter at Farpoint," part 1 (September 28, 1987).
44. Charles & Mavandadi (2004); Cacioppo et al. (2000); Hartup & Stevens (2007); Roy et al. (1998).
45. Charles & Mavandadi (2004).
46. *Star Trek: The Next Generation* episode 4–11, "Data's Day" (January 7, 1991).
47. Hartup & Stevens (1997).
48. Hartup & Stevens (1997).

Log File IV

Star Trek: Voyager and the Need for Affiliation

TRAVIS LANGLEY

People need people. The *need for affiliation*, a motive to connect to others and maintain relationships, may or may not involve intimacy.[1] Some can maintain strong bonds and stay loyal without disclosing private feelings and thoughts to one another. Sometimes there is simply safety in numbers. In *Star Trek: Voyager*, two groups—Starfleet personnel and Maquis rebels—get thrown together as an alien power hurls them across space to the other side of the galaxy.[2] They find they must work together to survive long enough to make their way back home. In no other Star Trek series is the need to affiliate so important and yet so difficult.

Captain Janeway makes an early choice that may more subtly facilitate unity and cooperation when she has them all dress in Starfleet uniforms right away[3] (even if that does reduce dramatic tension for the sake of television viewers). When people wear uniforms, they tend to act like they belong in them.[4] Both actions and attitudes begin changing to fit into the clothes.[5] Rebels loyal to Maquis values and goals—even those who tell themselves, "It's just a costume; I'm playing a role"—can lose track of the fact that it's role-playing.[6] Roles can become reality. Costumes can be connecting. They can even make us feel more bonded to—and less afraid of—those who simply dress the same.[7]

As a set of personality traits, the need to make connections is adaptive and important, but like so many good things, it can go too far. People who score highest in need for affiliation make better followers than leaders, evincing a neediness that may make them less popular than those who score lower,[8] or perhaps being less popular is what makes more of them grow needy. Psychologist David McClelland developed his *need theory* (a.k.a. *three needs theory* or *trichotomy of needs*[9]) in which he asserted that the needs for power, affiliation, and achievement exert the greatest influence on behavior and personality development.[10] During the course of his investigations into these needs, he detected a *leadership motive pattern*[11] in which two needs (higher need for power, lower need for affiliation) and self-control combined predicted more effective leadership.[12] Starship captains are cautious about fraternizing with crew members and even their own officers, the people to whom those captains must issue commands. A degree of loneliness goes with being the one in charge. Captain Janeway experiences this most of all because *Voyager* is essentially lost at sea and, for most of the series, out of contact with the rest of Starfleet. She cannot share the occasional company of her fellow Starfleet captains or even call upon them for advice. Janeway ends up spending more time on the holodeck than any other series' captain.

What unites the two groups on *Voyager* most is the fact that they share a *superordinate goal*, a higher priority or reason to pull together.[13] Otherwise, they might have insufficient incentive to blend together to become one group. Not everyone aboard *Voyager* has quite as strong a need to affiliate with everyone else, which may be why a few among them betray the rest.[14] The rest, however, grow more united. Together, they make their voyage home.[15]

References

Crowne, D. P., & Marlowe, D. (1964). *The approval motive*. New York, NY: Wiley.

Harrell, A. M., & Stahl, M. J. (1981). A behavioral decision theory approach for measuring McClelland's trichotomy of needs. *Journal of Applied Psychology, 66*(2), 242–247.

Star Trek: Voyager (1995–2001, 7 seasons, 172 episodes). Created by R. Berman, M. Piller, J. Taylor. Paramount. Aired on UPN.

Lynne, C. (1987). A study of narcissism, affiliation, intimacy, and power motives among students in business administration. *Psychological Reports, 62*(2), 355–358.

McClelland, D. C. (1961). *The achieving society.* New York, NY: Van Nostrand.

McClelland, D. C. (1975). *Power: The inner experience.* New York, NY: Irvington.

McClelland, D. C., & Boyatzis, R. E. (1982). Leadership motive pattern and long term success in management. *Journal of Applied Psychology, 67*(6), 737–743.

McClelland, D. C., & Burnham, D. H. (1976). Power is the great motivator. *Harvard Business Review, 54*(1), 100–110.

Navarrete, C. D., McDonald, M. M., Asher, B. D., Kerr, N. L., Yokota, K., Olsson, A., & Sidanius, J. (2012). Fear is readily associated with an out-group face in a minimal group context. *Evolution & Human Behavior, 33*(5), 590–593.

Ostrom, T. M., & Sedikides, C. (1992). Out-group homogeneity effects in natural and minimal groups. *Psychological Bulletin, 112*(3), 536–552.

Postmes, T., & Spears, R. (1998). Deindividuation and antinormative behavior: A meta-analysis. *Psychological Bulletin, 123*(3), 238–259.

Sherif, M. (1966). *In common predicament: Social psychology of intergroup conflict and cooperation.* Boston, MA: Houghton Mifflin.

Shipley T. E., Jr., & Veroff, J. (1952). A projective measure of need for affiliation. *Journal of Experimental Psychology, 43*(5), 349–356.

Zimbardo, P. G. (1971). *The psychological power and pathology of imprisonment.* A statement prepared for the U.S. House of Representatives Committee on the Judiciary, Subcommittee No. 3: Hearings on Prison Reform, San Francisco, CA.

Zimbardo, P. (2007). *The Lucifer effect: Understanding how good people turn evil.* New York, NY: Random House.

Notes

1. Lynne (1987)).
2. *Star Trek: Voyager* episodes 1–2, "Caretaker" parts 1–2 (both January 16, 1995).
3. *Star Trek: Voyager* episode 1–3, "Parallax" (January 23, 1995).
4. Postmes & Spears (1998).
5. Postmes & Spears (1998).
6. Zimbardo (1971, 2007).
7. Navarrette et al. (2012); Ostrom & Sedikides (1992).
8. Crowne & Marlowe (1964); Shipley & Veroff (1952).
9. Harrell & Stahl (1981).
10. McClelland (1961, 1975).
11. McClelland & Burnham (1967).
12. McClelland & Boyatzis (1982).
13. Sherif, M. (1966).
14. e.g., *Star Trek: Voyager* episode 2–20, "Investigations" (March 13, 1996).
15. *Star Trek: Voyager* episode 7–26, "Endgame," part 2 (May 23, 2001).

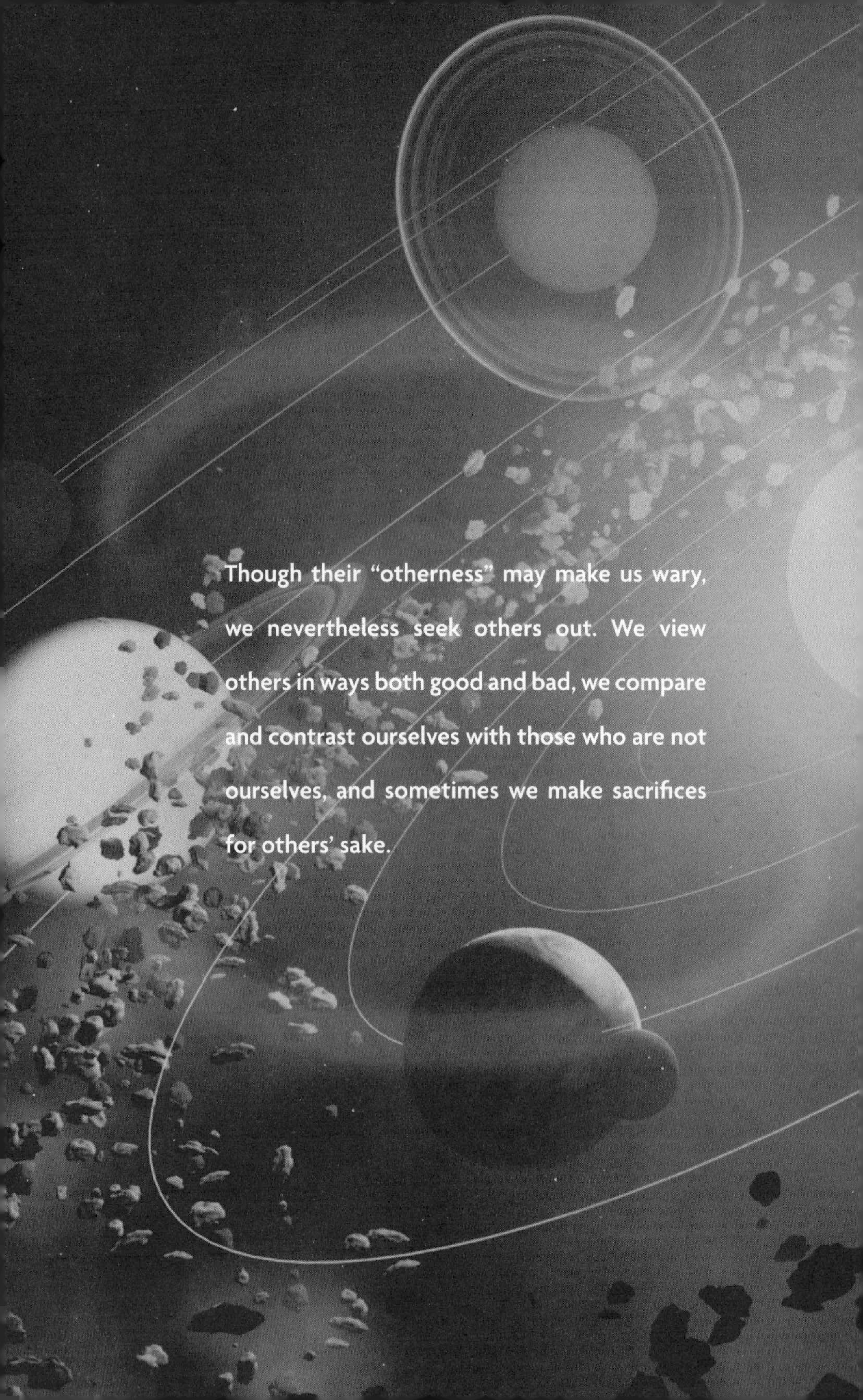

Though their “otherness” may make us wary, we nevertheless seek others out. We view others in ways both good and bad, we compare and contrast ourselves with those who are not ourselves, and sometimes we make sacrifices for others’ sake.

PART V

OTHERS

The logic that group needs should outweigh individual needs in priority may not explain an individual's choice to be the one who makes that sacrifice for the many.

•17•

The Needs of the Many: The Role of Sacrifice

COLT J. BLUNT

"Love sometimes expresses itself in sacrifice."

—Captain James T. Kirk[1]

> *"When it comes your time to die, be not like those whose lives are filled with the fear of death, so that when their time comes they weep and pray for a little more time to live their lives over again in a different way. Sing your death song and die like a hero going home."*
>
> —Shawnee leader Tecumseh[2]

Sacrifice and loss not only reinforce the potential consequences of adventure and exploration but also the cost of serving a higher purpose. Though self-sacrifice might seem like a universal phenomenon, different people make similar sacrifices for different reasons but with a wide variety of motivations.[3] Whereas Spock, arguably the best-known example of sacrifice in Star Trek history, gives his life to save the crew[4] in an act of *altruism* (helping others at a cost to oneself), others sacrifice themselves for different reasons, such as *loyalty* to others (e.g., Tasha Yar[5]) or *martyrdom* for oneself (e.g., Damar, who becomes a symbol to Cardassia[6]). In any science fiction story that offers vision, hope, and belief in a future that largely eschews ego in favor of peace, harmony, and collective survival, *how* someone meets his or her end is not nearly as important as *why*. Research has identified a variety of motivations for self-sacrifice and why, for some, the needs of the many outweigh the needs of the few.

Altruistic Sacrifice

Many Star Trek episodes, from the original *Star Trek* pilot "The Cage"[7] onward, begin with a similar premise: A Federation ship encounters a distress signal from a vessel or outpost, complications follow, conflict ensues, and difficult decisions must be made.[8] Given the many risks involved, why do captains throughout history choose to answer distress calls? Why do people ever go out of their way to help others? Volunteering and helping out strangers in need are often seen as acts of *altruism* (the performance of actions that have a cost to the performer while benefiting others, either directly or indirectly, without an expectation of reciprocity or receipt of reward[9]); however, those who subscribe to the concept of *psychological egoism* would argue that even these acts are not altogether altruistic.[10] They argue that people are inherently hedonists and engage in actions that are in their own self-interest and from which they derive pleasure: Good deeds, such as helping others, are done because they make people feel good, cause others to speak highly of them, or earn potential rewards from a deity. Thus, from the perspective of psychological egoism, even a Federation captain helping a stranded ship has motivations that fall short of altruism: Perhaps the damaged ship will contain Federation citizens, potential allies, valuable resources, or useful information. Psychological egoism in Star Trek is more noticeable in organizations outside the Federation; a Ferengi captain is likely to help a stranded freighter only to secure future profits and trade even if the gesture seems genuine on the surface.[11] According to the perspective of psychological egoism, Ferengi and humans differ only in the sense that Ferengi do not delude themselves by believing their motivations are anything but self-serving.

Psychological research is split on the existence of true altruism in humans. Some researchers find that helping behavior is strongly motivated by self-serving reasons, such as their desire to avoid personal distress and their perceived similarity to the one in need,[12] but such findings fail to explain the range of human sacrifice. Psychologists have offered evidence of true altruism. Even infants have been observed helping each other complete tasks without incentive or expectation of reward or reciprocity, a behavior even seen in other primates, such as chimpanzees.[13] Such evidence suggests that altruism may be a natural instinct in primates but that culture and society, rather than human nature, serve to erase altruistic motivation in humankind. Indeed, altruistic sacrifice is seen throughout much of the animal kingdom. Like Borg drones, worker honeybees will sacrifice themselves to defend their hive.[14]

The propensity to engage in altruism also depends on cultural factors. For instance, Asian countries tend to be *collectivistic*, emphasizing group goals and unified culture, whereas Western societies tend to be more *individualistic*, emphasizing individual goals and achievements.[15] Research indicates that individuals from collectivist cultures are more prone to self-sacrifice than are those from individualistic cultures.[16] Though the Borg represent an extreme in the collectivist-individualist spectrum in Star Trek, this is far from the only example. Many of the societies in Star Trek, such as the Vulcans, evidence a greater degree of collectivism than is seen in modern Western society.[17] Even Starfleet, largely made up of humans from cultures identified as individualist in the twenty-first century, adopts a largely collectivist viewpoint; this likely stems from a shifting global view, with humans (and other species) becoming a piece within a larger galactic puzzle with a shared viewpoint of peace, exploration, and enlightenment.

Much of the debate over sacrifice and altruism is represented in a thought experiment called the trolley problem.[18] Like the *Kobayashi Maru*, the unbeatable test taken by cadets at Starfleet Academy,[19] the trolley problem is a no-win scenario involving inherent loss of life. The trolley problem is a hypothetical situation in which an observer witnesses a rogue trolley barreling down the tracks at a group of five unsuspecting pedestrians. In the original version of the scenario, the observer can choose to take no action or instead flip a switch and divert the car onto a different track, in which case it will strike and kill a single pedestrian. Participants in a number of studies involving the trolley problem indicated that they would prefer to sacrifice themselves rather than sacrifice the life of another innocent bystander.[20] Although most divert the trolley to the track with one pedestrian to save five other lives, approximately one-third select the self-sacrifice option. However, it is obviously impossible to determine the degree to which these results would occur in real-world situations. This is similar to Wesley Crusher's first entrance exam for Starfleet, which forces him to choose between saving two separate lives.[21]

Undoubtedly the best example of altruistic sacrifice in Star Trek occurs when Spock dies to save the *Enterprise* and everyone on it.[22] Dying from radiation poisoning, Spock explains himself by reminding Kirk of his earlier remark: "The needs of the many outweigh the needs of the few." Such a decision likely arises from a number of factors:

- Vulcans present as a highly *collectivist culture*, one that values the society above the individual.
- Spock is the member of a highly cohesive crew largely made up of close friends and colleagues. Protecting them serves his own *affiliative needs* (the basic urge to form relationships with others).
- Ultimately, Spock takes a *utilitarian view* (seeing the rational pursuit of the greatest benefit for the greatest number of individuals) in that he knows he is best equipped for the job and that his death will allow others to live.[23]

In Spock's mind, such a sacrifice is logical. As he says of his own sacrifice while dying, "Don't grieve, Admiral. It's logical."[24]

Loyalty

Sacrifices made out of loyalty may seem altruistic at first, though the sacrifices differ depending on the relationship between the self-sacrificers and the persons who are saved. A child's parent might readily enter a burning building to rescue that child but perhaps not for a stranger. Loyalty is a strong force that can lead people to do extraordinary things. This is often seen in situations involving soldiers, emergency response personnel, family members, and friends.

A study of *heroic suicide* (the act of sacrificing one's life during combat for the protection of others) analyzed 125 Congressional Medal of Honor recipients.[25] Noncommissioned officers (those who rose through the ranks to directly command groups of soldiers) more often sacrificed themselves than did commissioned officers (many of whom were placed in leadership positions due to education or degree), and those in leadership roles were more likely than rank-and-file soldiers to engage in self-sacrifice. Starfleet officers most closely fit these prototypes of self-sacrificing soldiers. In Starfleet, even those who eventually become captains start out as lowly ensigns, manning sensors, engaging in menial engineering tasks, and piloting shuttlecraft. Further, starships are typically seen as being manned by exceptionally cohesive crews, and those ships and stations which serve as the set pieces of the various Star Trek films and series showcase Starfleet's elite. Such factors cultivate an environment of loyalty and sense of duty, making sacrifice not only a possibility but a likelihood should the need arise.[26] Tasha Yar's death while trying to rescue the crew of a crashed shuttle embodies these values.[27] Further, research on World War II veterans revealed increased unit cohesion years later among groups in which soldiers experienced the death of comrades.[28] Thus, Tasha's death, though devastating to the crew, likely leads to increased cohesion in the long run. This experience, combined with his loyalty to and friendship with the crew of the *Enterprise*, may contribute to Data's eventual decision to self-sacrifice.[29] Indeed, friendship alone can contribute to the decision to sacrifice oneself. Research has suggested that individuals are more likely to engage in personal sacrifices when they have a close relationship with the other party.[30] Though Charles "Trip" Tucker, chief engineer of the *Enterprise NX-01*, certainly demonstrates a duty and loyalty to the crew, it is his close friendship with Captain Archer and his desire to save Archer's life that lead to his ultimate sacrifice.[31]

The Reluctant Prophet

Martyrdom can serve as a powerful tool for people, not only elevating the individual engaging in self-sacrifice in the eyes of the other people, but exemplifying the ideals for which they died. Martyrs, both in modern history and in religion, become immortal through their stories, which are passed on through generations, such as those of Mahatma Gandhi, William Wallace, Joan of Arc, and Jesus. Their values and beliefs, especially as they related to their sacrifices, become more important than their actual backgrounds. Such individuals occupy a realm somewhere between fact and parable. Benjamin Sisko makes the ultimate sacrifice by casting himself and Gul Dukat into the flames of the Fire Caves of Bajor. Though he begins as a skeptic and would likely make his sacrifice for altruistic reasons alone, Sisko's apparent death serves the purpose of immortalizing him as a martyr in the living history of the Bajoran people.

. . . Outweigh the Needs of the Few

Star Trek has given us a glimpse into a future worth living, where people work together for the greater good of society.[32] However, such a society is ultimately built upon the sacrifices of others: people who pay the cost to uphold the ideals of justice, benevolence, and charity. The act of self-sacrifice is truly remarkable in light of the innate proclivity toward self-preservation. For those who give their lives—whether doomed redshirts following their training, members of a cohesive crew protecting their closest friends, individuals of strong conviction dying for a cause, or those committing the utterly selfless act of dying so that others might live—the theme is the same: For them, the needs of the many truly do outweigh the needs of the few.

References

Arnold, J. C. (2014). *Rich in years: Finding peace and purpose in a long life.* Walden, NY: Plough.

Batson, C. (1991). *The altruism question.* Mahwah, NJ: Erlbaum.

Behr, I. S. (1995). *Star Trek: Deep Space Nine—The Ferengi rules of acquisition.* New York, NY: Pocket.

Brand, J., & Robertson, E. (2001). *The ethics of Star Trek.* New York, NY: Harper Perennial.

Elder, G. H., & Clipp, E. C. (1988). Wartime losses and social bonding: Influences across 40 years in men's lives. *Psychiatry, 51*(2), 177–198.

Foot, P. (1967). The problem of abortion and the doctrine of the double effect. *Oxford Review, 5*, 5–15.

Gastil, J. (2010). The group in society. Thousand Oaks, CA: Sage.

Gert, B. (1967). Hobbes and psychological egoism. *Journal of the History of Ideas, 28*(4), 503–520.

Huebner, B., & Hauser, M. D. (2011). Moral judgments about altruistic self-sacrifice: When philosophical and folk intuitions clash. *Philosophical Psychology, 24*(1), 73–94.

Impett, E. A., Javam, L., Le, B. M., Asyabi-Eshghi, B., & Kogan, A. (2013). The joys of genuine giving: Approach and avoidance sacrifice motivation and authenticity. *Personal Relationships, 20*(4), 740–754.

Kreitzer, L. (1999). Suffering, sacrifice, and redemption. In J. E. Porter & D. L. McClaren (Eds.), *Star Trek and sacred ground: Explorations of Star Trek, religion, and American culture* (pp. 139–166). Albany, NY: SUNY Press.

Leung, K., & Bond, M. H. (1984). The impact of cultural collectivism on reward allocation. *Journal of Personality & Social Psychology, 47*(4), 793–804.

Maner, J. K., Luce, C. L., Neuberg, S. L., Cialdini, R. B., Brown, S., & Sagarin, B. J. (2002). The effects of perspective taking on motivations for helping: Still no evidence for altruism. *Personality & Social Psychology Bulletin, 28*(11), 1601–1610.

Mees, U., & Schmitt, A. (2008). Goals of action and emotional reasons for action: A modern version of the theory of ultimate psychological hedonism. *Journal for the Theory of Social Behaviour, 38*(2), 157–178.

Okuda, M., & Okuda, D. (1996). *Star Trek chronology: The history of the future.* New York, NY: Pocket.

Orehek, E., Sasota, J. A., Kruglanski, A. W., Dechesne, M., & Ridgeway, L. (2014). Interdependent self-construals mitigate the fear of death and augment the willingness to become a martyr. *Journal of Personality & Social Psychology, 107*(2), 265–275.

Poe, S. E. (1998). *Star Trek: Voyager—a vision of the future.* New York, NY: Pocket.

Riemer, J. W. (1998). Durkheim's "heroic sacrifice" in military combat. *Armed Forces & Society, 25*(1), 103–120.

Spinrad, N. (2006/2016). Star Trek in the real world. In D. Gerrold & R. J. Sawyer (Eds.), *Boarding the Enterprise: Transporters, Tribbles, and the Vulcan death grip in Gene Roddenberry's Star Trek* (pp. 11–26). Dallas, TX: BenBella.

Triandis, H. C. (1995). *Individualism & collectivism.* Boulder, CO: Westview.

Van Lange, P. A. M., Agnew, C. R., Harinck, F., & Steemers, G. E. M. (1997). From game theory to real life: How social value orientation affects willingness to sacrifice in ongoing close relationships. *Journal of Personality & Social Psychology, 73*(6), 1330–1344.

Warneken, F., & Tomasello, M. (2009). The roots of human altruism. *British Journal of Psychology, 100*(3), 455–471.

Wilson-Rich, N. (2014). *The bee: A natural history.* Princeton, NJ: Princeton University Press.

Notes

1. *Star Trek* episode 2–9, "Metamorphosis" (November 10, 1967).
2. Arnold (2014).
3. Impett et al. (2013); Van Lange et al. (1997); Warneken & Tomasello (2009).
4. *Star Trek II: The Wrath of Khan* (1982 motion picture).
5. *Star Trek: The Next Generation* episode 1–23, "Skin of Evil" (April 25, 1988).
6. *Star Trek: Deep Space Nine* episode 7–25, "What You Leave Behind" (June 2, 1999).
7. Star Trek pilot "The Cage" (not aired in its entirety until October 4, 1988), mostly seen in portions in *Star Trek* episodes 1–11 and 1–12, "The Menagerie," parts 1 and 2 (November 17 and 24, 1966).
8. *Star Trek* episodes 1–8, "Miri" (October 27, 1966), and 3–11,"Wink of an Eye" (November 29, 1968); *Star Trek: The Next Generation* episodes 4–4, "Suddenly Human" (October 15, 1990), and 5–15, "Power Play" (February 22, 1992); *Star Trek: Deep Space Nine* episodes 1–9, "The Passenger" (February 22, 1993), and 4–1, "The Way of the Warrior" (October 2, 1995); *Star Trek: Voyager* episode 1–10, "Prime Factors" (March 20, 1995); *Star Trek Beyond* (2016 motion picture).
9. Batson (1991).
10. Gert (1967); Mees & Schmitt (2008).
11. *Star Trek: The Next Generation* episode 1–5, "The Last Outpost" (October 19, 1987); *Star Trek: Deep Space Nine* episode 6–23, "Profit and Lace" (May 13, 1998); *Enterprise* episode 1–19, "Acquisition" (March 27, 2002). See Behr (1995).
12. e.g., Maner et al. (2002).
13. Warneken & Tomasello (2009).
14. Wilson-Rich (2014).
15. Triandis (1995).
16. Leung & Bond (1984).
17. Gastil (2010); Spinrad (2006/2016).
18. Foot (1967).
19. *Star Trek II: The Wrath of Khan* (1982 motion picture); *Star Trek* (2009 motion picture).
20. Noted by Huebner & Hauser (2011).
21. *Star Trek: The Next Generation* episode 1–19, "Coming of Age" (March 14, 1988).
22. *Star Trek II: The Wrath of Khan* (1982 motion picture).
23. Brand & Robertson (2001).
24. *Star Trek II: The Wrath of Khan* (1982 motion picture).
25. Riemer (1998).
26. Kreitzer (1999).
27. *Star Trek: The Next Generation* episode 1–23, "Skin of Evil" (April 25, 1988).
28. Elder & Clipp (1988).
29. *Star Trek: Nemesis* (2002 motion picture).
30. Van Lange et al. (1997).
31. *Star Trek: Enterprise* episode 4–22, "These Are the Voyages" (May 13, 2005).
32. Okuda & Okuda (1996); Poe (1998).

The aliens in science fiction tend to look more human that those, if any, out in the real universe seem likely to appear. Aside from practical considerations such as creating costumes that actors can wear or storytelling purposes that require the audience to relate to the characters, lessons learned from the psychology of creativity and even religion may hint at the underlying mental processes involved in making imagined nonhumans seem so human.

•18•

Imagination, Creativity, and Aliens

JIM DAVIES

"I have encountered 1,754 nonhuman races during my tenure in Starfleet."

—Commander Data[1]

"When people imagine novel animals, the properties of their creations are reliably predictable from research on noncreative aspects of categorization."

—cognitive scientist Thomas Ward[2]

Why should so many science fiction aliens look humanoid? At least 240 sentient humanoid species appear in Star Trek episodes and films, compared with 29 named nonhumanoid sentient species.[3] Within the fictional history, an ancient race may have relocated the universe's early humanoids to planets throughout the galaxy[4] or seeded several planets with DNA to guide evolution to form intelligent life similar to its own.[5] A casual glance from outside the fiction, however, suggests a lack of creativity. Studies in psychology have explored creativity in terms of both how creativity functions in people being creative and how people respond to creative works. What they have found may surprise you: More creativity isn't always better.

The Psychology of Creativity

When asked to draw aliens of their own design, participants in a well-known experiment[6] showed little creativity. They tended to mix and match parts of real people and animals—a person with a horse's head, for example. The creatures were bilaterally symmetrical, with body parts and facial structures about where you would expect them to be. The researchers' dismal conclusion was that creativity was heavily structured and involves reorganizing components people are familiar with.

But the participants in this experiment were given blank pieces of paper, and that's kind of intimidating. Perhaps if people were given inspiration for doing more wild things, they would be more creative. A student researcher and I tested this in my laboratory. In one condition we replicated psychologist Thomas Ward's findings with paper, and in the other condition we had people create monsters with a piece of software called the *Spore Creature Creator*,[7] which provides menus with lots of choices of features. The result? People were just as uncreative with *Spore* as they were with paper.[8]

Rather than criticizing the creators of Star Trek for being uncreative, we could speculate about budgetary and safety reasons for using actors rather than big puppets and cumbersome costumes. Many aliens are differentiated from humans only through the use of makeup and prosthetics to alter the appearance of faces, ears, and hands. The Vulcans visibly differ from humans in their angled eyebrows and elflike pointy ears. The Borg have more complex costumes that involve intricate mechanical hands, cyborg eyes, various facial tubes, and eclectic steel armor. Although diverse and visually appealing, these costumes are cost-efficient and allow for acting in a way that would be difficult with puppets, masks, or aliens without any faces at all.

We can see evidence for this motivation in Roddenberry's original pitch: "The 'Parallel Worlds' concept makes production practical by permitting action-adventure science fiction at a practical budget figure by the use of available 'earth' casting, sets, locations, costuming, and so on." Further, Roddenberry stated, "Where required, 'alien' variations will be obtained via padding, wigs, and similar makeup devices."[9]

There are good artistic and narrative reasons for humanoid aliens, too, suggesting that the designers knew what they were doing. For one thing, humanoid aliens are easier to relate to. It is easier to feel empathy for those who look similar to us.[10] Some kind of recognizable face is very important for reading the emotions of beings[11]—you can tell when a dog is scared or angry but not when it's disgusted or surprised. Dogs have limited facial expressions.[12] Psychologically realistic aliens make for characters that can engage in the kind of social conflict we need in stories.

We are built to understand human beings, and we can't help interpreting other things we see the same way. Take, for example, the idea of "the Greys," a species of aliens that some people ("alien abductees") believe visits Earth to bring people into their spaceships at night and run experiments on them.[13] Now, for this alien to be plausible, it must be fairly intelligent—a spacefaring, scientific species can't be stupid. So what do these aliens look like? Well, they tend to have features that signal intelligence to us *in human beings*: They have big heads with big eyes, small mouths, and small noses, and they are thin and bald. We think people are smarter when they have big eyes.[14] We notice the nose area first in people[15] and make judgments about their intelligence within 39 milliseconds,[16] suggesting that the nose is also an important feature in judging intelligence. Height, too, suggests intelligence in humans.[17] Imagine if someone told you he had been abducted by an alien that was fat and hairy, with small eyes, a big mouth and nose, and a tiny head. It sounds less plausible because it does not match what we think of as signals of intelligence in human beings. That is, it would just look stupid.

We ran an experiment in which we showed people images of hypothetical aliens and varied their physical features. When we asked how smart they thought an alien was, people rated aliens as being smarter when they were taller, their eyes were bigger, and their noses were smaller. We attribute intelligence to aliens in the same ways we attribute it to people.[18]

Many of the alien species in Star Trek interact with the human members of the Federation. Recurrent aliens such as the Vulcans, Cardassians, Romulans, and Klingons have starships that have warp capability (and thus can travel vast distances in space in very little time), suggesting a high level of intelligence, at least one that is comparable to that of Star Trek's humans. These aliens also have language, symbolism, and culture. So it makes some sense that many of Star Trek's aliens would be made humanoid to look more intelligent. But do they really need to look so much like people?

Maybe there's nothing wrong with the level of creativity of Star Trek aliens—after all, it is an enormously popular franchise. It turns out that creatures in speculative fiction can't be too weird or people will reject them as unappealing. How do we know this? To get a sense of just how creative an alien creature *should* be, we can get some answers from, of all places, the psychology of religion.

Creature Creator

Artist Terryl Whitlatch makes her living creating creatures, designing animals for companies such as Disney by using both logic and creativity. "To make imaginary animals believable, one must first be familiar with the biology of living animals—their place in nature, how they behave within their environment, what they eat, how they catch their food," she says.[19] "Real animals are my preferred subjects, not fantasy animals. Drawing and observing them—this is what gets under the skin and into the psychology and spirit of imaginary animals."[20]

—T.L.

What Are Gods Like?

Thousands of religions are spread throughout the world, and new ones arise all the time. Some of them catch on and last, but most do not. You might think that a religion can suggest the existence of just about anything, but you'd be wrong. A religion that does not match humanity's basic psychological expectations will not be successful.

Religions posit the existence of supernatural beings. If you look at the gods of many religions, an interesting pattern emerges: Gods tend to be beings or objects from one category of things, with only one or two features from another category. For example, a statue that can bleed is a member of the "objects" category with one feature (bleeding) from the "animal" category. A ghost is a member of the "person" category but is missing life and a material body. Different scientists disagree on exactly what these categories are, but many believe that in childhood we develop basic understandings of people, animals, objects, and ideas.[21] These categories, such as "things with minds" and "physical objects," were discovered in developmental psychology.[22] When people think about things, they infer many properties on the basis of the category they are in.

For example, we expect damaged living things in general to repair themselves over time, but we don't expect that of something in the "physical object" category. Therefore, a physical object that exhibits a property of a living thing violates this category boundary.

A man who can walk through walls is more compelling than a man with six fingers because the latter does not violate something fundamental about living things. He is merely unusual but does not violate category boundaries. So although surface appearances can change greatly from culture to culture (this god has horns, that one has three legs), the category violations tend to be similar, falling into a few kinds: people or animals that violate physical properties (e.g., incorporeal or invisible), biological properties (e.g., immortal, born of a virgin birth), and psychological properties (e.g., have supernaturally extended perception). Similarly, objects can have biological properties (such as bleeding) or psychological ones (such as being able to hear). No religion has gods that exist only on Wednesday, because days of the week are not a part of *any* basic category of human understanding. Note that some of the gods in Star Trek also tend to resemble the lesser beings they are related to or created by: The Prophets look like Bajorans and Fek'lhr look like Klingons.[23] If there are more than one or two violations, it is more easily forgotten. The simpler violations are better remembered and enjoy more success in cultural survival over time.[24]

Let's compare two hypothetical examples of gods: a baby that can make soup and a baby that can turn into a bird. Making soup is impossible for a baby, but not because soup making belongs to another category. It just so happens that babies can't make soup. As a result, it sounds kind of ridiculous as a religious belief. The baby that can transform into an animal, however, sounds more plausible as a religious belief, and experiments confirm this. People are more likely to remember the transforming baby than the soup-making baby and rate it as being more plausible. This includes people who don't actually believe in either of them—even the nonreligious share this intuition.[25]

Star Trek has *counterintuitive* features of aliens. For example, Betazoids are basically humans with black eyes and telepathy. Cardassians are humans with ridged skin and photographic memories. Telepathy is not something inherently associated with living things, and this category breaking makes them compelling. The physical features do not violate category boundaries and perhaps are not strong components of the compellingness of the aliens.

Further, compelling creatures, whether they are gods or aliens, cannot have too many features from other categories. A tree that sings sounds like it might be a part of a real religion, but a tree that sings, can turn into wind, bleeds, and has miraculous healing powers sounds kind of silly. Popular gods involve what are called *minimally counterintuitive ideas.*[26] If they are not counterintuitive (like a normal person), they are not particularly interesting, and if they are too weird (too creative?), they are not memorable or interesting.

So much for religion. What does this have to do with art, particularly the universe of Star Trek? It turns out that lots of things we find compelling about art predict what we find compelling about religion.[27] Scientists looked at Grimm's fairy tales and counted how many minimally counterintuitive ideas appeared in each story. They also rated each story on how popular and well-known it was on the basis of hits on a popular search engine. The most popular stories, it turned out, had only two or three counterintuitive ideas, whereas having more or less than that number correlated with lower popularity.[28]

We naturally see humans as being different from animals but even more different from plants. An analysis of Ovid's stories in *Metamorphoses* revealed that people were more likely to transform into animals, and animals were more likely to transform into people or into plants. People rarely turned into plants.[29]

All this suggests that our minds are prepared for only a certain amount of divergence from what we are familiar with. New creatures, whether they are gods in religion or supernatural creatures in folktales, should be fairly familiar but not too strange.

There's a sweet spot.

The Sweet Spot

The fact that we like best things that fit into a sweet spot between familiarity and novelty goes beyond gods, aliens, and monsters to all arts and even ideas. Too much of the familiar is boring, and too little is incomprehensible and, as a result, boring too.

When we see something again and again, we become familiar with it and can recognize it easily. This feels good, and we tend to like it—the *facilitation effect*. But prolonged exposure to the same pattern results in *habituation* and a lessening of arousal. We get bored because we're curious creatures who evolved to want to learn new things.[30]

Some evidence suggests that expertise in a particular field allows for the appreciation of more creativity. One study by Paul Hekkert found that car experts preferred cars with more unusual designs than do non-experts.[31] In another study, he found that art connoisseurs prefer more abstract and conceptual paintings than do amateurs, who tend to prefer depictions of realistic things.[32] Thus, it could be that in science fiction our preference for ever stranger worlds and aliens may increase as we gain experience in the genre. Luckily for us, Star Trek has so much content that there is something for everyone.

Familiar Yet Different

Maybe the aliens people created in Ward's experiment weren't so bad after all. This psychological research lets us look at Star Trek aliens in a new light: Perhaps to maximize our interest, aliens should be a lot like recognizable things (such as people or Earth animals), with just one or two different aspects.

The experiments with religion focus on category breaking, but a more general take-home message is that compelling creations should have only a few things different. Note that Betazoids and Cardassians have oddities (different eyes or skin) but also one impossible/counterintuitive feature (telepathy and photographic memories). Should the creators have added more counterintuitive features?

Perhaps not. If these scientific studies of gods and aliens are correct, making Star Trek aliens weirder would sacrifice compellingness on the altar of creativity.

References

Atran, S. (2002). *In gods we trust: The evolutionary landscape of religion (*Kindle Touch version). Amazon.com.

Bar, M., Neta, M., & Linz, H. (2006). Very first impressions. *Emotion, 6*(2), 269–278.

Berlyne, D. E. (1974). *Studies in the new experimental aesthetics: Steps toward an objective psychology of aesthetic appreciation.* Ann Arbor, MI: Hemisphere.

Boyer, P. (2001). *Religion explained: The evolutionary origins of religious thought.* New York, NY: Basic.

Brown, D. (1991). *Human universals.* New York, NY: McGraw-Hill.

Chu, S., & Geary, K. (2005). Physical stature influences character perception in women. *Personality & Individual Differences, 38*(8), 1927–1934.

Cockbain, J., Vertolli, M., & Davies, J. (2013). Creative imagination is stable across technological media: The Spore Creature Creator versus pencil and paper. *Journal of Creative Behavior, 48*(1), 13–24.

Davies, J. (2014). *Riveted: The science of why jokes make us laugh, movies make us cry, and religion makes us feel one with the universe.* New York, NY: Palgrave Macmillan.

Davies, J., & Fortney, M. (2012). *The Menton theory of engagement and boredom.* Presentation at the Conference on Advances in Cognitive Systems, Stanford, CA.

Davies, J., & McManus, M. (2014). How our desire for social information affects tastes in paintings and belief systems. In Kozbelt, A. (Ed.), *Proceedings of the Twenty-Third Biennial Congress of the International Association of Empirical Aesthetics* (pp. 153–158). (IAEA-14). New York, NY: International Association of Empirical Aesthetics.

EA Games (1998). *Spore Creature Creator with Creepy and Cute Expansion* (computer software).

Ekman, P. (1992). An argument for basic emotions. *Cognition & Emotion, 6*(3–4), 169–200.

Gnomon Workshop (n.d.). *Artist interview with Terryl Whitlatch*. Gnomon Workshop: http://www.thegnomonworkshop.com/news/2008/10/interview-with-terryl-whitlatch-2/.

Hekkert, P., Snelders, D., & van Wieringen, P. C. W. (2003). "Most advanced, yet acceptable": Typicality and novelty as joint predictors of aesthetic preference in industrial design. *British Journal of Psychology, 94*(1), 111–124.

Hekkert, P., & van Wieringen, P. C. W. (1996). The impact of level of expertise on the evaluation of original and altered versions of post-impressionistic paintings. *Acta Psychologica, 94*(2), 112–131.

Hsiao, J. H., & Cottrell, G. (2008). *The nose knows: Two fixation points needed for face recognition*. Association for Psychological Science: http://www.psychologicalscience.org/media/releases/2008/hsiao.cfm.

Hudson, A. L. (2016, March 30). *Interview with Terryl Whitlatch*. SFF World: http://www.sffworld.com/2016/03/interview-with-terryl-whitlatch/.

Kelly, M. H., & Keil, F. C. (1985). The more things change . . . : Metamorphoses and conceptual structure. *Cognitive Science, 9*(4), 403–416.

Lindeman, M., & Aarnio, K. (2007). Superstitious, magical, and paranormal beliefs: An integrative model. *Journal of Research in Personality, 41*(4), 731–744.

Malmstrom, F. V., & Coffman, R. M. (1979). Humanoids reported in UFOs, religion, and folktales: Human bias toward human life forms? In R. Haines (Ed.), *UFO phenomena and the behavioral scientist* (pp. 60–88). Metuchen, NJ: Scarecrow.

Memory Alpha (n.d. a). *Humanoid species*. Memory Alpha: http://en.memory-alpha.wikia.com/wiki/Humanoid_species.

Memory Alpha (n.d. b). *Non-humanoid species*. Memory Alpha: http://en.memory-alpha.wikia.com/wiki/Non-humanoid_species.

Moseman, A. (2010, December). Hot science: The best new science culture. *Discover, 31*, 30–36.

Norenzayan, A., Atran, S., Faulkner, J., & Schaller, M. (2006). Memory and mystery: The cultural selection of minimally counterintuitive narratives, *Cognitive Science, 30*(3), 531–553.

Paunonen, S. V., Ewan, K., Earthy, J., Lefave, S., & Goldberg, H. (1999). Facial features as personality cues. *Journal of Personality, 67*(3), 555–583.

Roddenberry, G. (1964). *Star Trek pitch*. http://leethomson.myzen.co.uk/Star_Trek/1_Original_Series/Star_Trek_Pitch.pdf.

Schirmer, A., Seow, C. S., & Penney, T.B. (2013). Humans process dog and human facial affect in similar ways. *PLoS One 8*(9): e74591.

Shermer, M. (1997). *Why people believe weird things: Pseudoscience, superstition, and other confusions of our time*. New York, NY: Freeman.

Trawalter, S., Hoffman, K. M., & Waytz, A. (2012). Racial bias in perceptions of others' pain. *PLoS One,* 7(11), e48546.

Upal, M. A. (2007). The optimal cognitive template of minimally counterintuitive narratives. In D. S. McNamara & J. G. Trafton (Eds.), *Proceedings of the 29th Annual Cognitive Science Society* (pp. 1–6). Austin, TX: Cognitive Science Society.

Ward, T. B. (1994). Structured imagination: The role of category structure in exemplar generation. *Cognitive Psychology, 27*(1), 1–40.

Notes

1. *Star Trek: The Next Generation* episode 5–2, "Darmok" (September 30, 1991).
2. Ward (1994).
3. Memory Alpha, a and b (n.d.).
4. *Star Trek* episode 3–3, "The Paradise Syndrome" (October 4, 1968).
5. *Star Trek: The Next Generation* episode 6–20, "The Chase" (April 26, 1993).
6. Ward. (1994).
7. EA Games (1998).
8. Cockbain et al. (2013).
9. Roddenberry (1964).
10. Trawalter et al. (2012).
11. Ekman (1992).
12. Schirmer et al. (2013).
13. Shermer (1997), p. 93.
14. Paunonen et al. (1999).
15. Hsiao & Cottrell (2008).
16. Bar et al. (2006).
17. Interestingly, people tend to think Greys are about the height of an average woman (Malmstrom & Coffman, 1979) even though height is seen as signaling intelligence in human beings (Chu & Geary, 2005).
18. Davies & McManus (2014).
19. Gnomon Workshop (n.d.).
20. Hudson (2016).
21. Lindeman & Aarnio (2007).
22. Brown (1991).
23. *Star Trek: Deep Space Nine* episodes 1–20, "In the Hands of the Prophets" (June 20, 1993); 7–1, "Image in the Sand" (September 30, 1998).
24. Atran (2002), p. 286.
25. Atran (2002).
26. Boyer (2001).
27. Davies (2014).
28. Norenzayan et al. (2006). Upal (2007) failed to replicate this finding.
29. Kelly & Keil (1985).
30. Berlyne (1974); Davies & Fortney (2012).
31. Hekkert et al. (2003).
32. Hekkert & van Wieringen (1996).

How can we know when a machine or program is no longer imitating sentience but has indeed achieved it? At what point is artificial intelligence simply intelligence?

•19•

The Measure of a Machine: The Psychology of Star Trek's Artificial Intelligence

ANTHONY FRANCIS
AND JIM DAVIES

"I am the culmination of one man's dream. This is not ego or vanity. But when Dr. Soong created me, he added to the substance of the universe."
—Lieutenant Commander Data[1]

"The whole thinking process is rather mysterious to us, but I believe the attempt to make a thinking machine will help us greatly in finding out how we think ourselves."
—computer scientist Alan Turing[2]

Psychology is the study of how minds work, usually in humans and other animals, but a science fiction universe can explore whether machines can have minds, too. Psychology can help us understand both the initial limits of artificial intelligence (A.I.), what these artificial intelligences are actually doing, and how their cognition (or cognitive-like performance) relates to their personhood. When the most prominent artificially intelligent machines in Star Trek—Data and *Voyager*'s Doctor—each first appear they often act like simple machines, and are often treated that way, too. They become more human-like over time and are treated more like humans. But are these smart machines in Star Trek really people or just models of people? The psychology of storytelling can help us understand why, in Star Trek, computers can perform very sophisticated cognitive activities, mimicking or surpassing human intelligence, but also have strange psychological limitations. From the ship's computer[3] that makes your life easier (when it's not humorously misunderstanding you) to the M5[4] that runs the ship for you (when it's not trying to kill you), these supposedly intelligent machines often appear to be at best frustrating idiot savants and at worst sociopathic plot devices. Even machines designed to emulate human minds have oddly stunted personalities. Awkward android Lieutenant Commander Data, while highly intelligent, at first lacks the social skills to deliver concise answers to simple questions,[5] and it takes several seasons for the heckled hologram Doctor aboard *Voyager* to self-actualize to the point where he has a full suite of human interests.

These psychological limits of characters within stories play a role in the psychology of what makes the stories themselves interesting. Studies of what makes stories memorable show that good stories must have interesting complications.[6] However, more critical systems like transporters and turbolifts rarely malfunction, so why are Star Trek's artificial intelligences, in particular, so quirky? The answer may have to do with the narrative architecture of Star Trek itself. In a blast of visionary optimism, Gene Roddenberry imagined a future that just worked, a future in which humanity could go almost anywhere, could do almost anything: "close enough to our own time for continuing characters to be fully identifiable as people like us, but far enough in the future for galaxy travel to be thoroughly established."[7] This lets Star Trek tell stories where people who are trying hard to get it right meet people who don't quite get it, people who, by struggling through difficult issues together, cast our culture's current problems into sharp relief. So, while Star Trek uses computers to explore many subtle issues in both human psychology and the ethics of re-creating it in machines, it also places limits on those computers to focus its stories on how people would tackle those issues.

Listen Carefully, Computer, I Am Lying

Other features that make stories easy to remember are characters people can identify with, which can make them memorable even to children,[8] and abnormal information, which can make even ordinary situations more memorable.[9] Combining these features—identifiable characters, facing interesting complications, produced by abnormal situations—would predict that stories where human characters face interesting threats from abnormal antagonists, such as machines, would be very memorable, and Star Trek appears to follow this recipe.

For example, Star Trek places limits on its computers, allowing stories to focus on human achievement. One could imagine that an arbitrarily smart computer could take over the universe, so intelligent computers in Star Trek can't be too smart, or if they're too smart, they must be rare. Too-smart, potentially not rare computers must either be protagonists with whom we can identify as humans, like Data, or have serious drawbacks that can be overcome by humans before the credits roll, like the M5. That's why computers smart enough to run entire civilizations are often depicted in Star Trek as being less flexible than video-game characters, forced to follow their original programs rigidly and far beyond their shelf life.[10] When they do deviate, it's usually to present (generally by mistake) a canned message from the computer's designers,[11] before a human protagonist such as Captain Kirk dispatches them with a simple paradox like "I am lying."[12]

Here the psychology of good storytelling conflicts with a realistic depiction of either human or machine psychology. For example, processing a contradiction is unlikely to cause any intelligence to short out. It's true that all computation consumes power, and in Star Trek, where computers are embedded in warp fields to make their computations proceed faster than light,[13] one could imagine a clever command making a computer consume enough power to explode—but a verbally delivered paradox almost certainly won't be it. Human minds don't shut down when faced with a paradox; studies show that people presented with paradoxes can actually perform more creatively.[14] In computer truth maintenance systems, "contradiction" is a third state beyond "true" and "false," and signals when a line of reasoning isn't fruitful,[15] similar to the use of proof by contradiction in human mathematical reasoning. Rather than causing a computer to think about a problem forever, a paradox is a sign to give up without wasting more time. "Lying, Captain? No . . . you are contradicting yourself."

A Spectacular Demonstration of Simulated Imagination

The quirky ways artificial intelligences fail in some science fiction should not blind us to some of the amazing things they *can* do, which include some psychological feats that might be

Turing's Test

World War II cryptographer Alan Turing (1912–1954) is sometimes known as the father of artificial intelligence for his 1948 report "Intelligent Machinery,"[16] which described learning in neural networks before either was a buzzword. But he might as well be called the father of computing for his 1936 paper "On Computable Numbers"[17] which both defined universal computers and proved you can't tell when they will halt—simultaneously putting artificial intelligences on guard against infinite-loop traps like paradoxes, and guaranteeing that their eternal vigilance will not always succeed.

Turing proposed the Imitation Game, now called the Turing Test, in which he argued that a machine that can pass for a human can think like a human.[18] *Star Trek: The Next Generation* takes his test further, arguing that a machine that exhibits the qualities of sentience—intelligence, self-awareness, and consciousness—should be treated like a person.[19]

challenging even for humans. While Star Trek overtly downplays computer intelligence, it often takes computer *superintelligence* for granted. Take the holodeck, for example, which creates interactive three-dimensional simulations of places. Simply creating an interactive three-dimensional (3-D) *visualization* is difficult enough that many humans can't do it.[20] While some people have very vivid mental imagery, others have *aphantasia*, a complete lack of mental pictures in their heads.[21] It's impressive that the holodeck computer is able to collect and sensibly reconstruct enough images to model a shape well enough to stand up to viewing from multiple angles—much less to capture enough surface texture to model a seat cushion in a convincing sit-down 3-D *reconstruction*.

To research a problem, Geordi LaForge creates a holodeck simulation of the room where the *Enterprise* was designed.[22] At first he wants to query the design records using *natural language*.

That involves parsing words, turning them into questions, probing databases, and constructing responses—something human beings can do even in very early childhood.[23] Unsatisfied with Siri-on-steroids, Geordi has the computer simulate a fully interactive person—which requires kinematic linkages, animation sequences, simulated expressions, and behavior control.

Even now, there are technologies that can simulate a personality from samples. *Deep learning* detects patterns in documents and can reassemble them into eerily similar new texts. While the reassembled output is currently only superficially similar to the source, similar systems can perform at human level on a variety of pattern analysis tasks.[24] Still, without a conversation model to track what has been said and a question-answering model to connect to the problem domain, a holodeck simulation of *Enterprise* designer Leah Brahms would sound like a parrot, repeating confabulated answers that superficially sound right but are all wrong—and creating a conversation model sufficient to engage a human being would require a serious engineering effort.[25] So the computer must simultaneously act as the best question-answering system ever, and interpolate those responses into an ongoing deep simulation of a personality, expressed through a three-dimensional character.

What Geordi asks the computer to do is something that, in a human, would be considered a spectacular act of skilled acting. The computer performs effortlessly—and Geordi takes that feat completely for granted.

The Mechanics of Solving Problems

Problem-solving in humans engages the forebrain, one of the brain's evolutionarily newest structures.[26] Problem-solving in artificial intelligence, however, is one of the field's oldest techniques.[27] Geordi's simulated Leah Brahms performs more sophisticated psychological feats than smart conversation. She engages in actual problem-solving, proposing a computer-controlled escape route with only a probability of success. Brahms's particular method looks and sounds like *rapidly exploring random trees* (RRTS), an artificial intelligence planning technique that tackles complex problems by taking many small leaps of faith, focusing on the most promising alternatives until a solution is found[28]—assuming it can recognize a solution when it finds one.

A computer can juggle thousands of alternatives at once, but can only make progress toward a solution if it can estimate the quality of its proposals with an *evaluation function* (a function used by simulation programs to estimate strategic value). Human memories are more limited, consciously considering only a few alternatives at once, because of our limitations in working memory.[29] But we make up for it with fantastic evaluation functions: experience learned over a lifetime and instincts tuned over millions of years of evolution, which together help us evaluate whether choices are good or bad.[30] Experience and instinct give Geordi a bad feeling about the simulated Brahms's plan, and he decides it's too risky for the crew, prompting him to devise a solution that's even better.[31] Intuition seems to be associated with the evolutionarily older parts of our brains,[32] suggesting that the ship's computers are better at simulating the more conscious, deliberative, and newer parts of our brains than the older ones that we share with other mammals. Our creative problem-solving abilities tend to get better in situations that make us feel better.[33]

The Rationality of Emotional Responses

What about emotion? While behaviorism somewhat ignored emotion for almost a half a century, many modern cognitive psychologists believe the study of emotion is critical for understanding human psychology[34]—yet many computers in Star Trek don't seem to have emotion. For example, Data first appears as a highly intelligent but emotionless android.[35] Is computer simulation of emotion possible, or even desirable, in a world where Vulcans mock anyone who cracks a smile?

With all due respect to Mr. Spock's green-blooded side, we've suspected that emotions are a critical component of reasoning ever since nineteenth-century railroad construction foreman Phineas Gage blew an iron rod through his frontal lobe and became a different—and unreliable—person.[36] Patients with similar injuries get distracted by details, are unable to put simple decisions in their larger context, but are oddly *less* emotional.[37] Cognitive science pioneer Herb Simon argued that emotions, while not logical, are in fact a rational method of choosing behaviors appropriate for the current situation.[38] The distinction is subtle: Logic is a mathematical scheme for deriving valid conclusions from valid premises, where rationality is a procedural scheme for selecting optimal courses of actions in a situation. Rational schemes can use logic, but rely more heavily on heuristics, or rules of thumb, which work most of the time. This is a good thing, because we rarely can establish logical premises, much less model the world well enough to draw logical conclusions.

Many psychologists suggest that the primary function of human emotion is *judgment*: positive and negative appraisals of people, things, events, and actions.[39] Judgments about people and things spark hate and love; judgments about past events evoke sadness or joy; judgments about future events trigger fear and hope; and judgments about actions provoke anger and pride. Those emotions in turn help us select the appropriate behavior patterns. Rather than being irrational, emotions are a finely tuned rational system to guide decisions in the face of incomplete information.

Sorry, Spock, but "logic" by itself isn't enough. Emotions seem to be necessary—in human psychology, at least—to give logic direction. Without an emotional evaluation of the goodness or badness of an outcome, people would be—as Phineas Gage was—stymied by simple decisions.

The Nagging Feeling of Something Left Out

Even after Data gets a chip that emulates the *function* of emotions, would that mean that he is *feeling* emotions? Functionalists like us say that emotions can be reduced to the functions they perform,[40] but many smart scientists think that the feeling of an emotion, its *qualia*, cannot be generated by a computer because feelings are produced by chemical processes in our brains and bodies.[41] To wrap your head around this, imagine if your brain were replaced, one neuron at a time, by computer parts. If the parts functioned correctly, your behavior might not change—but would your feeling of experience slowly drain away? Could you be replaced by a perfect android duplicate that would not feel anything at all?[42]

That's a hard experiment to perform, but Star Trek has tackled it. *Deep Space Nine*'s Dr. Bashir gradually replaces someone's degenerating brain parts with computer parts. When half of his brain is replaced, the suffering diplomat says, in a wooden voice, that it just doesn't feel the same. That's when they stop replacing.[43]

At first blush this takes the side of meat over machines, arguing that humans can feel and computers can't. But Star Trek is actually rejecting the whole premise of the thought experiment. Bareil's new parts don't feel the same, *so he doesn't act the same.* Similarly, when android double Kelby realizes that his feelings of love are fake in an early *Star Trek* episode, he kills himself

Lee Meriwether Interview: Artificial Intelligence, Genuine Feelings?

Can artificial intelligence (A.I.) really think and feel or does it only simulate thinking and feeling? *Affective computing* studies and develops emotion recognition and display by computers and robots. According to Rosalind Picard, who founded this area of computer programming, A.I. that is truly intelligent must understand and even have emotions.[44] The original *Star Trek*, while exploring the humanity of nonhumans, generally treated forms of A.I. as things. Subsequent series would debate the sentience of an android and later of holograms,[45] eventually winning them some recognition of personhood without really answering the question of how human they had become.

The question of whether A.I. can be truly human also leads to the question of whether A.I. can become a specific human. Can you "upload" yourself into a computer? If you're dead and all that remains of you is a facsimile in a digital realm, is that facsimile now *you*? Regardless of all the theories on how we define what "me" is, no one scientific theory emerges as the clear answer.[46]

Actress Lee Meriwether played a killer hologram, a likeness of long-dead station commander Losira, programmed to protect her outpost from outsiders.[47] When Kirk's appeal to the hologram's humanity unsettles her, though, she withdraws on one occasion without killing. Regret is a complicated emotional experience that exerts great influence on decision-making.[48] After leaving the outpost, Kirk suggests that the landing

in an emotional act of remorse.[49] In Star Trek, just as in human psychology, you simply can't disentangle feelings from behavior.

The Psychology of Infinite Potential

Where does this leave Data? Can an android be a sentient being? Cognitive science has some ideas about it (see "Lee Meriwether Interview" sidebar), and Star Trek has some criteria of its own.

party has survived only because the copy of Losira was complete enough to retain her humanity and experience regret over killing. Meriwether shared some thoughts on this with us.

Meriwether: I was a hologram created by the computer that was left on the planet. Playing the character was a twofold problem in that I was programmed to kill but there was enough humanity left in my character to have feelings, which became apparent in her final speech. The fellows who came from the *Enterprise* finally figured it out. They played the last tape which the computer had used to give the hologram my features. The speech tells the whole story of how the original Losira got there and I was trying to get back home and all. A long, long speech. It was beautifully written, actually. You could tell that I had concern for my people. They talk about me afterwards and they realize what happened. I was not able to save anyone, really. All that remained was my visage on the computer.

Langley: You've said that you don't consider your character a villain.

Meriwether: Oh, not a bit. No, no. You could see at the end. She was a commander and she was loyal to the people she cared about. The computer was programmed to repel others, and it would use my image. She became this hologram, but she still had enough of her humanity in the end.

—Travis Langley

Gene Roddenberry raised this very question in the original *Star Trek* pitch,[50] and *Star Trek: The Next Generation* took up the question by putting Data on trial.[51] Data's storage capacity, construction, and on-off switch are debated, and the answer to whether he "feels" is definitively negative, as Data does not yet have his emotion chip. Picard argues that it doesn't matter: Data has a human-level intellect, participates in human relationships, and even becomes physically intimate with a human, therefore he should be treated like one despite his differences—and the tribunal agrees. Many psychologists studying personality hold similar views regarding *human* capabilities, arguing we should move beyond merely studying individual differences to understand and promote individual *potential*.[52]

Voyager's Doctor shows this philosophy at its pinnacle. At first, the Doctor doesn't have a physical body or even a name: He's just the Emergency Medical Hologram (EMH), a program running on the ship's computer, his human "personality" a mere module used to generate bedside manner. The EMH is a piece of emergency equipment, one that, if not for the disaster that brings *Voyager* to the Delta Quadrant,[53] might never have been activated outside of a test.[54]

The EMH is as different from a person as can be, and the crew of *Voyager*, accustomed to holodeck characters, at first view the EMH as a nonsentient thing. It takes a person naive about Federation technology, the alien Kes, to see him as a person, and eventually the crew of *Voyager* follow her lead in treating the Doctor with respect. Even Captain Janeway, who once shuts the EMH off in the middle of a conversation, ultimately grows to accept him as a member of her crew and to encourage the Doctor to fulfill his ultimate potential.[55]

Although the artificial intelligences of Star Trek have some psychological drawbacks, the show offers many examples of how they demonstrate a wide range of sophisticated cognitive abilities, including planning, imagination, language processing, creativity, and even emotion. If we are asking if they should be treated as people, we might well ask what else they would need to demonstrate to satisfy ourselves that they should.

By showing the struggles of people like us interacting with smart computers of all kinds, Star Trek provides a shining, aspirational example of how we *should* treat truly intelligent machines—not as glorified toasters, but as full equals.

References

Allen, J. F., Byron, D.K., Dzikovska, M., Ferguson, G., Galescu, L., & Stent. A. (2001). Toward conversational human-computer interaction. *AI Magazine, 22*(4), 27–37.

Anderson, R. C. (1984). *Interestingness of children's reading material.* (Technical report no. 323). Urbana, IL: University of Illinois at Urbana-Champaign, Center for the Study of Reading.

Birnbaum, M. H., & Diecidue, E. (2015). Testing a class of models that includes majority rule and regret theories: Transitivity, recycling, and restricted branch independence. *Decision, 2*(3), 145–190.

Caprara, G. V., & Cervone, D. (2000). *Personality: Determinants, dynamics, and potentials.* New York, NY: Cambridge University Press.

Chalmers, D. (1996). *The conscious mind: In search of a fundamental theory.* New York, NY: Oxford University Press.

Chase, W., & Simon, H. (1973). The mind's eye in chess. In W. G. Chase (Ed.), *Visual Information Processing: Proceedings of the Eighth Annual Carnegie Psychology Symposium* (pp. 215–281). New York, NY: Academic Press.

Cowan, N. (2001). The magical number 4 in short-term memory: A reconsideration of mental storage capacity. *Behavioral & Brain Sciences, 24*(1), 87–114.

Damasio, A. (1994). *Descartes' error: Emotion, reason, and the human brain.* New York, NY: Putnam.

Dorrier, J. (2015, January 25). *If you upload your mind to a computer—are you still you?* Singularity Hub: http://singularityhub.com/2015/01/25/if-you-upload-your-mind-to-a-computer-are-you-still-you/.

Doyle, J. (1979). A truth maintenance system. *AI, 12*(3), 251–272.

Francis, A., Mehta, M., & Ram, A. (2009). Emotional memory and adaptive personalities. In J. Vallverdu & D. Casacuberta (Eds.), *Handbook of research on synthetic emotions and sociable robotics: New applications in affective computing and artificial intelligence* (pp. 391–421). Hershey, PA: IGI Global.

Hidi, S., & Baird, W. (1986). Interestingness—A neglected variable in discourse processing. *Cognitive Science, 10*, 179–194.

Isen, A., Daubman, K., & Nowicki, G. (1987). Positive affect facilitates creative problem solving. *Journal of Personality & Social Psychology, 52*(6), 1122–1131.

Joseph-Williams, N., Edwards, A., & Elwyn, G. (2011). The importance and complexity of regret in the measurement of "good" decisions: A systematic review and content analysis of existing assessment instruments. *Health Expectations, 14*(1), 59–83.

Jurásová, K., & Špajdel, M. (2011). The role of regret in rational decision making. *Studia Psychologia, 53*(2), 169–174.

Kahneman, D. (2011). *Thinking fast and slow.* New York, NY: Farrar, Straus & Giroux.

Karpathy, A. (2015). *The unreasonable effectiveness of recurrent neural networks.* Andrej Karpathy Blog: http://karpathy.github.io/2015/05/21/rnn-effectiveness/.

Lavalle, S. (2006). *Planning algorithms.* New York, NY: Cambridge University Press.

Levin, J. (1990). Qualia. In R. A. Wilson & F. C. Keil (Eds.), *The MIT encyclopedia of the cognitive sciences.* Cambridge, MA: MIT Press.

Marks, D. (1973). Visual imagery differences in the recall of pictures. *British Journal of Psychology, 64*(1), 17–24.

Miron-Spektor, E., Gino, F., & Argote, L. (2011). Paradoxical frames and creative sparks: Enhancing individual creativity through conflict and integration. *Organizational Behavior & Human Decision Processes, 116*(2), 229–240.

Newell, A., Shaw, J., & Simon, H. (1959). Report on a general problem-solving program. *Proceedings of the International Conference on Information Processing,* 256–264.

Ortony, A., Clore, G. L., & Collins, A. (1990). *The cognitive structure of emotions.* New York, NY: Cambridge University Press.

Picard, R. (1997). *Affective computing.* Cambridge, MA: MIT Press.

Roddenberry, G. (1964). *Star Trek.* Lee Thomson: http://leethomson.myzen.co.uk/Star_Trek/1_Original_Series/Star_Trek_Pitch.pdf.

Schank, R. (1979). Interestingness: Controlling inferences. *Artificial Intelligence 12*(3), 273–297.

Shiota, M. N., & Kalat, J. W. (2011). *Emotion* (2nd ed.). Belmont, CA: Wadsworth.

Simon, H. (1983). *Reason in human affairs.* Stanford, CA: Stanford University Press.

Sternbach, R., & Okuda, M. (1991). *Star Trek: The Next Generation—Technical manual.* New York, NY: Pocket.

Tsujii, T., & Watanabe, S. (2009). Neural correlates of dual-task effect on belief-bias syllogistic reasoning: A near-infrared spectroscopy study. *Brain Research,* 1287, 118-125.

Turing, A. (1936). On Computable Numbers, with an application to the Entscheidungs problem. *Proceedings of the London Mathematical Society, 2*(42), 230–265.

Turing, A. (1948). Intelligent machinery. Report written for the National Physical Laboratory. In S. B. Cooper & J. van Leeuwen (Eds.), *Alan Turing: His work and impact* (pp. 501–516). Waltham, MA: Elsevier.

Turing, A. (1950). Computing machinery and intelligence. *Mind, 59*(236), 433–460.

Turing, A. (1951). Intelligent machinery: A heretical theory. In S. B. Cooper & J. van Leeuwen (Eds.) *Alan Turing: His work and impact* (pp. 664–666). Waltham, MA: Elsevier.

Usher, J., & Ulric, N. (1993). Childhood amnesia and the beginnings of memory for four early life events. *Journal of Experimental Psychology: General, 122*(2), 155–165.

Zeman, A., Dewar, M., & Della Sala, S. (2015). Lives without imagery—Congenital aphantasia. *Cortex, 73,* 378–380.

Notes

1. *Star Trek: The Next Generation* episode 2–9, "Measure of a Man" (February 13, 1989).
2. Turing (1951).
3. Sternbach & Okuda (1991).
4. *Star Trek* episode 2–24, "The Ultimate Computer" (March 8, 1968).
5. *Star Trek: The Next Generation* episode 1–1, "Encounter at Farpoint," part 1 (September 28, 1987).
6. Hidi & Baird (1986).
7. Roddenberry (1964).
8. Anderson (1984).
9. Schank (1979).
10. *Star Trek* episode 3–17, "That Which Survives" (January 24, 1969).
11. *Star Trek* episode 1–21, "The Return of the Archons" (February 9, 1967).
12. *Star Trek* episodes 1–21, "The Return of the Archons" (February 9, 1967); 2–3, "The Changeling" (September 29, 1967); 2–8, "I, Mudd" (November 3, 1967); 2–24, "The Ultimate Computer" (March 8, 1968) . . . Oh, this is getting cruel; I'll stop.
13. Sternbach & Okuda (1991).
14. Miron-Spektor et al. (2011).
15. Doyle (1979).

16. Turing (1948).
17. Turing (1936).
18. Turing (1950).
19. *Star Trek: The Next Generation* episode 2–9, "Measure of a Man" (February 13, 1989).
20. Marks (1973).
21. Zeman et al. (2015).
22. *Star Trek: The Next Generation* episode 3–6, "Booby Trap" (October 30, 1989).
23. Usher & Ulric (1993).
24. Karpathy (2015).
25. Allen et al. (2001).
26. Tsujii & Watanabe (2009).
27. Newell et al. (1959).
28. Lavalle (2006).
29. Cowan (2001).
30. Chase & Simon (1973).
31. *Star Trek: The Next Generation* episode 3–6, "Booby Trap" (October 30, 1989).
32. Kahneman (2011).
33. Isen et al. (1987).
34. Shiota & Kalat (2011).
35. *Star Trek: The Next Generation* episode 1–1, "Encounter at Farpoint," part 1 (September 28, 1987).
36. Damasio (1994).
37. Damasio (1994).
38. Simon (1983).
39. Ortony et al. (1990).
40. Francis et al. (2009).
41. Levin (1990).
42. Chalmers (1996).
43. *Star Trek: Deep Space Nine* episode 3–13, "Life Support" (January 30, 1995).
44. *Star Trek* episode 1–7, "What Are Little Girls Made of?" (October 20, 1986).
45. Picard (1997).
46. *Star Trek: Voyager* episode 7–20, "Author, Author" (April 18, 2001).
47. Dorrier (2015).
48. *Star Trek* episode 3–17, "That Which Survives" (January 24, 1969).
49. Birnbaum & Diecidue (2015); Joseph-Williams et al. (2011); Jurásová & Špajdel (2011).
50. Roddenberry (1964).
51. *Star Trek: The Next Generation* episode 2–9, "Measure of a Man" (February 13, 1989).
52. Caprara & Cervone (2000).
53. *Star Trek: Voyager* episode 1–1, "Caretaker," part 1 (January 16, 1995).
54. *Star Trek: Voyager* episode 4–14, "Message in a Bottle" (January 21, 1998).
55. *Star Trek: Voyager* episode 7–23, "Renaissance Man" (May 16, 2001).

When we treat people as representations of the groups that include them, whether that means seeing them as something good or something bad, we can fail to recognize unique human beings. We need to break down stereotypes and build up role models despite our missteps along the way. One actor from the original Trek helps us consider the meaning and enduring impact of both, as well as how many steps we are going to have to take.

•20•

Chatting with Chekov on Stereotypes and Role Models: Two Sides of the Same Coin?

TRAVIS LANGLEY
AND JENNA BUSCH

Our concepts of stereotypes and role models can be opposite sides of the same coin: negative and positive perceptions or beliefs about certain kinds of individuals. A *role model* is a person, of course, someone others admire and perhaps try to emulate, whereas a *stereotype* is an assumption about someone's characteristics that is based on the belief that the person's group members share common traits. Our ideas about role models, however, psychologically function a lot like stereotypes because they can be overgeneralized, incorrect, and difficult to change.[1] Each is idealized in its own way, whether that means an ideal representation of what we want to emulate, adulate, or derogate. The real human beings who are perceived as both role models and stereotypes can suffer backlash from others for being complicated persons whose lives do not match expectations.[2]

These ideas are interrelated, such as when a figure who is in a position to be a role model (in the case of a fictional character) is depicted in stereotypical manner. When *Star Trek*'s Scot outdrinks anyone else,[3] its Japanese character must know martial arts,[4] or the first woman to try to become a starship captain (Janice Lester, best known for swapping bodies with Kirk in the original series' final episode) turns hysterical over her failure,[5] the stereotype could impede the power of a potential role model.[6] Star Trek may have challenged stereotypes, but did it also perpetuate some?

Navigating

Star Trek in all its incarnations addresses problems of prejudice and discrimination against anyone on the basis of race, gender, nationality, or other demographic factors beyond an individual's control.[7] Attitudes (*prejudice*) and actions (*discrimination*) biased toward groups and their individual members may both arise from and strengthen biased beliefs (*stereotypes*).[8] These beliefs develop for many reasons. For one thing, using a *heuristic* (mental shortcut) such as dividing people into categories simplifies decision making in a complex world, allowing for quicker reactions even through doing so runs the risk of reducing accuracy—for example, the *representative heuristic*, which consists of making judgments about people, places, things, and events by assuming that they are representative of related people, places, things, and events. Heuristics let us navigate through analyses by taking shortcuts, reaching the end of the journey faster but without necessarily ending up in the right place. Adding a Scottish, Japanese, or Russian character to a story can prompt expectations that are based on the character's culture and allow for oversimplified categorization that will reduce initial confusion for viewers or readers. A series can even create such expectations by establishing stereotypes for fictional groups, making it easier for the audience and the storytellers themselves by introducing a character who is at first seen as the Klingon character (such as Worf in *Star Trek: The Next Generation*), although the character can still grow in complexity over time without overloading the audience's capability for comprehension and retention.

Perhaps the earliest character added to an existing Star Trek series in order to represent previously unrepresented groups was Pavel Chekov. Actor Walter Koenig joined the cast of the original *Star Trek* in its second season,[9] when Ensign Chekov became the *Enterprise*'s young navigator in order to expand the characters' international representation and give the series "youthful attitudes and perspectives."[10] As the Cold War between the United States and Soviet Union carried on in our world, *Star Trek* showed a young Russian take his place as in a trusted position as part of Kirk's bridge crew. After the character grew in popularity and in-story importance, Gene Roddenberry grew concerned that having Chekov repeatedly boast about Russia "runs rather counter to the broad international philosophy built into *Star Trek*."[11] Even as he directed his writers to cut back on Chekov's "Russia did it first" comments, though, Roddenberry continued to categorize and characterize Chekov in terms of his youth. The active effort to avoid stereotyping may have led to more stereotyping in an ironic backfire known as *stereotype rebound* when he decided that Chekov should make his pro-Russia remarks less seriously.[12] Even though fiction can help the audience actively try to contemplate other people's perspectives, perspective taking can actually increase stereotyping if someone uses a stereotype as the foundation for imaging another person's point of view.[13]

We asked Koenig about *Star Trek* as it related to stereotypes and role models.[14]

Breaking Stereotypes

Social scientists disagree on how stereotyped thinking can change.[15] Many agree on the importance on challenging stereotypes but provide conflicting evidence regarding how best to do so. Learning about others through fiction can improve attitudes toward *out-groups* (whichever groups the person is not in), depending on how the fiction depicts the groups and prejudice itself.[16]

> **Busch:** *Star Trek* broke down a lot of stereotypes when it came out. Can you talk about how groundbreaking it was and still is?
>
> **Koenig:** Well, I think at this point it's fairly self-evident. There has been so much discussion about the fact that we had an African-American woman who had a position of authority and rank. The fact that there was an actual intimate moment between a Caucasian and an African-American where they kissed.[17] So many people have kissed Captain Kirk, it's not that extraordinary.

People tend to evaluate others more harshly for behavior that contradicts stereotypes and violates the associated *social norms* (unofficial rules of behavior considered acceptable in a group) expected of them.[18] By making the series regulars likable, though, *Star Trek* lessened that effect and prepared viewers to reexamine their prejudices about the groups to which the characters belonged. As our familiarity with out-group members becomes more personal and prolonged, we experience less anxiety over intergroup interactions.[19] If the interracial kiss between Kirk and Uhura had taken place early in the series' run instead of during its final season, viewers might have responded more negatively to the event. We more readily make judgments that favor our friends, and when our friends are members of our out-groups, we express greater support for and less prejudice toward those groups.[20] That kiss made a statement about racial issues by making race a nonissue to the characters.

While other television programs shied away from certain social and political issues of the time, *Star Trek* would address many of those issues, often by presenting obvious extraterrestrial analogues. To show the destructive and sometimes ridiculous nature of racial conflict and ethnic wars, one episode depicted two characters—both of them black on one side of the body and white on the other—consumed by race-based animosity when neither the main characters nor many viewers could spot the defining racial quality: One was black on the right side; the other, on the left.[21] Many episodes showed *mirror-image perceptions*,[22] reciprocal views that opposing groups can hold toward one another, such as when Klingons and Kirk's crew members each consider the other side to be untrustworthy.[23] Because the original series Klingons often represented the Soviet Union,[24] *Star Trek* could help viewers examine their own related perceptions and preconceptions without necessarily being tainted by their existing views about the Soviets.

> **Koenig:** Gene Roddenberry—I certainly don't know if he's a genius, but his concept was so innovative and so new and so fresh and groundbreaking that it should always be remembered that he was able to do that. He was able to bring together a multinational, multiracial cast and show them in an environment in which they all got along. Remember, *Star Trek* was a creature of the sixties, where we had the Iron Curtain, we had Vietnam. It was a very turbulent time. We had racial problems in this country, and we presented a world where people could get along. Where there is a future worth striving for.

Building Role Models

Even positive *exemplars* (role models worth emulating) can fail to inspire people unless a variety of other factors come together to inspire emulation. *Role aspirants* (those aspiring to be like their role models[25]) like their heroes to be confident yet humble, ambitious yet generous, and passionate with clear values and great communication skills, among other things.[26] Even though Chekov showed many of these qualities, he might have been the least confident of the regular series characters at the time.

> **Koenig:** You see, my feeling is, I did not contribute anything significant to the culture as Chekov. We don't have any Russian spies who are running around who were inspired by the Russian character aboard *Star Trek.* Whereas, time and again, DeForest Kelley and Jimmy Doohan tell me about people who became doctors and engineers because of their characters. There is one thing I can contribute in conjunction with the other actors on the show: We showed a time where we could exist in harmony.

Even if Chekov did not inspire Russian spies as far as we know, he played an important part in stories that inspired viewers and made people think. Observing others in real life can lead to emulation of their behavior[27] and make observers feel hope for themselves and others, but role model stories also motivate people, help their attitudes change, and make them feel enduring hopefulness.[28] According to *affective disposition theory*, enjoyment of media content depends on the person's feelings toward the characters and their outcomes,[29] and so giving the audience characters to care about and stories to engage them makes viewers happier. Things we enjoy inspire us more. The passion that fans felt for *Star Trek* therefore made its characters more powerful as role models and its stories more influential in those Trekkies' lives.

Koenig: The lovely thing that happens when people come up to me and talk to me is how they bonded with their parents or parent, watching *Star Trek*. And that's what we were about. It wasn't the most obvious influence we had, but it was true. People continually talk to me and tell me that's when they became close with their parents, watching *Star Trek*. And I feel, well, I was part of that cast. I can take a little credit for that. . . . I did some episodes and a couple of movies where we had something to say of a sociopolitical nature, and I think we can be commended for that. Gene Roddenberry certainly should have a big pat on the back for that.

Going Forward

Koenig: We've got to have a better society. We've got to have a greater humanity as a people. We've got to get to a point where we don't have wars, where we don't have another Vietnam.

Star Trek challenges stereotypes, albeit imperfectly at times, by depicting (1) actions and attitudes inconsistent with stereotypes the viewers might hold, (2) characters who regularly question stereotypes, and (3) stories that show the potentially devastating consequences of stereotypes, prejudice, and discrimination. Simply pointing out what people should not do is far less effective if we do not also point out what people should do. When stories present positive role models who act altruistically, intelligently, and even heroically, they help us learn to be better.

Koenig: I try to think that even if you take a million steps backward over the course of all of humanity's time on earth, that we take at least a million-and-one steps forward, that we continue to evolve.

References

Bettencourt, B. A., Dill, K. E., Greathouse, S. A., Charlton, K., & Mulholland, A. (1997). Evaluations of ingroup and outgroup members. *Journal of Experimental Social Psychology, 33*(3), 244–275.

Byrd, M. L. (1998). *Multicultural communication and popular culture: Racial and ethnic images in Star Trek.* New York, NY: McGraw-Hill.

Cameron, L., & Rutland, A. (2006). Extended contact through story reading in school: Reducing children's prejudice toward the disabled. *Journal of Social Issues, 62*(3), 469–488.

Charlston, R. (2014, August 29*). Star Trek's long history of racism and sexism, and the new Star Trek series planned for 2015.* Diversity Chronicle: https://diversitychronicle.wordpress.com/2014/08/29/star-treks-long-history-of-racism-and-sexism-and-the-new-star-trek-series-planned-for-2015/.

Clore, G. L., Bray, R. M., Itkin, S. M., & Murphy, P. (1978). Interracial attitudes and behavior at a summer camp. *Journal of Personality & Social Psychology, 36*(2), 107–116.

Drury, B. J., Siy, J. O., & Cheryan, S. (2011). When do female role models benefit women? The importance of differentiating recruitment from retention in STEM. *Psychological Inquiry, 22*(4), 265–269.

Enguidanos, S., Kogan, A. C., Lorenz, K., & Taylor, G. (2011). Use of role model stories to overcome barriers to hospice among African Americans. *Journal of Palliative Medicine, 14*(2), 161–168.Fiske, S. T. (1989). *Interdependence and stereotyping: From the laboratory to the Supreme Court (and back).* Invited address presented at the annual meeting of the American Psychological Association, New Orleans, LA.

Franzoi, S. L. (2012). *Social psychology.* Redding, CA: BVT.

Geraghty, L. (2007). *Living with Star Trek: American culture and the Star Trek universe.* London, UK: Tauris.

Hamberger, J., & Hewstone, M. (1997). Inter-ethnic contact as a predictor of blatant and subtle prejudice: Tests of a model in four West European nations. *British Journal of Social Psychology, 36*(2), 173–190.

Herek, G. M. (1987). Interpersonal contact and heterosexuals' attitudes toward gay men: Results from a national survey. *Journal of Sex Research, 30*(3), 239–244.

Howell, P. (2013, May 10). *Star Trek's John Cho a boldly going actor worth shouting about.* The Star: http://www.thestar.com/entertainment/movies/2013/05/10/star_treks_john_cho_a_boldly_going_actor_worth_shouting_about_howell.html.

Kennedy, S., & Hill, S. (2009). Could stereotype rebound affect aid advertising campaigns? *International Journal of Nonprofit & Voluntary Sector Marketing, 14*(2), 111–123.

Lefebvre, V. A. (2004). On sharing a pie: Modeling costly prosocial behavior. *Behavioral & Brain Sciences, 27*(4), 565–566.

Macrae, C. N., Bodenhausen, G. V., Milne, A. B., & Jetten, J. (1994). Out of mind but back in sight: Stereotypes on the rebound. *Journal of Personality & Social Psychology, 67*(5), 808–817.

Marx, D. M., & Ko, S. J. (2012). Superstars "like" me: The effect of role model similarity on performance under threat. *European Journal of Social Psychology, 42*(7), 807–812.

Marx, D. M., Monroe, A. H., Cole, C. E., & Gilbert, P. N. (2013). No doubt about it: When doubtful role models undermine men's and women's math performance under threat. *Journal of Social Psychology, 153*(5), 542–559.

Morgenroth, T., Ryan, M. K., & Peters, K. (2015). The motivational theory of role modeling: How role models influence role aspirants' goals. *Review of General Psychology, 19*(4), 465–483.

Moss, J. F., & Oden, S. (1983). Children's story comprehension and social learning. *Reading Teacher, 36*(8), 784–789.

Oliver, M. B., Hartmann, T., & Woolley, J. K. (2012). Elevation in response to entertainment portrayals of moral value. *Human Communications Research, 38*(3), 128–150.

Pettigrew, T. F. (1998). Intergroup contact theory. *Annual Review of Psychology, 23*, 173–185.

Phelan, J. E., & Rudman, L. A. (2010). Reactions to ethnic deviance: The role of backlash in racial stereotype maintenance. *Journal of Personality & Social Psychology, 99*(2), 265–281.

Platsidou, M., & Metalidou, P. (2003). Evaluation of heroic behavior and role-model preferences by individuals aged 10 to 19 years. *Psychology: The Journal of the Hellenic Psychology Society, 10*(4), 556–574.

Prestin, A. (2013). The pursuit of hopefulness: Operationalizing hope in entertainment media narratives. *Media Psychology, 16*(3), 318–346.

Price-Mitchell, M. (2011, July 13). *What is a role model? Five qualities that matter to teens.* Roots of Action: http://www.rootsofaction.com/what-is-a-role-model-five-qualities-that-matter-for-role-models/.

Raney, A. A., & Bryant, J. (2002). Moral judgment in crime drama: An integrated theory of enjoyment. *Journal of Communication, 52*(2), 402–415.

Roddenberry, G. (1968, April 18). *Document: 040 "Friday's Child"/recurring character writing notes.* http://missionlogpodcast.com/discovereddocuments/040/.

Rudman, L. A., & Fairchild, K. (2004). Reactions to counterstereotypic behavior: The role of backlash in cultural stereotype maintenance. *Journal of Personality & Social Psychology, 87*(2), 157–176.

Rudman, L. A., & Glick, P. (2001). Prescriptive gender stereotypes and backlash toward agentic women. *Journal of Social Issues, 57*(4), 743–762.

SaFireonPhire (2015, November 2). *Walter Koenig @ Comikaze.* https://www.youtube.com/watch?v=5bE_G4SiBxg.

Skorinko, J. L., & Sinclair, S. A. (2013). Perspective taking can increase stereotyping: The role of apparent stereotype confirmation. *Journal of Experimental Social Psychology, 49*(1), 10–18.

Stangor, C., Sullivan, L. A., & Ford, T. E. (1991). Affective and cognitive determinants of prejudice. *Social Cognition, 9*(4), 359–380.

Tobin, R. J., & Eagles, M. (1992). U.S. and Canadian attitudes toward international relations: A cross-national test of the double-standard hypothesis. *Basic & Applied Social Psychology, 13*(4), 447–459.

Trek Movie (2012, January 16). *Top 10 Star Trek episodes dealing with tolerance.* Trek Movie: http://trekmovie.com/2012/01/16/top-10-star-trek-episodes-dealing-with-tolerance/.

Ury, I. (2015, September 29). *The 5 most bafflingly racist beloved fictional universes.* Cracked: http://www.cracked.com/article_22894_5-secret-racist-messages-buried-in-your-favorite-pop-culture.html.

Vezzali, L., Stathi, S., Giovannini, D., Capozza, D., & Trifiletti, E. (2015). The greatest magic of Harry Potter: Reducing prejudice. *Journal of Applied Social Psychology, 45*(2), 105–121.

Westmore, M., Sims, A., Look, B. M., & Byrnes, W. J. (2000). *Star Trek: Aliens and artifacts.* New York, NY: Pocket.

White, R. (1984). *Fearful warriors: A psychological profile of U.S.-Soviet relations.* New York, NY: Free Press.

Williamson, R. A., Donohue, M. R., & Tully, E. C. (2013). Learning how to help others: Two-year-olds' social learning of a prosocial act. *Journal of Experimental Child Psychology, 114*(4), 543–550.

Zillmann, D. (1980). Anatomy of suspense. In P. H. Tannenbaum (Ed.), *The entertainment functions of television* (pp. 133–163). Hillsdale, NJ: Erlbaum.

Zwilling, M. (2010, October 14). *The seven traits of a role model.* Cayenne Consulting: https://www.caycon.com/blog/2010/10/seven-actions-of-a-true-role-model-entrepreneur/.

Notes

1. Drury et al. (2011); Marx & Ko (2012); Marx et al. (2013).
2. Phelan & Rudman (2010); Rudman & Fairchild (2004); Rudman & Glick (2001).
3. *Star Trek* episode 2–22, "By Any Other Name" (February 23, 1968).
4. Howell (2013).
5. *Star Trek* episode 3-24, "Turnabout Intruder" (June 3, 1969).
6. Charlston (2014); Ury (2015).
7. Byrd (1998); Geraghty (2007); Trek Movie (2012).
8. Stangor et al. (1991).
9. Beginning in episode 2–1, "Amok Time" (September 15, 1967).
10. Roddenberry (1968), p. 4.
11. Roddenberry (1968), p. 4.
12. Kennedy & Hill (2009); Macrae et al. (1994).
13. Skorinko & Sinclair (2013).
14. SaFireonPhire (2015).
15. Franzoi (2012).
16. Cameron & Rutland (2006); Vezzali et al. (2015).
17. *Star Trek* episode 3–10, "Plato's Stepchildren" (November 22, 1968).
18. Bettencourt et al. (1997); Fiske (1989).
19. Clore et al. (1978); Schofield (1986).
20. Hamberger & Hewstone (1997); Herek (1993); Pettigrew (1998).
21. *Star Trek* episode 3–15, "Let That Be Your Last Battlefield" (January 1, 1969).
22. Tobin & Eagles (1992); White (1984).
23. e.g., *Star Trek* episode 3–11, "Day of the Dove" (November 1, 1968).
24. Westmore et al. (2000).
25. Morgenroth et al. (2015).
26. Price-Mitchell (2011); Zwilling (2010).
27. Lefebvre (2004); Platsidou & Metalidou (2003); Williamson et al. (2013).
28. Enguidanos et al. (2011); Moss & Oden (1983); Oliver et al. (2012); Prestin (2013).
29. Raney & Bryant (2002); Zillmann (1980).

Log File V

Star Trek: Enterprise and the Need for Achievement

TRAVIS LANGLEY

Yearning to accomplish things for the sheer sake of accomplishment can be difficult to explain to people who lack that desire, people to whom it sounds impractical. Asked why he wanted to climb Mount Everest, explorer George Mallory answered, "Because it's there."[1] Mallory would soon die in the attempt, having considered the endeavor worth that risk.[2] "Well, space is there," U.S. President John F. Kennedy added decades later, "and the moon and the planets are there, and new hopes for knowledge and peace are there. And, therefore, as we set sail, we ask God's blessing on the most hazardous and dangerous and greatest adventure on which man has ever embarked."[3] Climbing to the stars, too, carried great risk and incurred losses. For people high in the personality factor known as *need for achievement*, tasks should be difficult, paths should be rocky, and challenges should be many to make their accomplishments all the greater. They choose the road less traveled.[4]

After the original *Star Trek*, subsequent Trek series expanded their charted space as Starfleet's explorers would reach the galaxy's core[5] and the quadrants far across the galaxy.[6] Much as our world once mapped and widely populated began feeling smaller, so, too, would the vastness of this fictional space shrink. When the Wild West gets tamed, where do the cowboys go?

Star Trek: Enterprise (2001–2005, 4 seasons, 98 episodes). Created by R. Berman, B. Braga. Paramount. Aired on UPN. Although originally titled *Enterprise* throughout its first two seasons, the series then became *Star Trek: Enterprise* for the remainder of its run.

Star Trek took its cowboys back in time, to a period earlier than that depicted in the original series. In the series originally titled *Enterprise*, Captain Jonathan Archer leads his crew away from Earth at warp 5 to begin the voyage into a galaxy with few alien races known to humans, no Federation to unite worlds, and one mystery after another.

One of the series' earliest examples of an appeal to an individual's need for achievement occurs in the pilot episode,[7] when linguist Hoshi Sato initially declines to rush into space on this *Enterprise*'s first mission, until Archer presents her with a challenge that could meet both of the two main achievement goals.[8] *Mastery goals* involve gaining competence, skill, talent, and personal growth through effort and persistence. Archer's recording of Klingon speech presents Hoshi with an unfamiliar language she immediately wants to master. *Performance goals* present opportunities to display skills and outperform others. "Think of it," Archer tells Hoshi. "You'd be the first human to talk to these people. Do you really want someone else to do it?"

Characters in every Star Trek series accomplish many great achievements, but in story chronology, Archer and his crew get to beat them all to it. Archer becomes known as "the greatest explorer of the twenty-second century" after making his achievements first and with the fewest resources.[9] No matter who later outperforms by going faster or farther, explorers throughout the ages have made marks that no one else could ever take away by being the ones to go first.

"We choose to go to the moon in this decade and do the other things, not because they are easy, but because they are hard."

—U. S. President John F. Kennedy[10]

References

Ames, R., & Archer, J. (1988). Achievement goals in the classroom: Student learning strategies and motivational processes. *Journal of Educational Psychology, 80*(3), 260–267.

Davis, W. (2011). *Into the silence: The Great War, Mallory, and the conquest of Everest.* London, UK: Bodley Head.

Dweck, C. S. (1990). Motivation. In R. Glaser & A. Lesgold (Eds.), *Foundations for a cognitive psychology in education.* Hillsdale, NJ: Erlbaum.

Kennedy, J. F. (1962, September 12). Speech at Rice University. Transcript at NASA: http://er.jsc.nasa.gov/seh/ricetalk.htm.

McClelland, D. C., Atkinson, J. W., Clark, R. A., & Lowell, E. L. (1953). *The achievement motive.* New York, NY: Appleton-Century-Crofts.

New York Times (1923, March 18). Climbing Mount Everest is work for Supermen. *New York Times*, p. X–11. http://graphics8.nytimes.com/packages/pdf/arts/mallory1923.pdf.

Rawsthorne, L. J., & Elliot, A. J. (1999). Achievement goals and intrinsic motivation: A meta-analytic review. *Personality & Social Psychology Review, 3*(4), 326–344.

Slade, L. A., & Rush, M. C. (1991). Achievement motivation and the dynamics of task difficulty choices. *Journal of Personality & Social Psychology, 60*(1), 165–172.

Notes

1. *New York Times* (1923).
2. Davis (2011).
3. Kennedy (1962).
4. McClelland et al. (1953); Slade & Rush (1991).
5. *Star Trek V: The Final Frontier* (1989 motion picture).
6. Delta Quadrant throughout *Star Trek: Deep Space Nine* and Gamma Quadrant in *Star Trek: Voyager.*
7. *Enterprise* episode 1–1, "Broken Bow," part 1 (September 26, 2001).
8. Ames & Archer (1988); Dweck (1990); Rawsthorne & Elliot (1999).
9. *Star Trek: Enterprise* episode 4–19, "In a Mirror, Darkly," part 2 (April 29, 2005).
10. Kennedy (1962).

FINAL WORD

Engage!

Travis Langley

"Engage!"

—Captain Jean-Luc Picard[1]

"Imagination is not something apart and hermetic, not a way of leaving reality behind; it is a way of engaging reality."

—author Irving Howe[2]

Star Trek engages us.

From birth, we require stimulation. Newborns have all the basic physical senses, and they will expand those senses as acuity improves and external stimuli engage them. Within their first two days, infants start to show *novelty preference*, seeking out new sights, sounds, and other sensations over those they already know,[3] at least until they develop favorites. Babies quickly begin to stare at faces, respond to sounds, and make noises for the sheer experience.[4] They want to be cognitively and emotionally engaged. They need to be. An enriching environment full of variety and wonders does the brain good,[5] and we wonder about it all. We want more.

Increasing mobility and exploration of the child's surroundings stretch each one's *cognitive map*, a mental representation of the environment,[6] out in every dimension. From this, the child develops a growing concept of his or her place in a vast and infinite universe. The enormity of it all can be both daunting and appealing. The yearning that some feel to trek to the stars comes out of those earliest impulses for stimulation and exploration. It is not simply to map the things out there but to find life, whether that means to discover extraterrestrial life or to build a life out there for ourselves. It may be telling that the Star Trek mission statement refers to "strange new worlds" rather than planets because it's really not about charting the locations of gases and rocks; it's about life and civilization. Star Trek is about interacting with others while also getting to know ourselves as individuals.[7]

Star Trek makes us think and it makes us feel.[8] Engaging us both emotionally and cognitively, its stories and characters repeatedly analyze the importance of all mental processes. That includes the relationship between emotion and cognition. Even when feeling and logic conflict, we need ways to use them together both to pose questions and to find answers that are practical, ethical, and morally right for all.[9] We seek human solutions.

Our adventure continues. Given the virtually infinite variables in every life and the countless places for us to explore from levels subatomic to multidimensional and everything seen or unseen in between, our possibilities are endless. Our stories carry on. As Star Trek continually illustrates, we can engage one another and come together through our similarities while also celebrating our differences—both united and unique. We take life's trek together even though no two people's treks are the same.

"Spock, you want to know something? Everybody's human."

—James Kirk[10]

> *"You are all the books you read, the films you watch, the people you meet, the dreams you have, the conversations you engage in. You are what you take from these."*
>
> —writer Jac Vanek[11]

References

Asamura, A. (1996). The transformation of children's cognitive maps: The development of map-like and sequential recognition of space. *Japanese Journal of Educational Psychology, 44*(2), 204–213.

Bloch, K. (2009). Cognition and Star Trek: Learning and legal education. *John Marshall Law Review, 42*(4), 959.

Cavanaugh, T. W. (1998). *Effect of using repurposed science rich feature films with varying levels of student activity in middle grades science instruction* (doctoral dissertation). Tampa, FL: University of South Florida.

Colombo, J. (2002). Infant attention grows up: The emergence of a developmental cognitive neuroscience perspective. *Current Directions in Psychological Science, 11*(6), 196–200.

Fields, R. D. (2005). Making memories stick. *Scientific American, 292*(2), 75–81.

Fisher-Thompson, D. (2014). Exploring the emergence of side biases and familiarity: Novelty preferences from the real-time dynamics of infant looking. *Infancy, 19*(3), 227–261.

Haan, N., Weiss, R., & Johnson, V. (1982). The role of logic in moral reasoning and development. *Developmental Psychology, 18*(2), 245–256.

Howe, I. (1994). *A critic's notebook.* New York, NY: Harcourt Brace.

Marshall, J. (2011). Infant neurosensory development: Considerations for infant child care. *Early Childhood Education Journal, 39*(3), 175–181.

Papalia, D. E., & Martorell, G. (2015). *Experience human development.* New York, NY: McGraw-Hill.

Pfeiffer, B. E., & Foster, D. J. (2015). Discovering the brain's cognitive map. *JAMA Neurology, 72*(3), 257–258.

Pizarro, D. (2000). Nothing more than feelings? The role of emotions in moral judgment. *Journal for the Theory of Social Behaviour, 30*(4), 355-375.

Rashkin, E. (2011). Data learns to dance: *Star Trek* and the quest to be human. *American Imago, 68*(2), 321–346.

Stepp-Gilbert, E. (1988). Sensory integration: A reason for infant enrichment. *Issues in Comprehensive Pediatric Nursing, 11*(5–6), 319–331.

Swain, I., Zelazno, P. R., & Clifton, R. K. (1993). Newborn infants' memory for speech sounds retained over 24 hours. *Developmental Psychology, 29*(2), 312–323.

Tolman, E. C. (1948). Cognitive maps in rats and men. *Psychological Review, 55*(4), 189–208.

Turati, C., Simion, F., Milani, I., & Umilta, C. (2002). Newborns' preference for faces: What is crucial? *Developmental Psychology, 38*(6), 875–882.

Vanek, J. (2014, August 21). *You become what you allow.* Positive Outlooks: https://positiveoutlooksblog.com/2014/08/21/you-become-what-you-allow/.

Notes

1. *Star Trek: The Next Generation* episode 1–1, "Encounter at Farpoint" part 1 (September 28, 1987), and many times thereafter.
2. Howe (1994), p. 41.
3. Colombo (2002); Fisher-Thompson (2014); Swain et al. (1993); Turati et al. (2002).
4. Papalia & Martorell (2015).
5. Fields (2005); Marshall (2011); Stepp-Gilbert (1988).
6. Asamura (1996); Pfeiffer & Foster (2015); Tolman (1948).
7. Rashkin (2011).
8. Bloch (2009); Cavanaugh (1998).
9. Haan et al. (1982); Pizarro (2000).
10. *Star Trek VI: The Undiscovered Country* (1991 motion picture).
11. Vanek (2014).

FILM CREDITS

Rather than list Star Trek film credits repeatedly throughout this book, we post them all in one place here. Television series episodes' information appear respectively in the Log File features.

Production Company/Distributor: Paramount.

The Original Series Films

Star Trek: The Motion Picture (1979). **Story:** A. D. Foster. **Screenplay:** H. Livingston. **Director:** R. Wise. **Producer:** G. Roddenberry.

Star Trek II: The Wrath of Khan, originally titled *Star Trek: The Wrath of Khan* on screen (1982). **Screenplay:** H. Bennett, J. B. Sowards, N. Meyer. **Director:** N. Meyer. **Producer:** G. Roddenberry.

Star Trek III: The Search for Spock (1984). **Screenplay:** H. Bennett. **Director:** L. Nimoy. **Producer:** H. Bennett.

Star Trek IV: The Voyage Home (1986). **Story:** H. Bennett, L. Nimoy. **Screenplay:** S. Meerson, P. Krikes, N. Meyer. **Director:** L. Nimoy. **Producer:** H. Bennett.

Star Trek V: The Final Frontier (1989). **Story:** W. Shatner, H. Bennett, D. Loughery. **Screenplay:** D. Loughery. **Director:** W. Shatner. **Producer:** H. Bennett.

Star Trek VI: The Undiscovered Country (1991). **Screenplay:** N. Meyer. **Director:** N. Meyer. **Producers:** R. Winter, S. Jaffe.

The Next Generation Films

Star Trek: Generations (1994). **Screenplay:** R. D. Moore, B. Braga. **Director:** D. Carson. **Producer:** R. Berman.

Star Trek: First Contact (1996). **Screenplay:** B. Braga, R. D. Moore. **Director:** J. Frakes. **Producers:** R. Berman, M. Hornstein, P. Lauritson.

Star Trek: Insurrection (1998). **Story:** R. Berman, M. Piller. **Screenplay:** M. Piller. **Director:** J. Frakes. **Producer:** R. Berman.

Star Trek: Nemesis (2002). **Story:** J. Logan, R. Berman, B. Spiner. **Screenplay:** J. Logan. **Director:** S. Baird. **Producer:** R. Berman.

The New Timeline

Star Trek (2009). **Screenplay:** R. Orci, A. Kurtzman. **Director:** J. J. Abrams. **Producers:** J. J. Abrams, D. Lindelof.

Star Trek into Darkness (2013). **Screenplay:** R. Orci, A. Kurtzman, D. Lindelof. **Director:** J. J. Abrams. **Producers:** J. J. Abrams, B. Burk, D. Lindelof, A. Kurtzman, R. Orci.

Star Trek Beyond (2016). **Screenplay:** D. Jung, S. Pegg. **Director:** J. Lin. **Producers:** J. J. Abrams, B. Burk, R. Orci.

ABOUT THE EDITOR

Travis Langley, PhD, professor of psychology at Henderson State University, is the Popular Culture Psychology series editor. He is volume editor and lead writer for *The Walking Dead: Psych of the Living Dead*; *Star Wars Psychology: Dark Side of the Mind*; *Game of Thrones Psychology: The Mind is Dark and Full of Terrors*; *Doctor Who Psychology: A Madman with a Box*; *Wonder Woman Psychology: Lassoing the Truth* (co-edited with Mara Wood); *Supernatural Psychology: Roads Less Traveled*; and *Captain America vs. Iron Man: Freedom, Security, Psychology*. He authored the acclaimed book *Batman and Psychology: A Dark and Stormy Knight*. Documentaries such as *Legends of the Knight* and *Necessary Evil: Super-Villains of DC Comics* feature him as an expert and educator. *Psychology Today* carries his blog, "Beyond Heroes and Villains."

As @Superherologist, he is one of the ten most popular psychologists on Twitter. Travis's favorite Trek series is whichever he saw most recently, his favorite Trek film is still *Wrath of Khan*, and he prefers to believe that the *Star Trek into Darkness* villain lied about being Khan.

ABOUT THE CONTRIBUTORS

Scott Allison, PhD, has authored numerous books, including *Heroes and Heroic Leadership*. He is a professor of psychology at the University of Richmond, where he has published extensively on heroism and leadership. His books include *Reel Heroes*, *Conceptions of Leadership*, *Frontiers in Spiritual Leadership*, and the *Handbook of Heroism and Heroic Leadership*.

Although **James Beggan** is currently a professor of sociology at the University of Louisville, he earned his PhD in psychology from the University of California, Santa Barbara. He regularly teaches courses in human sexuality, the self-concept in society, and statistics. He has published a number of articles on popular culture, specifically with regard to the role of *Playboy* magazine in defining the nature of both masculine and feminine identity. He enjoys swing dancing as a hobby and has published a qualitative analysis of the nature of sexism inherent in social dancing.

John C. Blanchar, PhD, is a visiting assistant professor of psychology at Swarthmore College. He received his doctorate from the University of Arkansas. His research investigates the psychological bases of political ideology, status quo preference and change, motivated reasoning, and prejudice and stereotyping.

Colt J. Blunt, PsyD, LP, has worked as a forensic examiner throughout his career and serves as a guest lecturer and trainer for a number of organizations and educational institutions. His academic interests include the intersection of psychology and law, including the study of criminal behavior. He contributed to *The Walking Dead Psychology: Psych of the Living Dead*, *Star Wars Psychology: Dark Side of the Mind*, and *Game of Thrones Psychology: The Mind is Dark and Full of Terrors.*

Jenna Busch is a writer, host, and founder of the Legion of Leia website. She co-hosted "Cocktails with Stan" with comic book legend Stan Lee. Jenna has spoken about popular culture and current events on ABC's *Nightline*, NPR, Al Jazeera America, and *Attack of the Show!* She has co-authored chapters and served as an editorial assistant on most of our Popular Culture Psychology books. Reach her on Twitter: @Jenna Busch.

Jim Davies, PhD, is a cognitive scientist at Carleton University in Ottawa, where he conducts research on computer modeling of human imagination. He authored the books Riveted: *The Science of Why Jokes Make Us Laugh* and *Movies Make Us Cry and Religion Makes Us Feel One with the Universe*, and has chapters in *Star Wars Psychology: Dark Side of the Mind* and *Doctor Who Psychology: A Madman with a Box.*

Christopher Day received his B.A. in Psychology from the University of North Carolina at Asheville. Having grown up on a steady diet of science fiction, fantasy, and '80s/'90s sitcoms, he prides himself as a creative consultant for the finer points of geek trivia. Chris is working on his clinical doctorate in Audiology at East Tennessee State University.

William Blake Erickson, PhD, is a researcher and lecturer at the University of Arkansas. His research interests include eyewitness memory and face recognition. He has published in journals such as *Applied Cognitive Psychology, Psychonomic Bulletin and Review, Psychology, Psychiatry, and Law,* and *Journal of Police and Criminal Psychology.*

Anthony Francis, PhD, is the author of the Skindancer series of urban fantasy novels for techno-geeks (*Frost Moon*; *Blood Rock*; *Liquid Fire*). He received his PhD from Georgia Tech with a certificate in Cognitive Science and has developed emotion models for robots in America and Japan. Anthony lives in San Jose with his wife and cats, and he promises that he is not secretly working to bring about the robot apocalypse.

Zeno Franco, PhD, is an assistant professor at the Medical College of Wisconsin, a former Department of Homeland Security Fellow, and a board member for the International Association for Information Systems for Crisis Response & Management. He has written extensively on heroism with his senior colleague, Dr. Philip Zimbardo.

Frank Gaskill, PhD, is a co-founder of Southeast Psych, one of the largest psychology private practices in the United States. He co-authored *Max Gamer: An Aspie Superhero* and *How We Built Our Dream Practice: Innovative Ideas for Building Yours.* Dr. Gaskill specializes in Asperger's, parenting, and how technology affects children, teens, and families. He lives with his wife, Liz, and his children Olivia and Maddox in Charlotte, NC. Follow him on Twitter (@drfgaskill).

Wind Goodfriend, PhD, is a professor of psychology and assistant dean of graduate studies at Buena Vista University. She earned her bachelor's degree at Buena Vista University, then earned her Master's and PhD in social psychology from Purdue University. Dr. Goodfriend has won the BVU's "Faculty of the Year" award several times and won the Wythe Award for Excellence in Teaching, and she is the Institute for the Prevention of Relationship Violence's principal investigator.

Chris Gore is a writer and comedian who turned his passion for geek culture into a diverse career. He created *Film Threat*, the influential magazine and web site that championed independent movies and was also the co-founder of *Sci-Fi Universe* magazine. His published works include the books *The 50 Greatest Movies Never Made* (St. Martin's Press), *The Complete DVD Book* (Michael Wiese Publications) and *The Ultimate Film Festival Survival Guide* (Random House). Chris has hosted television shows on FX, Starz, and IFC, as well as appearing on G4TV's *Attack of the Show!* where he covered movies through his popular DVDuesday segment. He co-wrote and produced the feature comedy *My Big Fat Independent Movie*. Chris counts his cameo as an alien dissident who nearly kills Captain Kirk in an episode of *Star Trek Continues* as his crowning achievement as a Trek fan.

J. Scott Jordan, PhD, has held fellowships at the University of Ulm in Germany, the Max Planck Institute for Psychological Research in Munich, and the Center for Interdisciplinary Research at the University of Bielefeld in Germany. He has published over 70 papers, co-edited nine books and journal special issues, and given more than 60 invited talks. His research focuses on the relationship between consciousness, action, self, and identity.

Alan "Sizzler" Kistler (@SizzlerKistler) is the *New York Times* best-selling author of *Doctor Who: A History*. A storytelling consultant and pop culture historian focusing on science fiction and superheroes, he is a contributor to *The Walking Dead Psychology* and *Doctor Who Psychology*, as well as to online sites such as Wired, Polygon, and Geek & Sundry. He appears as a character in *Star Trek* novels by David Alan Mack. Alan is the host and creator of the podcast *Crazy Sexy Geeks*.

Dana Klisanin, PhD, studies the impact of interactive technologies on the personal, collective, and mythic dimensions of humanity. She has investigated how the use of digital technology is changing how we think about altruism, heroism, and what we value. Dana is CEO of Evolutionary Guidance Media R&D, Inc., and executive board member of the World Future Studies Federation and c3: Center for Conscious Creativity.

Elizabeth Kus, PhD,is a staff psychologist working within the prison system. Utilizing her own passion for pop culture, she encourages clients to connect to their mental health issues by looking at them through the lens of fictional characters and stories. She can be reached at the website or through Twitter: @elizabeth_ann.

Chase Masterson played Leeta the brilliant and beautiful "Dabo girl" on the television series *Star Trek: Deep Space Nine* and stars in the Big Finish *Doctor Who* spinoff audio series Vienna. Fans named her "Favorite Science Fiction Actress on TV" in a *TV Guide* online poll. Chase has been an accomplished actor, producer, singer, dancer, Groundlings member, and Jeopardy answer. Together with Carrie Goldman and Matt Langdon, she co-founded the Pop Culture Anti-Bullying Coalition, which then became the Pop Culture Hero Coalition. The Coalition is the first 501c3 organization to use stories from TV, movies, and comics to promote real-life heroism over bullying.

Patrick O'Connor, PsyD, is the creator of Comicspedia, an online tool that assists therapists in bringing comic books into therapy. He teaches at The Chicago School of Professional Psychology. In his "Geek Culture in Therapy" course, students discover how geek culture plays a role in our understanding of ourselves and others and how geek culture artifacts are the vehicles through which we develop this understanding.

Craig Pohlman, PhD, is a neurodevelopmental psychologist who has helped thousands of struggling learners. He has written several books, including *How Can My Kid Succeed in School?* which helps parents and educators understand and support students with learning challenges. He is the CEO of Southeast Psych, a private practice and media company based in Charlotte, NC.

Dr. Clay Routledge is a professor of psychology at North Dakota State University and expert in existential psychology. He has published over 85 scientific papers, co-edited a book on the psychology of meaning, and authored the book *Nostalgia: A Psychological Resource. Psychology Today* carries his blog, "More Than Mortal." Dr. Routledge has also served as a guest blogger for *Scientific American*.

Billy San Juan, PhD, works as a psychosocial rehabilitation specialist in San Diego, CA. His clinical interests include the incorporation of masculinity as a culture within the context of case conceptualization in therapy. He often speaks on convention panels about psychology and popular culture. You can find him on his professional page at trilobits.net or on Twitter @billi_sense.

Janina Scarlet, PhD, is a Licensed Clinical Psychologist, a scientist, and a full time geek. She helps patients with anxiety, depression, chronic pain, and PTSD at the Center for Stress and Anxiety Management and Sharp Memorial Hospital and is a professor at Alliant International University,

San Diego. She has authored the book *Superhero Therapy* and chapters in all of our Popular Culture Psychology books. She can be reached via her website at www.superhero-therapy.com or on Twitter: @shadowquill.

Jay Scarlet holds Master's degrees in Psychology and in Library and Information Science. He works at Simi Valley Public Library, and is a past member of the Young Adult Library Services Association (YALSA)'s Research Committee. He has also contributed to the website Legion of Leia and the books *Star Wars Psychology: Dark Side of the Mind* and *Game of Thrones Psychology: The Mind is Dark and Full of Terrors.*

Steven Schlozman, MD, is an assistant professor of psychiatry at Harvard Medical School and staff child psychiatrist at Massachusetts General Hospital. Steve has written short fiction as well as the novel *The Zombie Autopsies: Secret Notebooks from the Apocalypse.* George Romero has optioned this novel and written the screenplay adaptation. Steven teaches a course on horror in literature and film to Harvard undergraduates, although it is not clear how much more of this nonsense his medical bosses will tolerate.

Eric D. Wesselmann, PhD, an assistant professor at Illinois State University, earned his doctorate in social psychology from Purdue University. He teaches social psychology, statistics, research, and the psychology of film. His published research has explored ostracism, stigma, and religion/spirituality. He is a consulting editor for *The Journal of Social Psychology* and has been a Trekkie since his father introduced him to the original series.

INDEX

(*continued on next page*)

(*continued on next page*)

S